How to sell
anything
on
amazon...
and make a fortune!

Michael Bellomo, JD/MBA
Joel Elad, MBA

McGraw-Hill

New York Chicago San Francisco Lisbon
London Madrid Mexico City Milan New Delhi
San Juan Seoul Singapore Sydney Toronto

The **McGraw·Hill** Companies

McGraw-Hill
2100 Powell Street, 10th Floor
Emeryville, California 94608
U.S.A.

To arrange bulk purchase discounts for sales promotions, premiums, or fund-raisers, please contact McGraw-Hill at the above address.

How to Sell Anything on Amazon... And Make a Fortune!

1234567890 CUS CUS 019876

ISBN 0-07-226260-5

Acquisitions Editor	Roger Stewart
Project Editor	Jody McKenzie
Acquisitions Coordinator	Agatha Kim
Technical Editor	Dennis L. Prince
Copy Editor	Mike McGee
Proofreader	Susie Elkind
Indexer	Karin Arrigoni
Composition	International Typesetting & Composition
Illustration	International Typesetting & Composition
Series Design	Michelle Galicia
Cover Design	Jeff Weeks

This book was composed with Adobe® InDesign®.

To William and Dottie Griffith for their inspiration.
To Jeff Bezos for his dedication.
And to Joel Elad for his perspiration.
Thank you all for one heck of a ride!

—Michael Bellomo

To my brother, Doron Jared Elad, for showing me the value of time.
To David Levitt and Delmar Janovec, for showing me the error of my ways
and encouraging me to go further.
To Jeff Bezos, for showing me and everyone the value of efficient and
data-conscious e-commerce.
And to Michael Bellomo, for showing me how to build on a dream.

—Joel Elad

About the Authors

Michael Bellomo holds an MBA from UC Irvine and a Juris Doctor in Law from the University of California, San Francisco. He has worked as an e-commerce manager and think-tank researcher studying how technology changes consumer markets. Michael worked on projects ranging from the analysis of the Columbia shuttle disaster to stopping bioterrorists. He is the narrator on a DVD presentation sent to Congress on the development of NASA's Orbital Space Plane. Currently, he is a Six Sigma Black Belt working at Baxter Bioscience in Los Angeles, California.

Michael has written 16 books and has been published in Italian, Portuguese, French, Dutch, German, Russian, and Chinese. He is the co-author of the Amazon bestseller *Microbe: Are We Ready for the Next Plague?*, a chilling work on how vulnerable we are to new, exotic diseases and acts of biological terrorism. He is also the co-author of two major technology books from McGraw-Hill: *eBay Your Business* and *How to Do Everything with TiVo*.

Joel Elad holds an MBA from UC Irvine and a BS in Computer Science & Engineering from UCLA. He has worked in various roles regarding technology and e-commerce for companies such as IBM, where he oversaw the development of internal Internet applications for thousands of employees and developed cutting-edge web applications for Fortune 500 clients. Currently, he is the Training and Special Accounts Manager for Net2Auction, an e-commerce company based in San Diego, California.

Joel is the co-author of the Amazon bestseller *eBay Your Business*, which helps businesses of all sizes navigate and profit from one of the leading Internet e-commerce sites. He also teaches e-commerce classes for the Learning Annex in cities such as Los Angeles and New York. He has presented at national conferences and held regional seminars on how to profit from e-commerce, and maintains his own e-commerce business, NewComix.Com, focusing on entertainment merchandise.

Contents

Foreword

As a rule, I've never much believed in get-rich-quick schemes—still don't. Today, though, if you were to ask if I believe in getting rich *easy*, I might need to pause and think a bit before I give you an answer. The world has changed and so has the premise of finding a promising "business opportunity."

In the early 1990s, I saw computers as not much more than newfangled typewriters without the ribbon and the carriage arm (that's because they were still pretty much "dumb" word processors). Although they were compelling in the hi-tech mystery, they weren't doing much more than allowing us to type without the need of correcting tape or liquid paper (remember that stuff?). But just a few years later, my eyes were finally opened to the true value and practical application of computers—they were the tool needed to surf the Internet. Sure, ARPANet had been around for years and years but that didn't mean much to me, and the fact that I wasn't a code-slinger meant I wasn't interested in conversing with a bunch of UNIX-fluent computer geeks (sorry, gang, but that's what you were—it's a badge you should wear proudly today, though). This all changed the day a co-worker introduced me to a PC application called *Mosaic*; he said I could use it to "surf the Net" and "cruise the Newsgroups." What did this mean and why should I care?

Back up about ten years and you'd see that, during the 1980s, I was an avid collector whose head was lost in baby boomer collectibles—toys, games, and movie goods—from my youth. I spent my time visiting collectible shows in my area and scouring *Toy Shop* magazine every time I could get my hands on one. I found plenty of whimsical goods from my charmed boyhood but, even though the stuff was cool, I always felt somewhat exploited—even violated—after buying from some dealer who laid down the facts that if I didn't buy at his price, well, he'd just raise his price and sell the item to another collector waiting in the wings. I hadn't a leg to stand on; I had *zero* bargaining leverage. The Internet and the Newsgroups changed all that. Quickly, I was making contact with other buyers and sellers in "real time" who would post the for-sale ("FS") and Wanted ads in the emerging ether of the World Wide Web. I found eBay thanks to the rec.collecting.toys newsgroup and, well, I've never been the same since.

Already comfortable with buying and selling over long distances (calling on *Toy Shop* ads or participating in the infrequent phone auction), my migration to dealing online was a simple one. The lid really blew off, though, when I started selling back in January 1996. Suddenly, *I* was the fellow at the head of the table, setting the stage for how the deal would go down. Actually, the bidders kept me in check there but, as the online realm was new and eBay was the greatest thing since the VCR, bids were high and sell-through rates were higher still. Unlike those arm-twisting dealers who lugged their wares to and from collectible shows or who found they'd have to wait another month to advertise new wares in a costly *Toy Shop* ad (or *Goldmine* or *Movie Collector World* or whatever), I was simply venturing into my nearby closet, attic, or garage and deciding what I would sell next. My overhead was practically nil at the time except for learning how to wrangle and master the eBay interface. For me, though, I saw that I, too, could go into business and not have to pay perverse monthly rent fees to the local strip-mall land baron.

Soon, the Internet grew busy with eager buyers and sellers, who found they now had the easy means to break down the former geographic barriers that prevented many of us from truly being able to engage in an entrepreneurial endeavor while learning how convenient online commerce could be. I shopped constantly at 800.com, a long-defunct DVD destination that was a personal favorite for a good couple of years. I frequented KenCranes.com, the former mail-order laserdisc success story that created an online presence to bolster and even surpass the sales activity Cranes himself had been enjoying at his brick-and-mortar establishment. In addition, I found a nifty new site from which to buy books and chart how my own were faring: Amazon.com. Like eBay, Amazon was early on the scene and was able to establish a desirable place in the mindshare of online shoppers. When I thought of books online, I thought of Amazon.

So where does this all lead? Well, I've found that almost everything I want or need is now readily at my fingertips, thanks to the Internet. Whether I seek to consume information or indulge myself in consumer delights, I turn to the Internet to satisfy my need. And, when that need becomes one of securing income, the earnings are just a few keystrokes and mouse-clicks away. Just as there are so many different web sites available for me and you to surf and shop from, so too are there many different profit-bearing (and fortune-turning) portals where we can set up shop quickly, easily, and practically risk free. You don't think so? Well, I do, and that's why I'm glad to see what authors Michael Bellomo and Joel Elad have done in this book—showing me and you the ins and outs of setting up shop and turning an enviable profit within the "world's biggest bookstore," Amazon .com. As much as I've been writing and teaching others about e-commerce within that big virtual auction parlor, I've been the attentive student of Michael and Joel as they've set about to explain the opportunities that await entrepreneurs who are either more drawn to the Amazon marketplace or—and better yet—are looking to expand their virtual presence within *multiple* marketplaces. The best news is that Michael and Joel have stepped forward to save me and you time—the veritable years it would take to harness the tools and techniques available at Amazon—and have discussed these tools in depth in this book. Better yet, you'll find they've saved you from making errors in approach and execution by guiding you away from the School of Hard Knocks. In the end, their timely text will get you on the fast path to fortune.

Although I can't promise you'll get rich quick, I do believe that with this book's help you can get from here to there much easier than if you were to try to tame the Amazon on your own.

Your fortune's waiting…

—Dennis L. Prince, Technical Editor

Acknowledgments

Joel Elad and I would like to acknowledge the hard work put in by Agatha Kim and Roger Stewart to ensure the quality of this book. We'd also like to acknowledge the talents of Jody McKenzie and her team for making our words flow so mellifluously.

In addition, we'd like to offer our best wishes to all the sellers working "on the river" who took time out from their busy schedules to speak to us about their experiences. Finally, we want to thank Dennis Prince, whose work and care as an editor leads us to conclude that he is very aptly named indeed.

—Michael Bellomo

Introduction

How to Sell Anything on Amazon...And Make a Fortune! is designed to be an informative, comprehensive, "how-to" guide to help steer you through all the steps one should go through to properly take advantage of the Amazon.com site and the benefits it can offer an eager and motivated seller or a business.

In this book, we don't just jump into the site and push you through it. There are lots of books out there that will teach you how to register and list items. But a successful run on Amazon doesn't happen without some planning, and that's where we come in. We spend the first part of the book explaining the structures and offering strategies on taking advantage of Amazon's wide marketplace. We then take you into each money-making arena with practical, how-to advice. We follow that up with a variety of marketing techniques and tricks to improve your sales and increase your audience. We finish by providing you with a set of advanced processes and techniques to help vault your sales to the next level.

Whether you're into selling used and new books, DVDs and VHS movies, computer software and electronics, or a huge variety of your own specialty goods, this book can benefit you. You don't need to already have a presence on the Internet. However, you'll find you get the most out of this book if you fall into one of the following categories:

- You're an entrepreneur or a business that already sells online, but are looking for a new avenue to sell different kinds of merchandise.

- You've got access to an array of products ranging from books, movies, and music, to electronics, computer software, and household items, and you're looking for a way to sell them quickly and efficiently online.

- You're an executive manager of a company and you're responsible for expanding sales, adding sales channels, and increasing ROI.

Part I

Set Up Shop on Amazon

Chapter 1

Get Your Business Up and Running on Amazon

Obsess about customers, not the competitors.

—Jeff Bezos, founder of Amazon.com

Amazon.com is more than the premier online shopping site. Its brand name, along with a tiny handful of others, such as Yahoo and eBay, is the public face of e-commerce to the world at large. Of that handful, Amazon is arguably the most important in terms of the state of e-commerce. That's because Amazon has pioneered an impressive data analysis and customer service model that helps people shop quickly and securely, and uses both their past buying and browsing patterns to predict and recommend new purchases. They have given a positive, pleasing face to e-commerce and that's why many people now think of Amazon as their best place to shop online.

Yahoo, for all its innovations, is still primarily seen as a search engine. eBay requires a bit more financial savvy to understand its online auction system than many casual users possess. Amazon.com, in contrast, is wonderfully simple. Just point and click and you can buy practically anything, from books to barbeques, to DVDs and dishwashers.

A Short History of Amazon.com

Amazon was founded in 1995 by Jeff Bezos, a classic overachiever and the youngest vice president of his investment banking firm. At 37, he quit his job and headed west to Seattle to try his hand at his business idea. Bezos and his handpicked team of software designers had spent a year in planning before they launched their company, one that they believed would revolutionize the way everyday folks find and purchase high-volume goods like books, music, and videos.

In July 1995, Bezos hired his first four employees, and began working in his Seattle garage. As Bezos and his staff would pack boxes while kneeling on the garage floor, Amazon's reputation grew and the increase in orders necessitated hiring more people, eventually forcing them to purchase a separate warehouse for their inventory. By 1999, *Time* magazine named Bezos "Person of the Year," calling Amazon the "poster-child of e-biz." During the dotcom crash, when hundreds of fledgling companies ran out of funds, profits, and investors, Amazon.com continued standing tall. While it *was* losing money during this period, investors were confident that Amazon had built the right model and that their efficiency and customer loyalty would net them a profit once they achieved a high volume.

While that confidence wavered every time another negative quarter was reported, Amazon's volume grew and their position began to solidify as other players abandoned the market.

By the year 2000, more than 60,000 other web sites were linked to Amazon .com. The number is likely triple that today. Amazon's sales for 2004 rose to almost $2 billion. This number is so far above any other online shopping site as to make comparisons difficult or meaningless.

Amazon.com Partners

Jeff Bezos saw that his customers liked the shopping experience they were getting from Amazon. His investment in customer service and I/T was obviously paying off, given that customers were returning. That's when he started thinking about how to capitalize on that trust. Since his vast inventory allowed people to find that rare book, CD, or video, how about Amazon helping its customers unearth other rare or hard-to-find items? That meant expanding into other categories so Amazon could transform from "Earth's Biggest Bookstore" to "Earth's Biggest E-Tailer." As Amazon expanded into other categories outside of printed, visual, and audio media, they began to develop partnerships with other companies and sellers, to limit their costs, and "test the waters" to see if a category was a right fit for Amazon's customer set. These partnerships fell into two specific categories: corporate and trusted partners.

Corporate Partners

Big suppliers such as Toys R Us, The Gap, and Circuit City helped Amazon.com move their brand image from "this is the place to shop for books" to the broader online marketplace that it is today (although, many of us still immediately think of "books" when we think of "Amazon"; few people think about the sprawling river cutting through South America). The company involved may place their entire catalog online with Amazon, or only offer a limited selection of their products. Typically, these products are displayed along with similar ones from competing firms and even Amazon.com itself. The distinguishing characteristic of these sellers is that they sell their own merchandise using a buying and selling interface provided by Amazon. A typical corporate partner's store is shown in Figure 1-1.

Corporate partnerships work out for both parties involved: Amazon gets to expand the selection they offer to their customers without investing money in inventory, while the corporate partner gets to benefit from Amazon's loyal customer base and extensive infrastructure. One excellent partnership has been

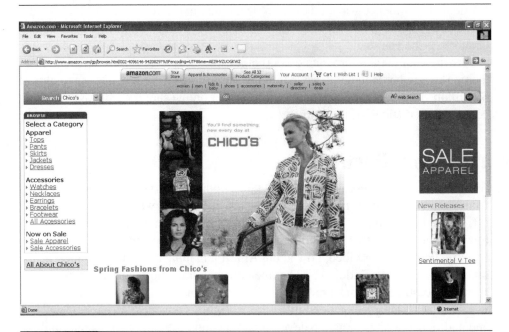

FIGURE 1-1   An example of an Amazon.com corporate partner's store

the Toys R Us deal. When Toys R Us first pushed into the Internet retail space, they got slammed with orders their first holiday season and the end result was countless orders arriving after Christmas and lots of angry customers. Toys R Us came to Amazon and now Amazon handles the distribution of Toys R Us Internet sales, with significantly higher customer satisfaction and revenue.

Trusted Partners

Trusted partners offer products that Amazon has chosen not to carry, such as watercraft or medicine. Amazon researches the company in question and links to them as a partner site. Essentially, Amazon.com does the homework for the consumer and certifies that the partner is trustworthy enough to do business with. Among the vast array of Amazon trusted partners are companies such as CarsDirect.Com, Kodak, Hotwire, and others. You can visit the current list of trusted partners by going to the Amazon site and typing in **Trusted Partners** in the Help section. A page similar to that shown in Figure 1-2 will appear.

While the partner will display the Amazon Partner logo on their web site, as in Figure 1-3, the consumer is not purchasing the merchandise at Amazon.com.

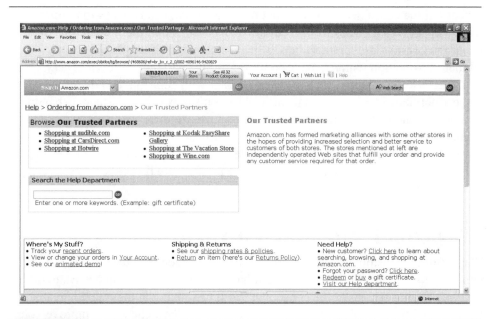

FIGURE 1-2   Amazon's trusted partners

FIGURE 1-3   The Amazon Partner logo

It does tell the consumer, however, that this is a site Amazon wishes to partner with, which gives it one level of credibility. Because one of the foundations of Amazon is ease of use, partners benefit from customers already having stored all their information with Amazon, so they don't have to reenter it with every new purchase. This helps "lock in" the customer with Amazon, and therefore, any partner networked with Amazon. As Amazon's network of partners expands, customers benefit from a greater selection, and Amazon (and their partners) helps capture more revenue and retain their loyal customers. Therefore, Amazon is always on the lookout for valuable new categories to serve as well as partners to help them achieve those goals, whether those partners are businesses or savvy entrepreneurs.

How Amazon Is Opening Up Their Catalog

The 47 million customers that Amazon.com sells to each year hasn't tempted the company to rest on its laurels. Instead, it has pioneered some unique ways to offer multiple buying options to the consumer. We'll be looking at these three areas in the book, with an emphasis on the ones that stand the best chance to improve your business sales on Amazon.com.

Amazon Marketplace

One interesting innovation is the Amazon Marketplace, which allows Amazon.com consumers to buy and sell used or collectible items directly from a new product's detail page. An example of this link is shown in Figure 1-4. Amazon notes the number of these available items and groups them by price and item condition.

The Last Of The Mohicans: Original Motion Picture Soundtrack [SOUNDTRACK]
Randy Edelman, Trevor Jones

List Price: $19.98
    Price: $14.99 & eligible for FREE Super Saver Shipping on orders over $25.
    See details.
You Save: $4.99 (25%)

Availability: Usually ships within 5 to 7 days

46 used & new from $9.95

Share your own customer images

▸ See more product details

FIGURE 1-4   The Amazon Marketplace link

Amazon has given their Marketplace idea considerable prominence via its "Sell Yours Here" link listed at the top of many pages. This type of link, however, won't be found everywhere on the site. In fact, it's found only in the following site "store" areas:

- Amazon.com Books

- Amazon.com Music

- Amazon.com DVD/Video

- Amazon.com Computer & Video Games

- Amazon.com Electronics

- Amazon.com Tools & Hardware

- Amazon.com Sporting Goods

- Amazon.com Camera & Photo

While providing excellent web "real estate" for people or small retailers who wish to sell their used or collectible items, this can be a fairly inefficient way for larger businesses to sell new merchandise, both due to the limited nature of the listings and the competition with small sellers who may offer lower quality (used and refurbished items) at a lower price. Larger businesses might consider their own virtual storefront to help sell their goods using their brand name, for example.

Amazon.com Auctions

Amazon has wisely decided to move into the online auction territory to tap into the same selling excitement and experience that defines the loyal eBay community. Amazon's rates for sellers are quite competitive—only a dime per listing. In addition, Amazon.com waives all auction listing fees for sellers who establish a Pro Merchant Subscription for $39.99 (as of this writing). A typical auction page on Amazon.com, as in Figure 1-5, looks remarkably similar to an eBay auction page.

Unlike eBay, Amazon offers a feature to their auction sellers called CrossLinks. With a CrossLink listing, the seller can insert a link to their listing directly on an Amazon.com product detail page.

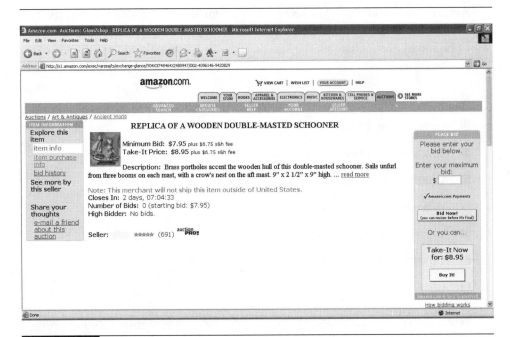

FIGURE 1-5 An Amazon auction page

Finally, if the auction attracts a winning bidder, the fee charged to the seller is based on the amount of the winning bid. Amazon's fees are shown in brief in Table 1-1.

Auctions can also play a part in your Amazon.com strategy. They are particularly useful for selling legacy items which may not be pulling in as many buyers to your retail channels as you'd like. Such retail channels can range from a traditional brick-and-mortar storefront to your company's web site.

Winning Bid Amount	Amazon's Fees
$0.01 to $25.00	5 percent
$25.01 to $1,000.00	$1.25, plus 2.5 percent of any amount greater than $25
$1,000.01 or more	$25.63, plus 1.25 percent of any amount greater than $1,000

TABLE 1-1 Fees on Amazon's Sliding Scale

zShops

Amazon.com's zShops essentially offer merchants who want to sell with Amazon a virtual storefront, such as in Figure 1-6. Buyers on Amazon.com can browse zShop stores while searching and browsing the zShops listings. By itself, this concept isn't new. Other sites have also positioned themselves as e-commerce hubs on the Internet. For example, web portals such as Yahoo and Infospace currently host merchant web stores. In 2000, Yahoo listed some 6,000 shops in its Yahoo Stores, including Tower Records and bookseller Barnesandnoble.com.

Where Amazon.com differs is in the close affiliation of its brand name with its zShops merchants—for example, the URL for any storefront follows the format http://www.amazon.com/shops/nickname. Additionally, Amazon offers more valuable web "real estate" by allowing zShops merchants to promote their goods on Amazon's product pages. As with the Amazon Marketplace, this means that a used bookseller can promote their pre-owned copies of a book on a new book page.

There is significant potential in utilizing zShops for your business on Amazon.com. It can mean activity similar to what Wherehouse is achieving with its music shop and what eLearningCenter is discovering with their software store.

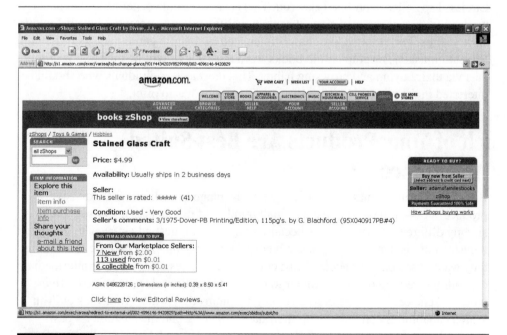

FIGURE 1-6   A sample Amazon zShop page

For that reason, we'll go over the setting up and marketing of a zShop storefront in great detail in Chapter 6. For now, it's just best to recognize the potential that zShops offer in enhancing visibility of the goods you want to sell and how it can serve an important role in your money-making plans.

Amazon's Data Gathering Gold Mine

You may have thought about the sheer number of eyeballs attracted to Amazon, and its vast brand-name recognition, as major advantages to helping your business move more merchandise. This sounds excellent, but don't forget Amazon's world-class ability to gather and analyze customer data, not to mention how you can leverage the site's efforts to propel your own e-commerce endeavors.

Tens of millions of shoppers have already shared their personal shopping habits with Amazon, which is done by collecting and analyzing many things, including the Internet protocol address used to connect the purchaser's computer to the Internet, the user's buying history, the zShops visited, the user's Auction history, and their page interaction information. This would include scrolling, clicks, mouse-overs, and methods used to browse outside of the page.

Amazon aggregates this customer information to create features such as Purchase Circles, Top Sellers, and Just Like You. This is an incredible benefit for merchants working with Amazon.com since it can prequalify and route potential buyers to your store's items. For example, purchasers interested in specific genre items (say, Civil War–era muskets, or pulp comic books from the 1950s), will be picked out of the data via their buying and browsing habits. This preselects individuals who should be interested in the specific merchandise your company has to offer.

Which of Your Products Are Best Suited for Amazon.com?

Broadly speaking, Amazon offers the best advantage for sellers with extensive product lines—or those that have a small number of products that sport several slightly different models. This is because one of the biggest advantages to selling at Amazon.com is that Amazon makes it easy for the customer to find the exact items they want based on their needs. Most company web sites offer basic or intermediate capabilities, relying on the customer to browse the entire selection of disk drives, wool jackets, or silverware before finding the items they want. Amazon's built-in search capabilities combined with their data gathering and the customer's past purchase history allow customers to go directly to the model they are looking for, thus reducing the number of clicks it takes for a customer to make a purchase.

Move Both Ends of Your Inventory, Hot and Cold

Amazon, by its very nature as a virtual marketplace, also offers you the best opportunity to make sales from the "tail" end of your merchandise. The "tail" might best be described as the 80 percent of your inventory which is not in as high demand as, say, your latest model of product. However, while you may have difficulty gaining shelf space with a brick-and-mortar store that can only show the top-selling models, on Amazon you can make the entire line of products available for people to shop from—and their buying habits will be different when they have a greater selection of products to choose from.

An example of how Amazon.com helps you "sell from your tail" would work as follows. Let's say your business makes laser printers. Your 5000X model is selling very well, and it's getting prime shelf space in the retail world. Because it's getting this sort of attention, you have several hundred 4000X model printers sitting in the warehouse not getting sold. Although the difference in features is marginal, the 4000X model just isn't selling.

This is in large part because only 1 or 2 people at any given electronics store are asking for it—too small a number for a retailer with limited space to devote a spot on the shelf to it. However, with Amazon, the space limitations are essentially infinite. If the customer is searching for your 4000X model (or, rather, wants a 5000X model with fewer bells and whistles), they can find it at Amazon—the one place that can connect them with your stockpile of B-model printers.

If you look around the Internet, you can find similar models in services such as NetFlix. The DVD rental site allows people to choose from millions of titles because they don't have to invest in retail stores and shelf space like Blockbuster and Hollywood. Amazon allows people to browse through millions of items that don't have to compete for shelf space, because they all sit in remote warehouses yet share one common database. This increases customer loyalty because people begin to search using Amazon and usually find what they're looking for before moving on.

Sell Inventory that Can Compete on Price

Finally, Amazon offers a tremendous advantage if you can compete on price. If your business sells a "commoditized" product like a computer part or DVD, the buyer rarely cares about who they get the product from—there is very little "vendor loyalty" in commodity items. Their primary concern is with the price, speed of delivery, and (if the item is pre-owned) the condition. This is a particular boon if your company sells refurbished or off-brand products.

For example, say that your business resoles hiking boots. Rather than pay twice the price for a "brand name" resoled boot, the customer may not particularly care to pay the "premium" for the brand, and would rather go with a less expensive make. Since the customer knows what they want and you have the merchandise, Amazon is able to put you and the buyer together by allowing them to shop on price point and not purely by established brand name.

It's that relationship, that connecting of buyer and seller, that can help you make your fortune using Amazon. Now that we've given you an idea of what can work on Amazon, let's dive right in and get started with the registration process.

Setting Up Your Amazon Account

If you've already been buying stuff on Amazon, your account is created and is filled with your shopping history, personal recommendations, your profile information, and much more. However, let's walk through the process of setting up an account to use for your selling history.

> **TIP**
>
> *You may want to set up a new account even if you already have a personal account, so information between the two doesn't get intermingled. For example, you don't want feedback from a personal transaction to potentially impact your record as an Amazon seller. On the other hand, if you've built up a positive record with your own transactions, you may consider building onto it for your main selling activities. Amazon encourages the use of multiple accounts because they recognize the different buying habits of the personal buyer and corporate user.*

Whenever you sign up for an account online, there needs to be a "unique identifier," a piece of information that will distinguish you from all the other people who have accounts with their system. This basically boils down to two elements of information commonly used by most sites: a userid and your e-mail address. The userid is a special identifier that you create, and is checked against the current member list to make sure more than one person isn't using the same userid. The e-mail address is also unique, since there usually aren't two people receiving e-mail at the exact same e-mail address. While there may be 100 Bob Nesmiths, bobnesmith@ yourcompanyname.com and bob.nesmith@yourcompanyname.com are two unique identifiers.

In the case of Amazon, they use your e-mail address as the unique identifier for your account. If you go to Amazon's home page at www.amazon.com and click Your Account, for example, you're presented with the screen shown in Figure 1-7 to get started in creating your account.

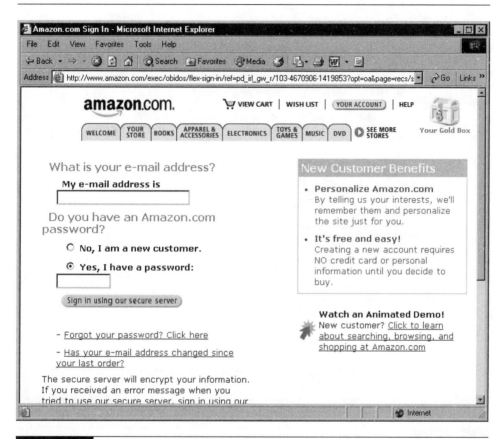

FIGURE 1-7   Creating a new account on Amazon. Step 1: Entering your e-mail address

TIP

For a corporate situation, think about asking your IT folks to create a special e-mail address, like amazon@yourcompanyname.com, or amz_orders@yourcompanyname.com, so you can monitor your Amazon selling activity without it getting mixed into someone's personal account. This is a good idea, too, should the original coordinator happen to change jobs or leave the company.

Enter the e-mail address you're planning to use to coordinate your Amazon selling activity. Then, when it asks "Do you have an Amazon.com password?" click the radio button next to the option of "No, I am a new customer." Afterward, click the button that says "Sign in using our Secure Server" to continue. You'll then be taken to Step 2 of the registration process, as shown in Figure 1-8.

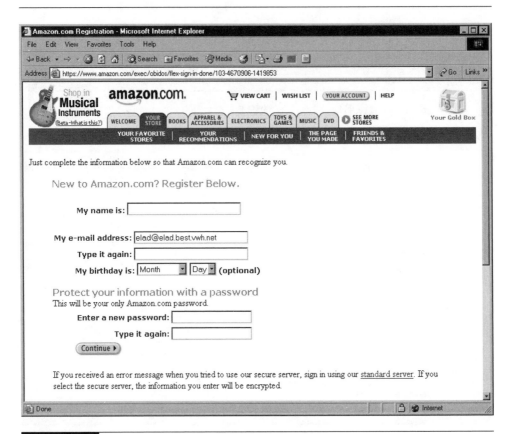

FIGURE 1-8   Step 2 of your registration: name and password

First, you'll be prompted for your name. You may want to consider putting the name of the company, instead of your personal name, since this information will be displayed in all the screens you see when logged into the site. Next, you'll be asked to confirm the e-mail address you gave initially by entering it a second time in the box provided. You're also given the option of providing your birthday. In most cases, you probably shouldn't provide a birthday if you're representing a company, but there's no real harm in doing so. Just expect to see some colorful messages when that day comes up and you log into Amazon.

Finally, you'll be asked to pick a password to use when logging into your account. Pick something that will be easy to remember for you and your co-workers, but not too easy for the outside world to guess. We recommend you don't use any personal passwords you're using elsewhere, unless you're the only person who'll have access to this account. There aren't too many rules as to what the password must be, so you have some flexibility in using letters, numbers, familiar words, and so on. Be sure to enter the password twice in the fields below, and when ready, click the button to Continue. You should see the Recommendations page, as shown in Figure 1-9.

Setting Up a Corporate Account on Amazon

If you want to add the ability to have a corporate account on Amazon, you can do so using the same e-mail address and password you just set up. Every time someone logs in with this combination and purchases something, Amazon will determine at the checkout phase whether it's for personal or corporate use and only allow the designated account managers access to the corporate area.

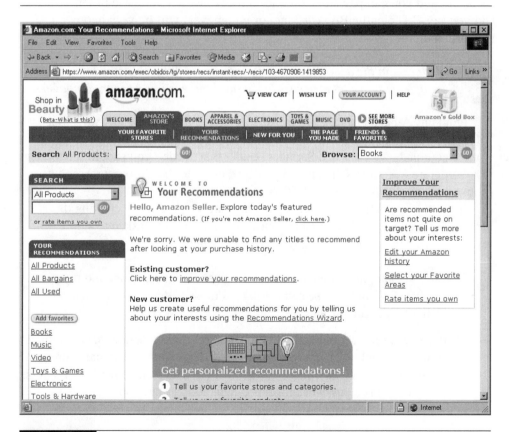

FIGURE 1-9   Your Account is created, and Amazon is ready to make recommendations.

Amazon designates the "Primary Account Manager" as the person who creates the corporate account. Only this person has the ability to edit the profile regarding the institution, business, or account name. More importantly, only this person has the ability to apply for an Amazon corporate credit account. This corporate credit account allows you to pay for your purchases using a corporate purchase order instead of a regular credit card. Therefore, decide now who should hold the rank of Primary Account Manager and have that person complete the following step.

If you're wondering who should be the Primary Account Manager, the answer could be this simple: Who do you go to at your office to get reimbursed when you buy something for the company? Go to that person and give them this pitch: "Hey, Bob, you know all those expense reports you have to process because we're all buying books and software for the business? Well, if you sign up for an Amazon corporate account, we can charge everything to one account, and you can pay Amazon once a month with a purchase order. What do you say?" Typically, Bob (or Jane, or whomever) will be very happy to participate.

> **NOTE** *Later on in the account creation process, you'll be able to add other people and give them access to the account, even as Account Managers.*

From any Amazon page, click the link at the top of the page that says "See More Stores" in order to see the Store Directory. Scroll down the page and look for the column header marked Services. Under that header, you should see the link for Corporate Accounts. Click it and you'll be taken to the Corporate Accounts home page, as shown in Figure 1-10.

In the top-left part of the screen, you can start the process by clicking the orange button marked Open A Corporate Account. You'll be asked to sign in to create a corporate account. You have two options here:

- Choose the option "I am a returning Amazon.com customer and my password is" and use the same e-mail address and password you used earlier to log into the site.

- If you want to keep separate accounts entirely, create a new, separate-mail address through your Internet e-mail provider, and then use that address in the space provided and pick the option "I am a new customer." You will be asked to create a password for this e-mail address later on.

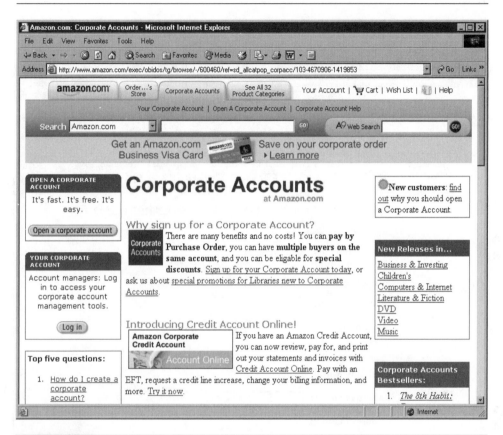

FIGURE 1-10   The home page for Amazon Corporate Accounts

Once you've made your selection, you'll be taken to the first page of the four-part account creation process, as shown in Figure 1-11. At this phase, you're asked for account information. First, complete the fields for your title (as the Primary Account Manager) and insert your contact phone number. Next, you're asked for basic info about your company: business name, address, phone number, and type of business. Finally, you'll need to give an official name to your account, instead of just your personal name. It's advisable to use your company name, but you can further distinguish it by adding a subdepartment name or something to help identify the types of products you'll be selling on Amazon. For example, if you hope to sell clothing in the Apparel section, you could name your account "Clothes by Company X." Once all this info is complete, click the Continue button to move to Step 2.

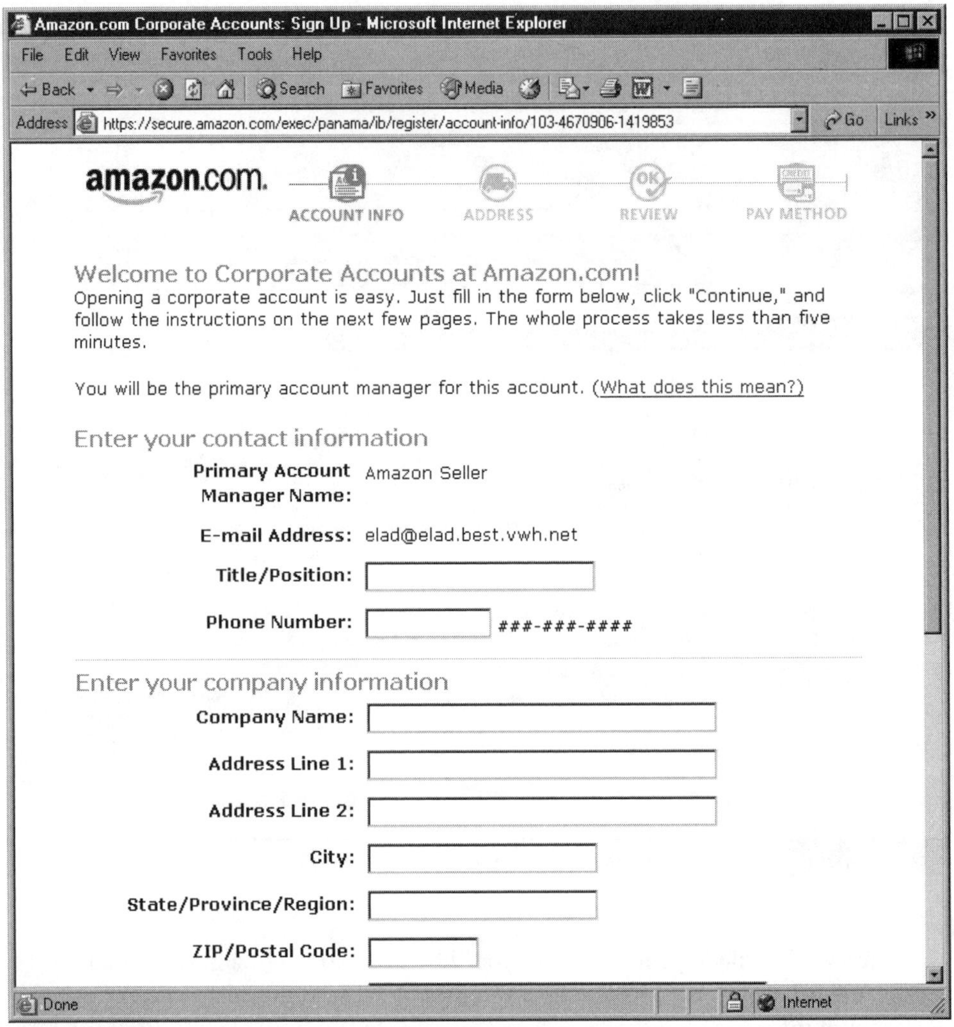

FIGURE 1-11   The Amazon Corporate Account Info screen

In Step 2, you're asked to determine the shipping address to be linked to your corporate account, mainly for purposes of where to ship any products purchased by this account. You can leave the address you entered in Step 1, or enter a different shipping address in the fields provided, as shown in Figure 1-12. This is particularly helpful if your billing and shipping addresses are different, or you need items shipped to a central warehouse while account management concerns must go to the head office.

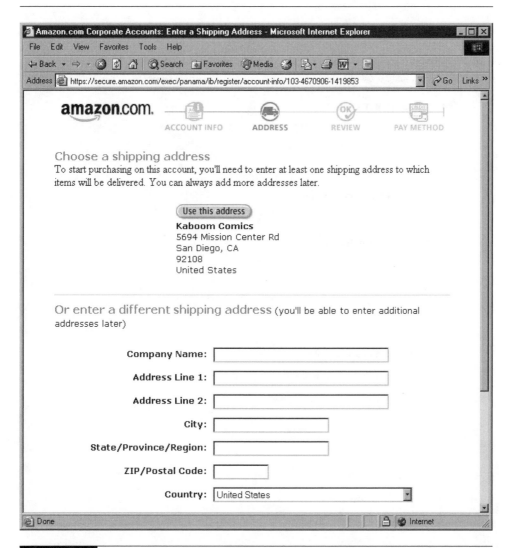

FIGURE 1-12   The Amazon Corporate Account Shipping Address page

If you want to keep the address you gave, click the Use This Address button. Otherwise, complete the information and click the Continue button at the bottom of the page. Either action will take you to Step 3.

Now that you've set up all your account information, you're asked to verify it in step 3. Review the information presented (it should like that in Figure 1-13), and make changes to the account name or shipping address if needed. When it all looks the way you want it to, press Continue to proceed to the fourth and final step!

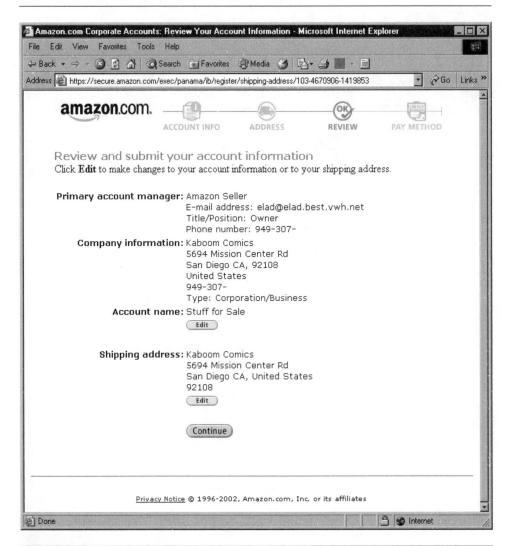

FIGURE 1-13   The Amazon Corporate Account confirmation page

Okay, now that they know all about you, here comes the important part—how to pay for your purchases! From this screen, you're asked to either provide a credit card, or to apply for a credit account. If you apply for a credit account, you'll be able to have your employees pay for purchases with a purchase order instead of credit cards, review all purchases made by you and your employees in one monthly statement, and have individual invoices and their corresponding purchase orders at your fingertips. Just click the Apply For A Credit Account button near the top of the screen to continue.

Let's assume you're applying for a credit account. If so, you should see a screen like the one in Figure 1-14. Now you've got to start answering questions about your business, including such things as the "Doing Business As" name, the Parent Company (if applicable), Years in Business, Legal Type of Business, and so on.

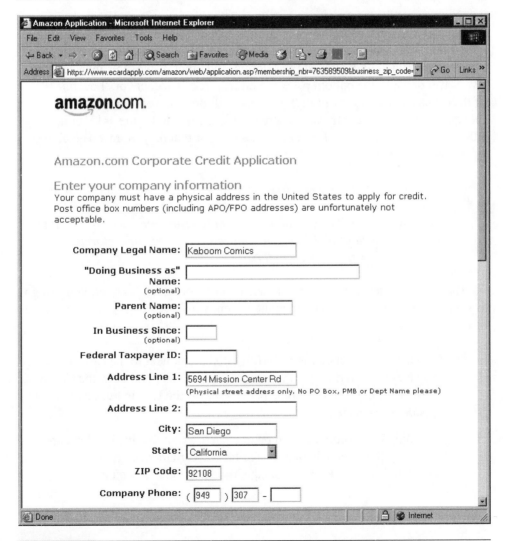

FIGURE 1-14   The Amazon Corporate Account Business Information page

Answer only those questions you feel comfortable with. You can leave any optional questions blank. This information helps Amazon and Citibank (their credit issuer) determine whether to grant this account. Consult with the appropriate people in your company to get the necessary information, especially the Federal Taxpayer ID.

NOTE   *If you are a sole proprietorship, chances are your Federal Taxpayer ID is your Social Security number, especially if you don't have any employees on the payroll.*

Once all the information is entered, click Continue to move on. You must review the terms and conditions of the Corporate Account before you can proceed. You'll be presented with interest rates, terms, and other disclosures mandated by law. Scroll down to the bottom page and either click "I accept" or "I decline" (if the terms are not to your liking). Amazon will process your application on the spot and return with a confirmation screen, like the one in Figure 1-15, either telling you that additional information is needed, or that they've received all the information and your answer will arrive shortly.

CAUTION   *Remember, until your credit account is fully approved, you cannot use your Amazon account to purchase anything. If you provide a valid credit card, Amazon will allow you to make purchases, and once your credit account is established, you can remove your credit card information or switch over your payment preference.*

That's it! Whenever you want to manage your Corporate Account, you just go to your Manage Your Corporate Account screen, which you can get to in a couple of ways:

- From any screen, click the See More Stores link next to the category tabs. From there, scroll down to the Services subheading and click the Corporate Accounts link. From that home page, look for the Log In button along the left side of the page.

- Click the Your Account button on any page. From the display that appears, look along the right side of the page for a box marked Corporate Accounts. You should see a link titled Manage Your Corporate Account.

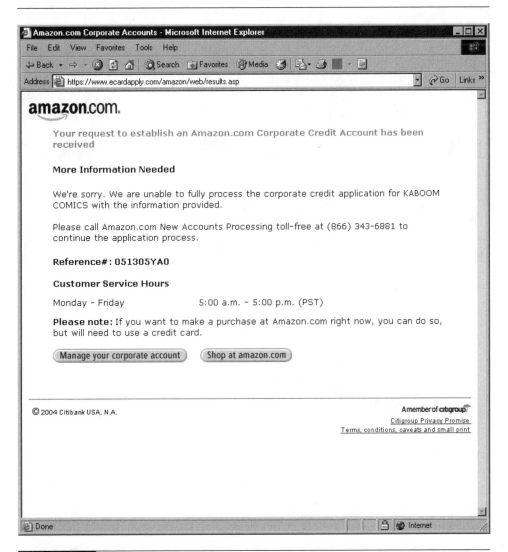

FIGURE 1-15   The Amazon Corporate Credit Account Confirmation screen

By following either of these instructions, after logging in you'll be presented with your "home page" for managing the Corporate account, as shown in Figure 1-16. From here, you can add purchasers and account managers to your account, track purchases, and make changes to your settings and/or profile information. Use this page as a handy guide to keep track of your company's use of Amazon purchases.

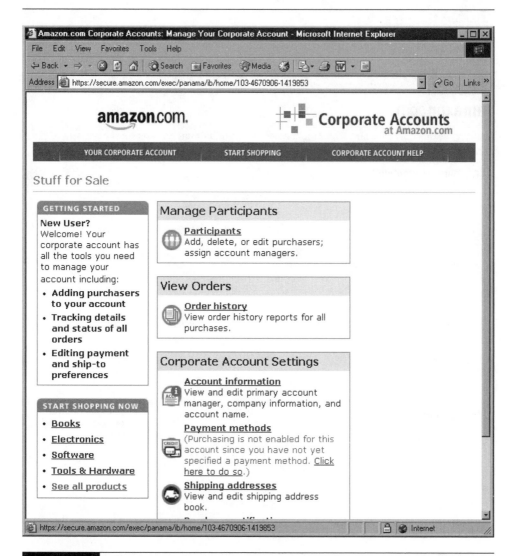

FIGURE 1-16   The Amazon Corporate Account summary screen

Now that you have your Corporate Account, be sure to log in often and recommend to your Primary Account Manager that he/she review the purchase history in order to see if there are ways to reuse past purchases and save money. After all, your Corporate Account could tell you in a hurry whether your employees are all buying the same book, when they could be sharing those books. If utilized properly, your Corporate Account can save you money.

Amazon Payments

One of the ways that Amazon differentiates itself from other e-commerce sites such as eBay is that they usually coordinate the payment process between buyer and seller instead of letting the two parties handle it directly. Basically, Amazon Payments is their intermediary and it works as follows:

1. A buyer decides to purchase one of your items on Amazon (a Marketplace, Auctions, or zShop item) and clicks the Order button.

2. Amazon charges the buyer's credit card for the full amount.

3. Amazon Payments "deposits" your proceeds into your Amazon Payments account, meaning your sales price minus any commissions or fees, plus a shipping credit.

4. Every two weeks, Amazon Payments will transfer the accumulated credit sitting in your account to the bank account that you designate in your Amazon Payments account information. They will also notify you with an e-mail that the transfer has occurred.

This way, neither party is privy to the other's sensitive financial information, such as credit card numbers. Buyers gain an additional benefit from having this service in place. All purchases of merchandise through Amazon Payments come with a $2,500 "A to Z Guarantee," which protects buyers in case their purchase never shows or is materially different from what they thought they were ordering. We'll talk about guarantees more in the next chapter.

Sellers reap several benefits from this system. First and foremost, there are no transaction fees for using Amazon Payments. Other online payment systems, like PayPal, can charge up to nearly three percent per transaction, just to receive money. Here, your customers can use their credit cards safely and securely, and you get all of your money directly without those incremental fees.

Also, sellers can ship items directly to the buyer knowing that the item is paid for and they can't be immediately "chargebacked" through their own merchant credit card system. They can also download reports to use in tracking and evaluating their sales, and handle refund processes online without much fuss or trouble.

NOTE   *In some cases, mainly when you're dealing with an Amazon "merchant," like Target or Toys R Us, you'll most likely pay that merchant directly instead of using Amazon Payments.*

Registering with Amazon Payments

When you sign up for your Amazon account, you're on your way to getting an Amazon Payments account. However, you still have to register your Payments account and tell Amazon your bank account information so they know where to deposit your money. As far as registration, you have two options:

■ Wait until you sell an item through Amazon, at such a point they'll prompt you to update your Payments account with the valid information.

■ Go directly to the application for registering an Amazon Payments account.

We're going to go ahead and walk you through the process of registering for your Amazon Payments account now so you don't have to worry about it later. Finding the actual link to get started isn't as obvious to locate, so here are some shortcuts:

■ You can enter the direct link by typing the following URL into your web browser: http://s1.amazon.com/exec/varzea/register/login/pipeline-type%3Dpayee

■ Alternately, you can click the Help word near the top right of any Amazon screen. In the screen that appears, scroll down to the bottom of the page and, in the text box below Search Our Help Department, type **Applying & Payments Basics**. In the screen that appears, as shown in Figure 1-17, click the link in the middle of the screen titled Complete An Application.

After you're prompted to sign in with your e-mail address and password, you'll be asked to enter your credit card information, as shown in Figure 1-18. Currently, Amazon accepts Visa, Mastercard, American Express, Diner's Club, Carte Blanche, and JCB credit cards. They ask for a credit card in order to help identify you as the seller since Amazon Payments will deposit the buyer's payments into your account.

Next, you're taken to the screen where they ask you for your billing address. The key here is to provide the billing address that's associated with the credit card you just filed in the last step. This helps Amazon verify that you are the legal owner of that credit card and, therefore, verifies your identity. Fill out all the fields,

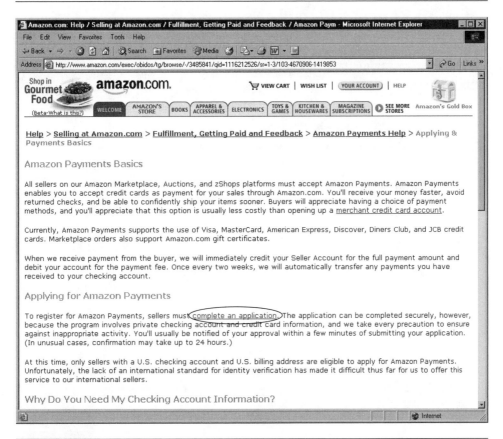

| FIGURE 1-17 | Finding the link to register for an Amazon Payments account |

as shown in Figure 1-19, including the home phone and daytime phone. Even if they're both the same number, don't leave any field blank (except for the Address 2 and Extension fields, that is, because those are optional).

Once you click Continue, you're taken to the third screen, where, after verifying the credit card and address you've just provided, you're asked to come up with a nickname, read (and agree to) their Participation Agreement, and decide whether to file your checking account information now or later, as shown

FIGURE 1-18   The Amazon Payments registration screen—Credit Card Info

in Figure 1-20. You should pick a nickname that reflects either your business or the primary type(s) of goods you plan to sell on Amazon. This is because the nickname is what buyers will see as your name when you sell on Amazon. Make your name count; it'll help in your branding and selling activity, which we cover more in depth later in the book.

CAUTION   *Don't use any trademarked names in your nickname, such as* bestamazonseller *or* ebaydvds, *since that will void the Participation Agreement.*

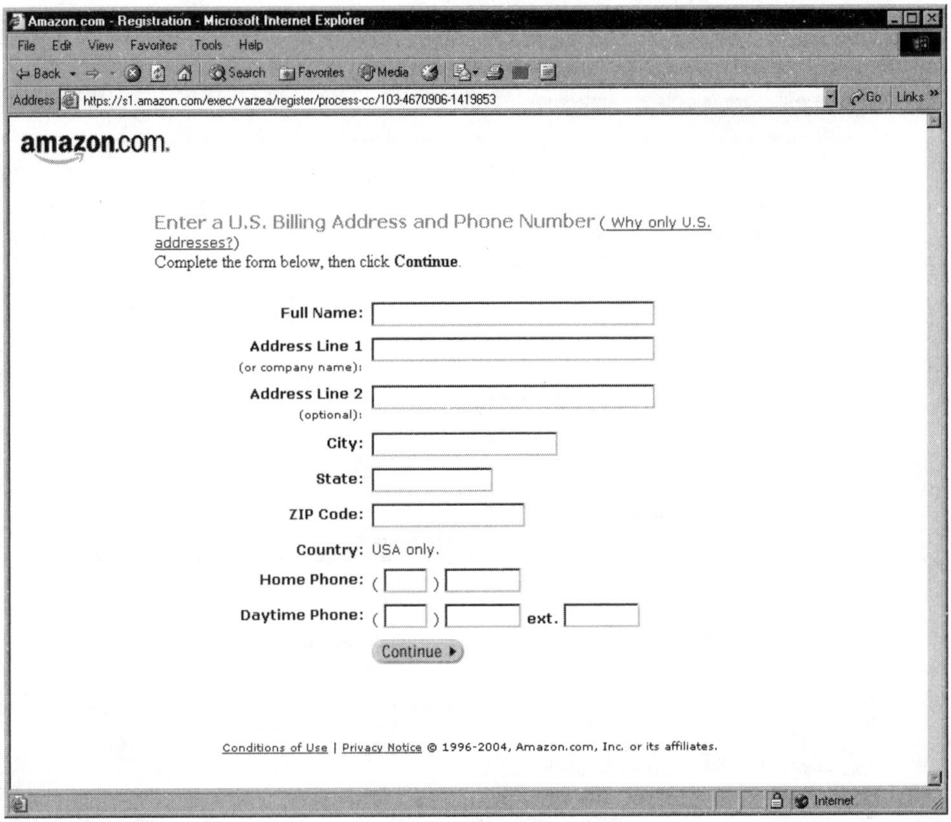

FIGURE 1-19   The Amazon Payments registration screen 2: the Billing Address

Be sure to check the box next to the line about the Participation Agreement to state that you agree with its terms, once you've had a chance to read it. Also, for our purposes, we're going to assume that you plan to file your checking account information now, so make sure the radio button is checked next to the option that says, "Enter my checking account information **now**." Once that's done, click Continue to move on.

At this point, you should get a sample check ready to enter all your checking account information. Remember, you can use either a personal or business checking account, but be sure to pick the account where you want the proceeds from your Amazon sales activity to end up. Amazon guides you through the process, as you

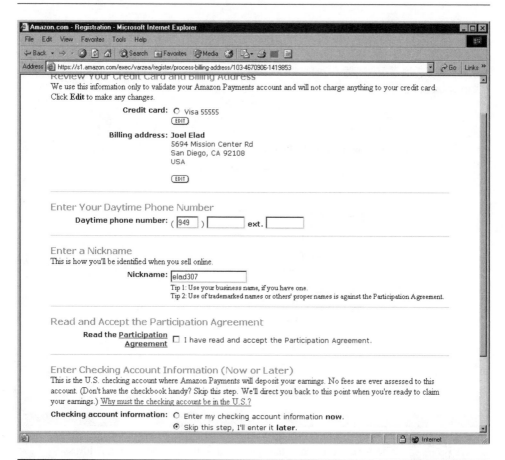

FIGURE 1-20 Amazon Payments registration screen 3: Nickname and Agree To Terms

can see in Figure 1-21, to find your Routing Transit Number (RTN; sometimes referred to as your ABA or Routing Number) and your Checking Account number. They'll also ask for all the numbers along the bottom of your check and the Name on the account. Once that's all filled in, click Continue to proceed.

TIP *Most financial institutions and credit card issuers offer some sort of liability protection when you use that information online. Check with your provider to find out exact terms, and go with the institution that gives you the best coverage or lowest liability.*

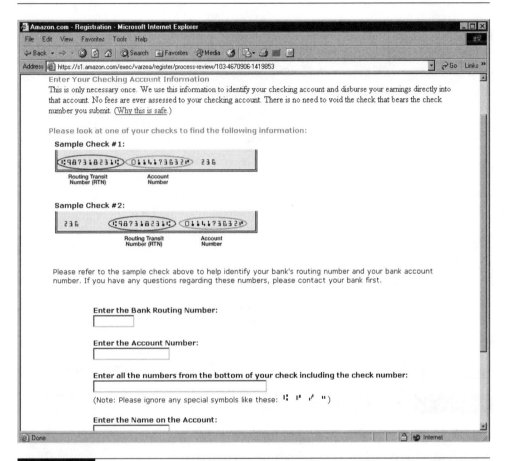

FIGURE 1-21   Amazon Payments registration screen 4

That's it! You should see a confirmation screen similar to that in Figure 1-22. You are now set up to receive your payments for any and all Marketplace, Auctions, and zShops sales that you make on Amazon. Remember that you can change this information at any time by following the links to edit your Amazon Payments information. It is recommended, however, that you do not change the information right before a scheduled transfer of funds, as the Automated Clearinghouse (ACH) transmission system that the banks use require a few days for transactions to fully post. The ACH system is simply the bank's way of moving the money securely, and to do this, they take the information they're given and don't accept most updates to protect your information and money.

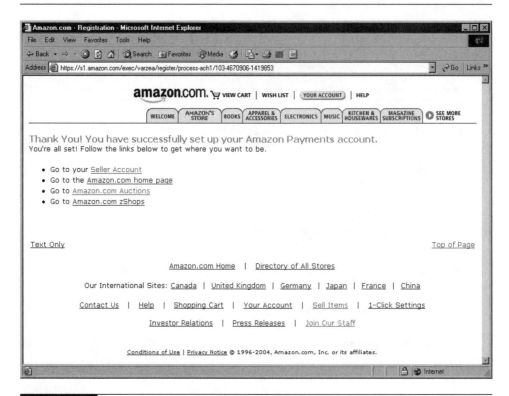

FIGURE 1-22   The Amazon Payments Confirmation screen

Getting Paid with Amazon Payments

As we mentioned earlier, any credit or funds in your Amazon Payments account will be automatically deposited into your checking account at the end of every two weeks. The only exception to this is that, if there is less than $1 in your account when that time occurs, the remaining balance is carried over onto the next statement.

Every payment period, Amazon Payments prepares a statement which details all the income you've made, minus any fees they've collected in regards to your sales, plus any additional seller fees and buyer refunds that you may have issued, and at the end displays a closing balance. One interesting feature of this statement is that you'll see the breakdown of income by area of sales, such as Marketplace, Auctions, and zShops. You'll get an e-mail similar to the statement shown in Figure 1-23, for example, that details your various sales activities and shows which venues are doing better than others. You can also log into your account and view statements for the

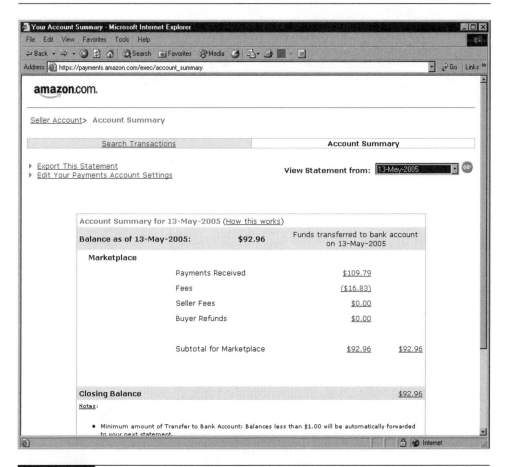

FIGURE 1-23   The Amazon Payments Statement screen

last four months as well, which will help you get a handle of the volume of business you're getting. Once we get into Part IV (Chapter 10 specifically), we'll talk about managing this business more carefully, but for right now, we're showing you this function so you can always have a top-level snapshot of your business.

To Sum Up

We've given you the basics of the site, pointed out the key areas and partners to watch for, and helped you get set up with the various accounts. Now it's time to dive into Chapter 2 and learn about all the great categories available on Amazon.com!

Chapter 2

Understand and Use Amazon's Categories

What we want to be is something completely new. There is no physical analog for what Amazon.com is becoming.

—Jeff Bezos, founder of Amazon.com

Coming from any other dot-com mogul, the preceding quote might be dismissed as mere puffery. Yet Bezos was truly on to something when he said that there was no "physical analog," or non-Internet counterpart for Amazon. Currently, there is no "brick-and-mortar" retailer or business that can be compared to how Amazon operates. This is especially true when it comes to infrastructure—Amazon is able to offer more products, in less space, than any other merchandizing arena in history. And yet, this overflowing and ever-expanding array of products and options for the consumer, organized into a dynamic, changing category structure means that it is critical to understand and use Amazon's web structure to your advantage.

Where to Find Everything

Amazon.com's main web page is an interesting contradiction. Why? Because although it has been lavished with praise, it has also by and large been passed over for awards for great web design. Without going into too much detail—though you can certainly read about it in the sidebar in the middle of the chapter—the reason is that Amazon.com realized early on that customers did not come to their site for the coolest, graphic-intensive, feature-heavy, eye-popping web design. Instead, web shoppers want the quickest, easiest way to find the product they want and, if it's at a reasonable price, purchase it.

NOTE   *One school of web surfing abides by the "three clicks" rule. That is, if it takes a user more than three clicks to locate a product or information, more and more people will "give up" and go elsewhere. While some people initially feel that this might be a slight overstatement, Amazon is a great example of the underlying philosophy: make it as simple as possible for the user while providing the greatest number of options. Their "one-click" checkout method is a patented concept, and a competitive advantage for Amazon.*

The Amazon.com home page breaks down into a few main areas that allow users to navigate through it depending on whether they wish to type in specifics, zoom to a featured item/category, or browse through lists to narrow the field. These areas, which are called out in Figure 2-1, include:

- ■ **The Top Navigation Bar**   This is where you'll find the clickable tabs that allow you to access the major categories. This is also where you'll find the four shopping tools (Your Account, Cart, Wish List, and Help).

- ■ **The Subnavigation Bar**   The colored bar immediately beneath the tabs is where you can jump to areas such as Top Sellers and New Releases. It also houses the Search field.

- ■ **Center and Right Sections**   The center and right-hand side of the screen are typically reserved for special deals and featured categories Amazon.com decides to offer. These normally change on the basis of an especially hot commodity (say the release of a new Harry Potter book) or a seasonal need

The Subnavigation bar   The Top Navigation bar   Center and Right sections

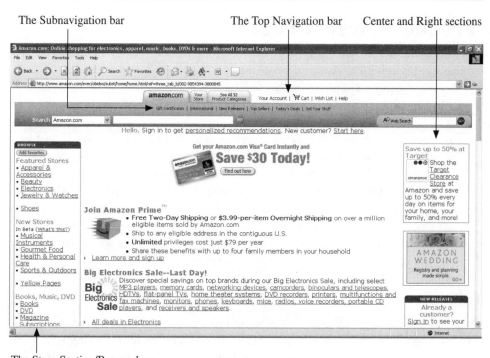

The Store Section/Browse box

FIGURE 2-1   Amazon's main web page, with subsections called out

(back-to-school supplies in August and September). These sections can give prospective sellers an up-to-date, immediate idea of what Amazon is promoting, which they can then use as "insider industry knowledge" when deciding what to sell on Amazon.

- ■ **The Store Section/Browse Box**   The important, left side of the screen is allocated to Amazon's many stores. The topmost section is where you'll find Featured Stores, which again might be stocked with the same hot products or seasonal goods as promoted in the center section of the home-page display.

The remaining sections list New Stores, commodity categories, Featured Partners, and links where budding new merchants (that's you) can learn how to join the Amazon.com family and make money. If you enter a subcategory of Amazon.com searching for, say, electronics or apparel, this store listing will change into a Browse box that more closely matches what you may be searching for.

The Product Category Page

In a sense, the Product Category page can be thought of as the "launch pad" for navigating through all of Amazon's categories.

To view the page, simply click the See All Product Categories tab, like that shown in Figure 2-2.

NOTE   *Amazon.com used to list their categories across the top in several tabs, such as Books, DVDs, Music. However, as Amazon's reach has continued to grow and prosper, this became too cumbersome and confusing to the site's visitors. As of this writing, the tab actually reads See All 32 Product Categories. Doubtless, that number will increase over the next few months. Because Amazon is constantly analyzing and improving their site due to customer interaction, orders, and feedback, expect to see more changes and more ways Amazon can benefit all their users.*

Tabs

Once you decide which category you want to browse, just click any of the categories displayed on the product category page. The category chosen for browsing will appear as a tab at the top of the screen, as in Figure 2-3. As can be seen from the name of the tab, in this figure it's the Sports & Outdoors product category.

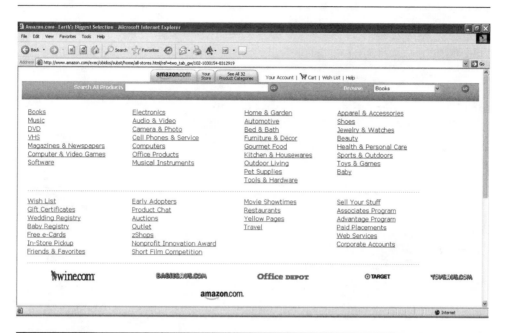

FIGURE 2-2   The All Product Categories tab

FIGURE 2-3   The sample product category page: Sports & Outdoors

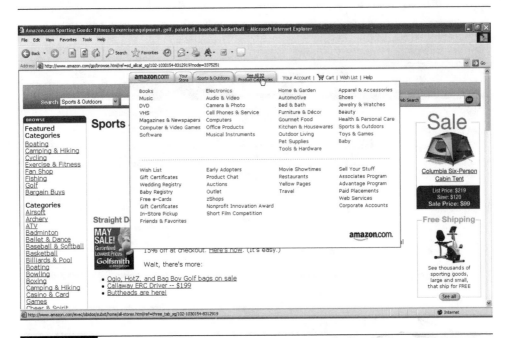

FIGURE 2-4   The See All Product Categories pop-over window

To return to the product category page, you don't have to click the "Back" button on their browser, or start back at the Amazon.com home page. One of Amazon's wonderful navigational shortcuts works as follows: just move your mouse pointer over the See All Product Categories tab, and all the categories will appear as a pop-over window, as shown in Figure 2-4.

Subnavigation

Each category has its own unique subnavigation area, which are the menus of options that appear below the tabs. For example, in the Sports & Outdoors area shown in Figure 2-3, the subnavigation choices are specific to what you would expect to find interesting in this category of goods: apparel, camping & hiking, exercise & fitness, fan shop, footwear, golf, paintball, and treadmills.

Compare this to Figure 2-5. Notice that in the Baby category, the subnavigation bar includes Baby Registry, Browse Categories, Browse Brands, Gift Ideas, Resource Center, Baby Outlet, and a special link to the Amazon.com partner, BabiesRus.com.

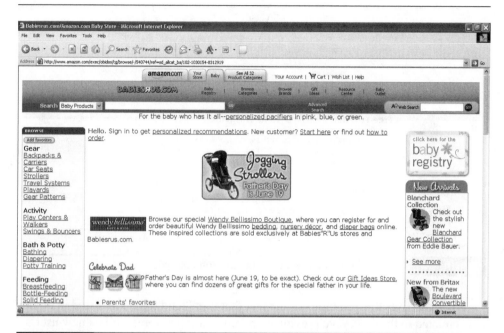

FIGURE 2-5   A different example of a product category. Notice the differences in the subnavigation area compared to Figure 2-3.

As you can see, not all subnavigation choices are the same. In the previous two examples, there were a different number of choices in the Sports & Outdoors submenu than in the Baby submenu. Depending on which category your company's merchandise falls into, you should "drill down" into the subcategories to see how many clicks it would take to get to your product line.

Why do we recommend doing this kind of research? Remember, if it takes more than three clicks for the user to get to your product, they may not complete the process. Therefore, learning the subnavigation structure will help you pick the products most accessible to your buyers. This is one of the first steps to optimizing your inventory to making that fortune!

The Center and Right Sections

The center and right-hand side columns highlight main items for sale. It's true that this is reserved for specific promotions or to bring attention to certain features and programs which users find popular. However, yet another testament to Amazon.com's customer-centric design is evident once the user has purchased something from Amazon.com: the user's home page changes to reflect their purchase.

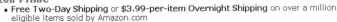

Join Amazon Prime™
- Free Two-Day Shipping or $3.99-per-item Overnight Shipping on over a million eligible items sold by Amazon.com
- Ship to any eligible address in the contiguous U.S.
- Unlimited privileges cost just $79 per year
- Share these benefits with up to four family members in your household

▸ Learn more and sign up

Big Electronics Sale--Last Day!

Discover special savings on top brands during our Big Electronics Sale, including select MP3 players, memory cards, networking devices, camcorders, binoculars and telescopes, HDTVs, flat-panel TVs, home theater systems, DVD recorders, printers, multifunctions and fax machines, monitors, phones, keyboards, mice, radios, voice recorders, portable CD players, and receivers and speakers.

FIGURE 2-6   A new user's center and right Amazon.com page sections

---

Amazon bases this principle on the fact that users tend to be interested in buying items related to those they've previously purchased. Therefore, while a new user's Amazon.com home page might look like Figure 2-6, a user who purchased, say, books on business and biology might get specific recommendations and offers on their home page, such as in Figure 2-7.

YOU

Amazon.com
If there ever was a pair of docs who can make the small intestine seem truly intriguing, here they are. Dr. Mehmet Oz is an alternative-medicine... Read more
(Rate this item) More top sellers

Join Amazon Prime™

- Free Two-Day Shipping or $3.99-per-item Overnight Shipping on over a million eligible items sold by Amazon.com
- Ship to any eligible address in the contiguous U.S.
- Unlimited privileges cost just $79 per year
- Share these benefits with up to four family members in your household

▸ Learn more and sign up

Lions Don't Need to Roar

From Publishers Weekly
As in society at large, reflecting the priority of packaging over content or performance, the emphasis of this guide to business success by Benton,... Read more
(♀Recommended: Why?)

FIGURE 2-7   A user with purchasing history. Notice the specific product and shipping recommendations.

Learning from the Pros: How Amazon.com Does Web Design Right—and What You Can Learn for Free

Amazon.com has probably spent more time researching the best way to design a web site than anyone in the e-commerce business. This is, in part, a result of the data gathering techniques noted in Chapter 1, which go down to the level of tracking what your mouse pointer lingers on. In addition, Amazon's very survival depended on an easy-to-use web site since the Internet was their only access to customers due to the fact that they have no physical presence, or "brick-and-mortar" store, to attract customers. Therefore, since they focused on e-commerce more than community-building functions, they strove to make e-commerce the centerpiece of the site, which all other functions revolved around and supported.

Why should you be interested in this information? Well, first because once you feel ready to link up with Amazon.com, you'll most likely want to have a web site of your own that offers the same high quality where you can sell your goods to returning customers directly—without paying a fee for each sale, as you must through Amazon. Second, you can make use of the considerable man-hours and money Amazon has spent on research and development in responding to customers and their shopping patterns. And third, you can avoid the kind of site "overdesign" that's usually foisted on a company by an overenthusiastic web guru simply by following a few tips culled from Amazon's site when designing your own company's e-commerce web site, such as those in the following:

■ Amazon doesn't use memory- and graphics-intensive features like Macromedia's Flash, which allows people to see animation clips when they arrive at a web site The consumer's ability to view and buy from your site should not be influenced by whether they have the latest software for their Internet browser, like a Flash plug-in.

■ Amazon doesn't use sophisticated encoding languages like DHTML to build their web pages. Amazon.com considers them too unreliable to use because not everyone's computers can translate the sophisticated languages properly, and it can cause certain computers to malfunction when being viewed on a web page.

(continued)

■ Amazon doesn't design links so that clicking them opens a new window, like the many pop-up ads you see today. Instead, it replaces your previous page with the web page you've selected, keeping you focused and not forcing you to keep track of multiple Internet browser windows.

■ Amazon doesn't use pictures that dance and sing to you on the screen, like animated GIFs. These increase the load time of the page and are extremely distracting when it comes to buyers making purchases.

■ Amazon doesn't use a splash page to introduce their site. Splash pages, which open up and give a little presentation to introduce someone to your site, are little more than exercises in company vanity.

The Browse Box

Finally, the box on the left side of the screen will offer the next level of subcategories, based on where the user is browsing. Just as with the center and right sections of the page, this area updates itself as you're browsing to help you drill down to specific subcategories.

The Browse box is similar to the subnavigation bar, because for both features your options are independent of whether you've shopped on Amazon. By contrast, the center and right sections of the screen change based on your purchases, to help guide you to your next potential purchase. The combination of features like the Browse box and the site's forever-updating sections allows Amazon.com to create a store that revolves around the user while giving them a familiar and constant structure for shopping.

Types of Categories on Amazon

As mentioned earlier, Amazon has established 32 different categories of merchandise (as of this writing), which they offer to their consumers. Amazon has used a variety of strategies to arrive at this current configuration, and it's important for you to understand the main types of product categories and the specific rules associated with each. Understand that the term "categories" here isn't about the difference between books and CDs but, rather, whether Amazon relies on its own warehoused inventory, a collection of merchants' inventory, or a single dominant partner, to power its deep selection in the category.

NOTE

Remember, regardless of the number of categories, Amazon can carry a virtually unlimited number of items within each, due to their strategy of combining inventory from various merchants and their own warehouses. Even if there is no specific category, an item may be stored in a related category.

"Amazon-Owned" Categories: Books, Movies, and Music

Despite all the categories Amazon hosts today, the site is primarily regarded as the biggest online bookstore on Earth, boasting "Earth's Greatest Selection." Books make an excellent product for online sales. They are pretty much uniform, based on their ISBN number (the same book you buy online is the same book you can find in a bookstore), and aren't as heavy as, say, large appliances, pet food, and other goods that weigh hundreds of pounds, so they're easy and inexpensive to ship anywhere. Plus, books typically aren't considered a major purchase, so customers feel more comfortable buying and paying for them online. Amazon uses all their information technology and data-gathering techniques to guide customers to the book (or books) of their choice, and offer tons of recommendations for that customer to try other similar or interesting books. Amazon has used this base and strategy to expand into similar categories, such as DVDs, music CDs, and videos.

One of the biggest distinctions of what we like to call the "Amazon-owned" categories is that, here, you are actually competing against Amazon itself. They still maintain distribution centers across the U.S. (and the world, for that matter) and buy and sell new books, DVDs, music CDs, and videocassettes. Customers who shop these categories will always be offered the "Amazon" new copy first, but they are also immediately presented with the option to peruse other new, used, or collectible items concurrently offered by sellers such as you. In this way, customers can immediately perform a price and merchant comparison and see the potential of price savings from picking this option!

Your power lies in the fact that books are usually the same regardless of where they're purchased. The book that sits on a bookshelf in Barnes & Noble is the exact same book that someone can order from Amazon.com, and by extension, the book they can order from you. Customers don't have to worry about the specific variety or look and feel, they just want to open their package and get their item. They don't care whose warehouse shelf it was retrieved from, as long as it's the book they ordered. As far as they're concerned, in most cases, "a book is a book is a book." (Of course, this does not apply to collectible, first edition, or signed books.)

Their main concern is price, followed up by condition. If you can provide a competitive price and a consistent condition of the item, you get to piggyback on the complex and intelligent design of Amazon, for a modest fee.

The key here is to focus on a good price (which we'll discuss more in the next chapter) and to advertise the correct condition and version of the item, so there are no surprises when the buyer opens their package. Because their profit margin may be less in these categories than in others, most sellers compensate by going after volume. Whether you maintain a deep selection of the hottest sellers or a broad selection (the "long tail" we discussed earlier) of less popular but higher-margin goods will depend on your individual situation.

There are also specific rules based on the condition and numbers of your item:

- ■ **Used** If your item is used, Amazon dictates that you MUST set your price at or below the price Amazon offers for the new product, even if Amazon is currently out of stock of the new item.

- ■ **New** If your item is brand new (still shrink-wrapped, no marks or blemishes, unread, and so on), then Amazon states for these types of categories (books, DVDs, cassettes, CDs) the price you set must also be at or below the Amazon price for a new item.

- ■ **Collectible** If your item has a special quality that makes it collectible (for example, you have a first-edition book or the item is signed), then Amazon states you must price your item *above* the list price for that item.

- ■ **Multiple Items** If you have multiple copies of the same item, *in the same condition*, you must create only one listing stating the quantity. If, however, you have copies of the same item, each in a different condition, you must create a separate listing for each item.

NOTE *Amazon recommends no more than five different product listings for any given product. They don't want potential customers to be confused when shopping with a given seller.*

"Collection of Merchants": Electronics, Software, and More

Books, DVDs, and music are great "commodity" items to sell, but if you're looking for something with a higher average selling price and better margin, Amazon has got you covered.

They've expanded their category selection to include lots of great items, from Consumer Electronics, Computers and Software, to Video Games, Home and Garden, and Apparel & Accessories. Most of these categories were built on what we like to call a "collection of merchants." Amazon partners with several large featured merchants, and in some cases, they buy up inventory and resell it directly under their banner, like they do with books, movies, and music. They have recently opened up the field in most of these categories to allow any seller to sell their item along with both themselves and the featured merchants.

Becoming a featured merchant certainly gains you several advantages. First and foremost, a featured merchant's items can (and usually are) featured in the main part of the category home page. Second, when customers are clicking around to see all the Used and New Marketplace copies of an item, featured merchants will always appear at the top of the page. For example, Figure 2-8 shows what happens if a customer wants to buy the new Star Wars: Revenge of the Sith video game for the X-box. When the customer clicks the Used And New link, they're brought to

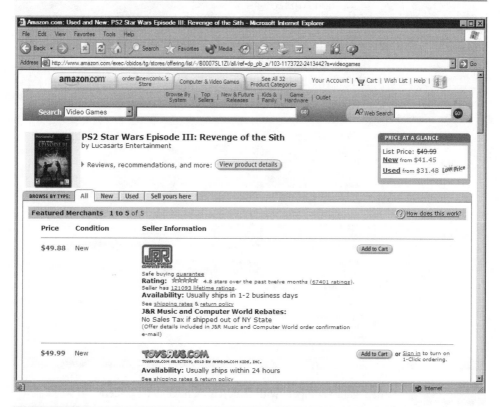

FIGURE 2-8   Featured merchants get the top spots in certain categories.

a screen where the first five items listed are those offered by featured merchants. The interesting thing to note here is that, while Toysrus.com has an exclusive partnership agreement in the Toys & Games category, it only peripherally includes this video game (which is why they are #2 on this list and not in the top spot) because they are slightly more expensive than the top featured merchant.

However, the "little guy" is not down and out in this system. Typically, small- to medium-sized sellers can compete when it comes to one very effective component—price! The featured merchants are typically locked into selling their items at the "Amazon-approved" price, which is usually retail or something close to it. Non-featured merchants, however, can place their items in the Marketplace and sell it for any price less than retail that they can accept. Using the same example of the Star Wars: Revenge of the Sith game for the X-box, Figure 2-9 shows that Amazon sellers are selling it for up to 40 percent off the retail price, or $29.57.

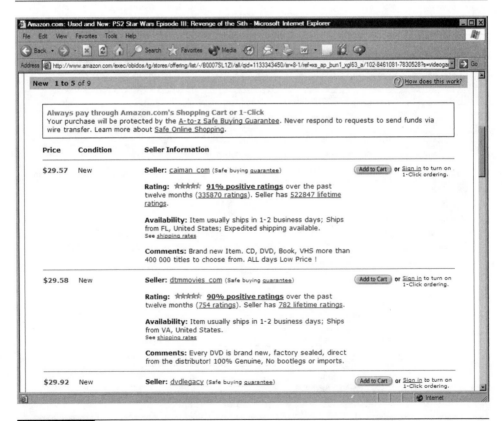

FIGURE 2-9 Sellers get to compete with featured merchants on price.

With the volume of customers that come through Amazon looking to buy their game and move on, regular sellers can pick up an amount of that traffic and still benefit from things like the Amazon "one-click" easy checkout system.

Other rules the seller should be aware of in categories such as this are those regarding pricing. Amazon does allow you to sell refurbished items at or below Amazon's listed price for a given item. Also, Amazon does allow flexibility in how you price new Computer & Video Games items. However, you are only allowed to list those items when Amazon is currently out of stock on the same item. Once Amazon gets a new shipment of items for a given product, they will keep your inventory listings until they have expired, and not allow you to add new listings while Amazon is in stock of the item.

When it comes to selling your items in the Marketplace in general, the current list of participating Amazon stores/categories besides the "Amazon-owned" categories discussed previously are

- Computer & Video Games

- Computers

- Software

- Electronics

- Office Products

- Tools & Hardware

- Camera & Photo

- Kitchen & Housewares

- Outdoor Living

- Sports & Outdoors

- Musical Instruments

- Cell Phones & Service

- Everything Else

However, because of fraud concerns with large electronics purchases, Amazon has recently updated the rules for selling on a few of its categories. As of May 2005, Amazon must pre-approve the seller for any Marketplace sales in the Computers and Cell Phones & Service categories. Additionally, the seller must be pre-approved to sell the "top listed products" in the Electronics, Software, and Computer & Video Games categories as well. All sellers can continue to sell other Marketplace items in those three categories, but Amazon must pre-approve you before you can sell the top items. We advise you to check with Amazon to see if they've updated this policy. Unfortunately, there is currently no application process to get pre-approved. Amazon will notify you if they feel you are eligible, after reviewing such criteria as your length of sales with Amazon, feedback record, and returns/refund rates.

> **TIP**
>
> *If you're interested in getting pre-approved, the best thing you can do, according to other Amazon sellers, is to sustain a lot of positive transactions in other categories, earning enough sales and positive customer feedback to show Amazon you're a professional and responsible seller.*

> **NOTE**
>
> *While you cannot sell these items in the Marketplace if you're not a pre-approved seller, you can still sell most of these items through a zShop or Auction listing.*

"One Merchant" Categories: Toys, Baby, and More

As Amazon ramped up their product selection, they also began discussing partnership options with key merchants, coming up with beneficial partnerships that helped both sides. One notable example of this is Toys R Us. As the big toy retailer began suffering drops in revenue and customers, they embarked on an ambitious online strategy, which failed miserably during the key holiday shopping season of 1999. They decided to turn to Amazon to help them reach and service the online customer. Amazon got the opportunity to virtually "stock" and carry millions of different units of toys and related products, while Toys R Us gained a reputable partner to handle e-commerce ordering, customer service, and distribution.

The result was that Toys R Us and their baby store, Babies R Us, now provide the largest portion of inventory in the Toys & Babies categories at Amazon.com. Now, when someone on Amazon orders a toy, that order will be filled by Toys R Us and the customer has the option of picking it up at their local Toys R Us store or having it shipped to their house. As you can see in Figure 2-10, the subnavigation bar for the Toys & Games category is branded by Toys R Us, and their targeted ads appear beneath that. The title of the page is not the "Amazon Toy Store," but actually, "Toysrus.com/Amazon.com Toy Store."

What does this mean to you? It means that most of the items in that category are currently off limits to newer sellers, which means new sellers cannot offer competing units of the items Toys R Us offers through their Amazon co-branded site.

FIGURE 2-10   The Toys R Us Branded toy store at Amazon

You are no longer competing with Amazon, but their targeted merchant. That does *not* mean you are out of opportunities. First off, certain peripheral categories have been opened up, like Video Games. If you remember our example from Figures 2-10 and 2-11, the Star Wars: Revenge of the Sith game for the X-box is categorized in two different places: Toys & Games and Computer & Video Games. Because Computer & Video Games is not a single merchant-powered category, Amazon has allowed other sellers to offer new and used copies. The key here is to check the items you have to sell and see how they're categorized by Amazon, and if other sellers can sell those items.

While some categories may be currently limited to sellers, another big opportunity for other sellers comes with categories that evolve and expand. Office Depot has been, and continues to be, a big partner with Amazon. At one point, the Office Supplies category was single-handedly powered by Office Depot, branded as the Toys & Babies categories are today. Today, however, Office Depot no longer controls this category. When you go to the Office Products category, shown in Figure 2-11, you see an unbranded category, where items such as the HP Photosmart 8750 printer (shown as a featured item) are sold not only by Office Depot, but by other sellers as well. However, click the Office Depot box in the top-right corner of that page and you're taken to the Office Depot branded store, as shown in Figure 2-12, which offers their full range of products and lets customers pick up their purchases at a local Office Depot store.

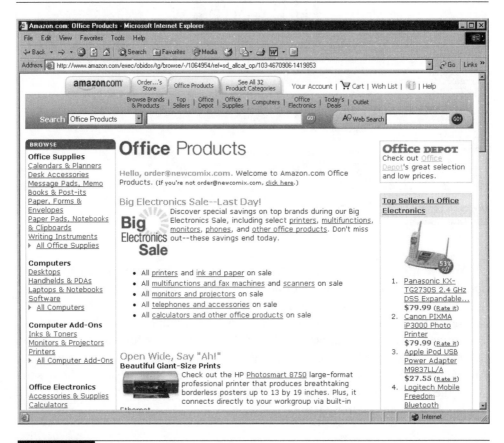

FIGURE 2-11   Amazon's Office Products category

FIGURE 2-12   The Office Depot branded store within Amazon

Beta Categories

Of course, Amazon didn't grow by sticking to these three previously discussed types of categories. As they've seen opportunities to expand their selection, they've tested the waters by introducing a beta category while they figure out what the best method is to service their customers. As an example, as of the writing of this book, Amazon is beta testing four new categories: Gourmet Food, Health & Personal Care, Musical Instruments, and Sports & Outdoors. They take special care to mark these categories as beta categories and offer an explanation to consumers as to what that means.

NOTE   *Beta is a term that indicates advance. In this case, a beta category is something being offered in a test mode, in advance of the official launch.*

They also apply some of their inherent advantages to introduce their users to these new categories. One method uses some of Amazon's most valuable real estate—the Browse box on the left side of their web page. Figure 2-13 shows a typical Amazon home page, but note in the Browse box, Amazon has grouped the New Stores together, right under Featured Stores, to bring attention and (hopefully) customer traffic to their fledgling categories. Amazon will also employ special graphics and feature boxes to bring their customer's attention to any relevant cross-traffic Amazon can generate while customers browse their site. This cross-traffic generation allows Amazon to grow new categories, which can benefit sellers by opening up new categories where they can sell as well.

Listing of new stores

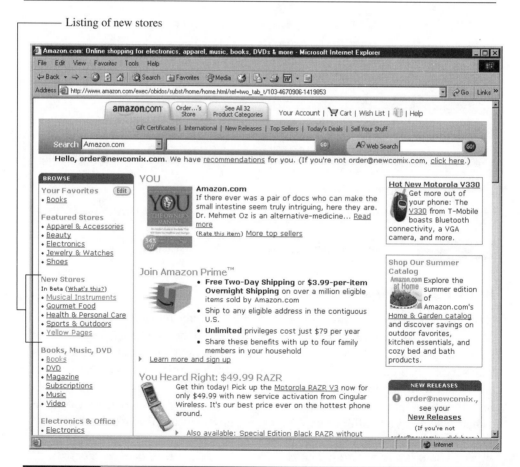

FIGURE 2-13   Amazon's new stores get prime placement on their home page.

Amazon Expands into Jewelry

A short while back, Amazon decided to beta test a Jewelry & Watches category. Their response was so good that they decided to make it a full-fledged category. Founder Jeff Bezos wrote an open letter to the community explaining why Amazon decided to open this new category. The following is taken from their web site:

Dear Amazon.com Customers,

During the beta test of our new Jewelry store more than 100,000 customers ordered jewelry at Amazon.com, and we are now officially opening the store with a commitment to offer low prices on high-quality jewelry.

Traditionally, jewelry markups are high. Typical jewelers purchase a piece for $500, and depending on how hard you negotiate, sell it to you for $800 to $1000—a markup of 60 percent to 100 percent (there is even a term for doubling: it's called "keystoning"). At Amazon.com, the costs of buying, handling, and shipping a piece of jewelry aren't much higher than those of selling a book, so we can pass significant savings on to our customers.

Our typical markup in diamond jewelry is less than 15 percent of our product cost, and significantly less for more expensive diamonds. A diamond for which we pay $500 therefore costs you $575. We provide the industry standard grading information you need to compare with other stores and verify prices in a no-sales-pressure environment. For example, check the specifications on our selection of diamond engagement rings or on our bestselling pair of diamond stud earrings.

We've also invited a select group of third-party jewelers to offer their products for sale on Amazon.com. They provide greater selection than we could offer on our own, ranging from inexpensive, fun fashion jewelry to expensive one-of-a-kind designer pieces.

We are working to create the best possible jewelry shopping experience with the lowest possible prices, and we hope you enjoy the new store. Thank you for being a customer.

On behalf of Amazon.com,

Jeff Bezos

Founder and CEO

How Beta Categories Are Introduced

There are several ways that new categories get introduced on Amazon. Sometimes, they get a prime opportunity with a key vendor to offer a product that would be suitable and interesting to the Amazon customer base. Other times, they sense a need for their customers and find a way to fill that need. In still other cases, like the Segway Human Transport store, they simply find a cool product they want to carry.

Amazon will communicate their ideas for new categories in different avenues. Besides features on their home pages and selected pages, they will usually post announcements on their different message boards, to give their customers and sellers a heads-up and gather feedback on these decisions. They occasionally use devices like targeted e-mails and the very occasional pop-up window to bring attention to new efforts they are undertaking. They understand that their communication with the customer needs to be efficient, discreet, non-invasive, and relevant to their activities. Their decision to launch new categories is the result of meeting these high customer-centric standards. Amazon supports these decisions by using featured advertising on key real estate on their web pages to communicate new categories, which allows observant sellers like yourself to pay attention and be ready to capitalize on these new opportunities.

Selling in a Beta Category

Since Amazon carefully plans any new category they add to their catalog, and gives that new category a lot of promotional push, it's important that you as a seller be able to capitalize on that attention and push and enter any relevant products as soon as possible to profit from that customer traffic.

The best part is that Amazon will typically ask for their sellers to participate and add to their category, since that's their overall strategy. Let's go to the Gourmet Food section. If you scroll down to the bottom of the page, you should see a box asking people to "Join Our Store!"

When you see an opportunity like this, click the link titled Send Us Your Comments. You'll be taken to a comment form like the one shown in Figure 2-14. This form allows you to identify the products you'd like to contribute to Amazon's catalog, along with the opportunity to identify yourself as the seller and/or manufacturer of that item. Amazon reviews all these entries and will usually extend an invitation to qualified sellers to add the item to their catalog, as long as it is not illegal to sell and not previously included in their catalog.

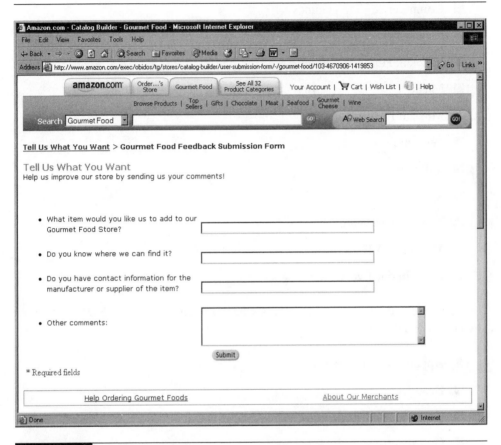

FIGURE 2-14   Tell Amazon what you want to add to their new category.

Not in Any Category? Create Your Own

If you just can't find your item in the Amazon catalog, it's time to create a product detail page for that item. Here, we'll talk about determining if this needs to be done, and the steps to take in creating this product detail page.

What Items Can I (or Can't I) Sell?

The following are the list of categories where you can create your own product detail page:

- ■ Books
- ■ Camera & Photo

- Computer & Video Games
- Electronics
- Kitchen, Home & Garden
- Music
- Musical Instruments
- Pet Supplies
- Software
- Sporting Goods
- Tools & Hardware
- Video & DVD
- Items in our Everything Else store

Conversely, the following are stores where you currently CANNOT create your own product detail page:

- Apparel & Accessories
- Beauty
- Cell Phones & Service
- Gourmet Food
- Health & Personal Care
- Jewelry & Watches
- Magazines
- Office Products

| TIP | *It's important to check with Amazon to see if this list has changed. The easiest way to find out is to go to their Help page, and under Search Our Help Department, type* **Create a Product Detail Page Product Restrictions**. |

Recall that there are some categories, such as Electronics and Toys & Babies products, where your listing options are limited. If you have an item for sale that is currently *not* being sold by Toys R Us or Babies R Us, for example, you are allowed to add your product detail page beside their catalog listing. This is different from adding your item to a page where they are just Out of Stock. At a later date, you may be able to sell items they currently stock, alongside their offerings, just like most of the other categories on Amazon. You can always keep track of new changes by searching Amazon's help pages for information about Creating A Product Detail Page.

Creating Your Product Detail Page

Once you've identified that your product is in an eligible store, and isn't present in the Amazon catalog currently, you're ready to create your own Product Detail page. In short, it involves a five-step process:

1. Classify your product.

2. Add detail to your page.

3. Preview the page.

4. Create the page.

5. Sell your item on that page.

When you're ready to add your page, go to the link using this process:

a. Type in the following link:

http://s1.amazon.com/exec/varzea/sdp/sai-identify/

b. Go to the Help section, and under Search Our Help Department, type

Create a Product Detail Page

Click the first link, scroll down the page to the section Creating A Page, and click the Click Here To Get Started link.

NOTE

In order to add your own Product Detail page, you need to have a Pro Merchant Subscription, which we cover in greater detail in Chapter 6. This subscription, at $40 per month, is useful for anyone planning to sell a medium to large quantity of items on Amazon on a regular basis.

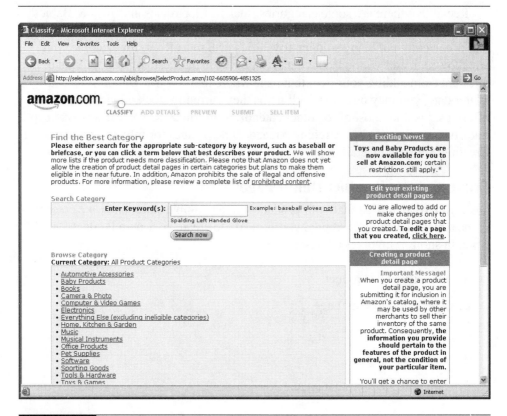

FIGURE 2-15 Classifying your new product

In Step 1, you'll use the links provided on the web page, as shown in Figure 2-15, to help classify and determine where to place your product. Once that's been determined, pick the appropriate store and go to Step 2.

Based on the product type you determined in Step 1, Amazon will know what pieces of information to ask you for in the second step of this process. Expect to see a series of screens asking for details on your new product, as shown in Figure 2-16. This can range from the Product Name, Manufacturer, and Brand Name, to the Description, Serial Number, Color, Weight, and other determining factors. Also, you will be asked to provide a picture of this item for the Detail Page. Given the visual nature of e-commerce shopping, it's absolutely crucial you have a photo of your item available. If you're representing a manufacturer, consult with them to help get this photo, but only use that photo if it accurately reflects the condition of the items you'll be selling for that manufacturer.

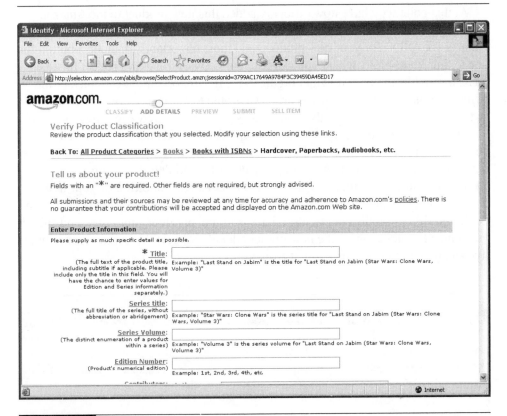

FIGURE 2-16   Adding information to your product detail page

This is especially true for items that are sold new, shrink-wrapped in their original box. Once you've entered all the details asked for, click Continue to move to Step 3.

At this point, Amazon has collected all the information for this new product and, as the third step, is presenting you with a preview of the detail page it's about to create for the product. It's important to look over the entire page and make sure all the information is correct. Remember, once this product is listed on Amazon, other people will be able to sell the same product alongside yours. Also, if you're going to the trouble of creating this product detail page, you want it to be a compelling page that will urge customers to buy one, and by association, your copy or version of this product. Use the other pages as a guide for the type of information Amazon customers are looking for in a product. Once you've determined that the preview represents the page you want to create, click Submit to move to the fourth step.

At this point, you have now officially added this new product to the Amazon catalog. The confirmation screen will point out the Amazon Standard Identification Number (or ASIN) for your new product, and most importantly, include a button for you to Sell Yours Here, where you can list your copy of this new product for sale on Amazon, like the one shown in Figure 2-17. It's important to keep track of the ASIN for this new product, so you are always able to automatically list new copies of this item when your currently listed copies get purchased by eager buyers.

In the fifth and final step, you will complete the fields necessary to sell your copy or version of this new product to Amazon customers. We will go into greater detail in Chapter 4 about how to properly describe and detail your item for sale, but for now, just know that you'll be asked to enter the condition of your item, any pertinent comments about it, and the price you want to sell it for on Amazon. Once you fill out all the data fields, click Continue, preview your entry, and submit your entry for inclusion on the new product detail page. At this point, your item is live and people can start ordering it from you.

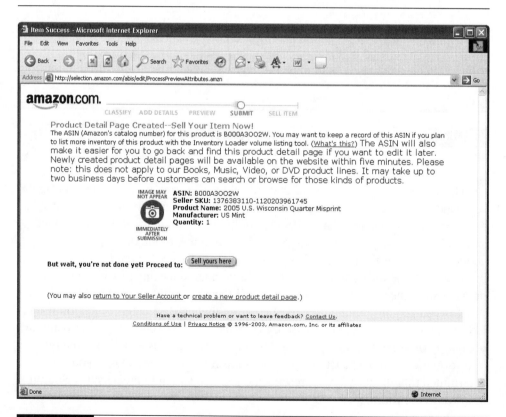

FIGURE 2-17 Your new product detail page has been created!

The "A to Z Guarantee Protection" Plan

One of the biggest barriers to e-commerce has been the issue of trust. Consumers are being asked to buy something without being able to hold it, touch it, "kick the tires," or try it on. They're being asked to transmit sensitive financial information over the Internet and wait for a shipping company to eventually bring their new purchase to them. Thankfully, all the companies involved have been working overtime to reduce these barriers and concerns, which improves the overall shopping experience. Likewise, credit card companies like Visa and MasterCard have introduced extensive fraud and liability protection programs, software makers have introduced Secure Socket Layer technology to protect your financial information, while shippers such as UPS and the Post Office have added tracking technology to allow customers to see the progress of their item.

Amazon is also leading the good fight to protect their customers and ensure a safe and happy shopping experience. One way they do this is by offering the "A to Z Guarantee Protection" plan. In essence, this plan works as follows: If a consumer buys something worth $2,500 or less, and either the product does not arrive, or the product is "materially different" than what the customer was expecting, then the customer gets a full refund. No deductible is taken, and the limit is quite high given the average purchase price at Amazon.

NOTE   *This protection does not extend to featured merchants who operate on Amazon, such as Babiesrus.com, Borders.com, eBags, Eddie Bauer, eLuxury, Imaginarium.com, Marshall Fields, Mervyns, Newport News, Nordstrom, Spiegel, Target, Toysrus.com, Ultimate Outlet Brands (or Spiegel Clearance), Virginmega.com, Waldenbooks.com, and Warehouse Deals.*

This Guarantee plan covers you as a seller as well, because Amazon extends this guarantee to also include your customers. We'll discuss how this benefit impacts you as a Marketplace seller, specifically, in Chapter 4. Just understand that this is another program that Amazon institutes to help bring customers to your items.

To Sum Up

We've walked through the basic structure of the web site, shown you how to access the various features and categories there, and explained the types of categories and how featured merchants and Amazon itself will affect your selling in these categories. Now it's time to discuss listing and pricing strategies for selling on Amazon!

Chapter 3

Develop Listing and Pricing Strategies to Beat the Competition

There are two kinds of companies, those that work to try to charge more and those that work to charge less. We will be the second.

—Jeff Bezos, founder of Amazon.com

Odd as it may seem, many prospective Amazon.com businesses never follow the e-commerce adage *"think before you list."* There is a great deal of value in doing your homework to get better returns on the items you plan to showcase. Once you've identified what you want to sell on Amazon, your next step should be to accurately gauge what you think the product will sell for.

It's important to do research to set your expectations correctly. Otherwise, you could end up wasting time and Amazon fees on items that won't sell, or cut into your profit margin by pricing items too cheaply. A little research will also help you set your overall pricing strategy, decide if you want to utilize Amazon's auctions to sell your items, and estimate how much page space you should spend on describing the item.

Thankfully, one of the best avenues for determining acceptable prices is right in front of you: Amazon itself. With the millions of items for sale every day on Amazon, the site is constantly adding incredible amounts of valuable data. By searching through what Amazon.com has available online, you can quickly determine what many given products will sell for, based on the type of item, its general availability, and its particular characteristics.

Know Your Product

At first glance, the idea of "knowing your product" might seem too simplistic. After all, who else knows your product better than you? Well, the answer might surprise you, particularly if you're used to thinking in terms of product lines or extensions. In reality, relatively minor things about your product—its condition (new or pre-owned), collectibility (limited edition or mass market), and even its packaging can increase—or decrease—your chosen price.

Start by checking to see if your product—or your type of product—is widely available on Amazon already. Compare their listed products with your items. Determine if your product can compete on price, features, or even distinguishing characteristics—does your magazine have the same cover artwork, or does your laser printer allow for extra shades of blues compared to what is listed?

An Example of Collectibility

Collectible items go far beyond baseball cards or children's toys. In fact, even relatively mundane items can have a special "limited edition" quality to them which buyers will pay extra for. Amazon.com allows you to showcase these special items with minimal difficulty.

For an easy-to-understand example of how this can affect your bottom line, let's look at Amazon's core market: books. Of course, at first glance it might be inconceivable that a bookstore or publisher can compete with Amazon, particularly on price or availability. However, Amazon's book listings now provide a link to two other types of books: new and used editions.

What isn't as apparent is that there are actually *three* types of product that can be listed: new, used, and *collectible*. For example, in Figure 3-1, the listings are for a book that retails in new condition for 15 percent less than what is shown for a collectible version.

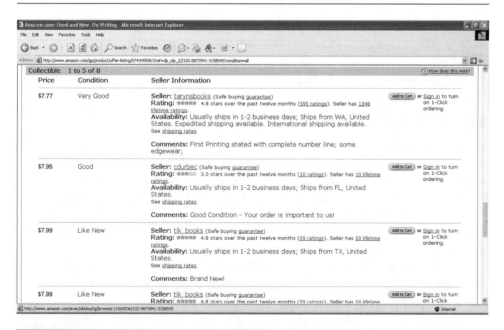

FIGURE 3-1   The listing for a collectible edition of a book

Still other items can increase the value of a book, even if it is used. For example, booksellers across the country know that the following items can greatly enhance the price they ask for a given text.

- Advance reading copy

- Limited or special edition

- Author signed

- Collectible bookplate

- Errata sheet

Even if your company doesn't sell books, these ideas are still applicable. If you sell motorcycles, a special chrome accelerator might be a bonus that increases the product's value. If your firm sells clothing, a limited-edition blouse with a special logo might be the ticket. And if your company sells graphic novels, special variant covers can command a premium.

 *You should only use the Collectible label when you have a true collectible item. Some sellers use the label indiscriminately for any item they have, in order to charge a higher price. This usually causes a negative reaction from most of their buyers.*

An Example of Refurbishment

A second example of how you can better compete by knowing your product is through understanding how Amazon lists other products besides their core staples such as books and music. Instead of a Collectible listing, most other product categories include a Refurbished listing, as in Figure 3-2. A *refurbished* item can be a legacy product (in other words, an old or previous version of one of your products) from your company's line which you have renovated or repaired to return to the general consumer market.

You should note, however, that not all products are high-value enough to be refurbished, particularly items that are pure commodities (computer memory cards), consumables (gourmet coffee), or are disposable by nature (plastic razors). But for the items that are valuable enough to sell for used prices, refurbishment can pad your bottom line when selling on Amazon.

If you're wondering whether you have an idea that isn't worthy of refurbishing, consider that the main differences between commodities, consumables, and disposable items are as follows: Commodities are not worth refurbishing, because

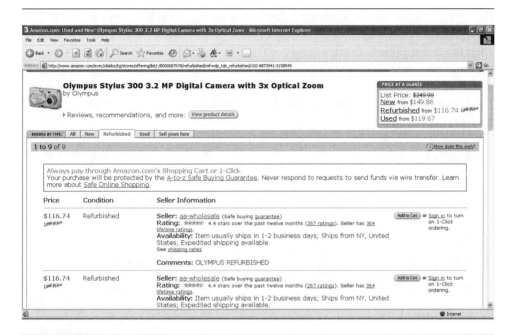

FIGURE 3-2   Listings for a refurbished digital camera model

the cost of a new item will usually be the same or less than the cost of refurbishing an old product. Consumables get "used up" or ingested, so there's nothing to refurbish, and items that are disposable usually aren't safe or recommended to be refurbished.

Used items generally sell for less than new ones. However, refurbished items from your product line will typically command a higher price than pre-owned ones, even if the items do not have a distinguishing collectible aspect or feature, mainly because you've ensured that the product is functional or in working order, whereas a "pre-owned" item does not imply this extra work has been done.

> TIP   *Refurbished items sell particularly well—and generally for higher prices—if they are items from your product line which are expensive, or come with some sort of written guarantee of quality or a repair warranty.*

Evaluating Your Product's Condition

Whatever the condition of the products you have to sell, Amazon.com allows merchants to list items at any price, regardless of the Amazon.com price or its list price.

However, you should always follow Amazon's detailed condition guidelines that they give for each product category. This will not only allow you to more precisely "dial in" the appropriate price for your item, but it will also protect you from potential consumer complaints if it is clear what a "used" versus a "refurbished" item really is.

Amazon lists specific information for evaluating product conditions in the following categories:

- Books
- Music
- Videos & DVDs
- Video Games
- Electronics
- Tools & Hardware
- Camera & Photo
- Kitchen & Housewares

- Software & Computer Games
- Outdoor Living
- Office Products
- Computers
- Cell Phones & Service
- Toys and Games
- Baby
- Everything Else

The detailed guidelines for each category can be found at the following web page: http://www.amazon.com/exec/obidos/tg/browse/-/1161242/.

Appraising the Worth of Collectible Items

It's an axiom in the hobby and collector's markets that authenticated or graded items command much higher prices. If an item is authenticated, buyers can be certain of what they're getting, so they'll pay more, and auction bidders will usually bid higher. Items that are professionally graded also command higher prices since buyers and bidders know with confidence that they're receiving an item of a certain confirmed quality. It fact, in many areas (coins and valuable antiques come to mind) serious buyers or collectors won't even consider items that haven't been graded or authenticated.

Sellers at Amazon.com can offer potential buyers something especially valuable: third-party authentication and grading. Third-party grading services stake their reputations on the items they authenticate. Once an item is registered and appraised or graded, you'll know exactly how to gauge its value for sale.

Amazon's Pricing Advantage for Grading Coins

One service that Amazon.com provides is a tremendous boon should your company be involved in the relatively popular niches of coin collecting or sports memorabilia. Amazon gives merchants direct access to coin grading and counterfeit detection experts at the Numismatic Guaranty Corporation (NGC). The NGC is the official grading service of the American Numismatic Association, the largest coin hobby organization in America.

According to Amazon, the following services are made available to you:

- Coins are graded and certified with complete impartiality.

- Coins are sonically sealed in archival-quality, tamper-evident safety holders.

- Coins are returned to you along with crisp digital images of each coin.

Amazon's Pricing Advantage for Sports Cards

Amazon gives you access to the sports-card grading experts at the Sportscard Guaranty Corporation (SGC). SGC offers a clear, iron-clad grading guarantee in the industry for sports and non-sports trading cards of all types and sizes. If you have a problem with something you get graded by the SGC, you can dispute it directly with them and ask them to regrade the item.

According to Amazon, the following services are available:

- Sports cards are authenticated with complete impartiality.

- Sports cards are graded with complete impartiality.

- Cards are sonically sealed in archival-quality, custom-fitted, tamper-evident safety holders.

- Cards are returned to you together with registration numbers and crisp digital images.

For either service, the digital images are excellent for listing products at Amazon's new Auction services or on Amazon's zShops. As an added bonus, Amazon has negotiated a ten-percent discount in the fees charged for the listed services, giving an additional competitive advantage to others who need items assessed, graded, or appraised.

Know the Hot Products

You can also determine what products are "hot" on Amazon.com by utilizing their Top 100 or Top Seller lists. Given that Amazon is essentially a giant database of products, it's relatively easy for the e-commerce giant to list items by sales rank. For example, whichever books on their two-million-plus list sells the most copies in a given 24-hour period (combined with some past sales data) end up with the top spots.

Given that Amazon.com's core business is books, it's no surprise that the lists in that specific category are more detailed and subdivided than in others. For example, the Top 100 are the books that have sold the most directly from Amazon .com. It's updated on an hourly basis. An example of this list, which is accessible from a link on the upper toolbar on any book-related page, is in Figure 3-3.

By contrast, Amazon also lists the books that top the *New York Times*' best sellers list, as in Figure 3-4. This list is available from a tab in the upper toolbar once you start exploring the Top 100 category. Additionally, the left-hand column displays subcategories of books where the top sellers in that specific niche reside.

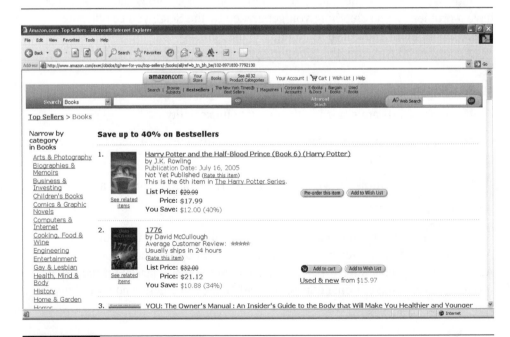

FIGURE 3-3   Amazon.com's Top 100 list of books

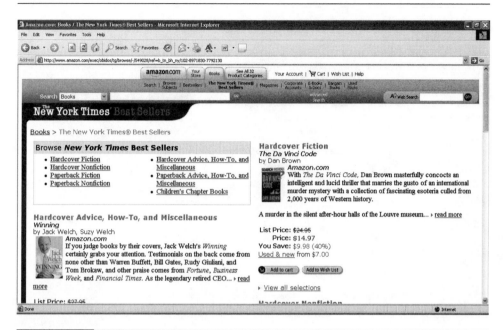

FIGURE 3-4   The *New York Times*' best-sellers list. Note the left-hand columns showing where you can find best sellers in other subcategories.

Finally, if your business doesn't sell in Amazon's core areas, you can see what is hot by going to any one of Amazon's 32 categories. On the category page, one of the links in the top toolbar will always be Top Sellers. If you see a consistent high ranking in the Automotive category for, say, tire gauges (as in Figure 3-5) or engine oil products, then you're seeing the easiest-to-read indicator of what the consumers are buying in quantity.

The main thing to learn from these hot products is to see what aspects they share with one another. In other words, what is it about these specific "hot" products that makes them so hot? What appeals to you, as a potential buyer perhaps, when looking at them? Which hot items could you potentially stock immediately? We've asked you to go through this research to prepare you for our next step: determining how best to list an item on Amazon. Take away any key style designs you see, specific words or phrases used over and over again to entice you to buy, features that are described, and so on. And with that, let's dive into preparing your hot listings!

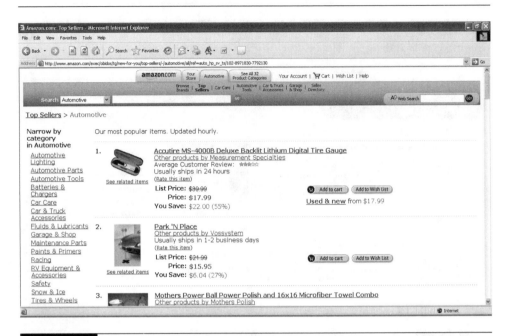

FIGURE 3-5   The Top Sellers in Automotive

How to Describe an Auction on Amazon

When it comes to describing an item you are going to put up for auction at
Amazon, there's more freedom and flexibility when it comes to the description
than there is when listing something in the Marketplace or in your own zShop.
The benefit is that you can distinguish your item and highlight all the positive
features to generate sales. The downside is that it involves some extra work and
takes a bit longer than the other methods.

In Chapter 5, we're going to walk through all the steps and procedures of
preparing an auction listing, and we'll talk about the capabilities and limitations of
each field. Right now, however, we want to talk about the basics as far as information
gathering, along with any research that will help you in your auction listing.

First, don't overestimate the usefulness of the product's manufacturer and/or
distributor. Almost every company has a web presence today, which means easy
online access to graphics, product descriptions, benefit analyses, and so on. Within
reason, learn from how they position their product and use those same techniques

when describing your auction listing. Sometimes, a detailed explanation on the benefits of the product will help sell it more than a bulleted list of the characteristics of the item.

Second, when it comes to graphics, honesty is the best policy. Manufacturers' stock photos are used all the time, especially on Amazon, so don't be afraid to use them as part of your strategy. If your item is still brand new, shrink-wrapped, untouched, and so on, attaching a clean picture that the manufacturer uses to sell the product is an honest representation. Similarly, including a picture of what the item looks like out of the box is an acceptable inclusion, especially if you note that the picture is from the manufacturer. After all, why open the package and potentially ruin the item, just to get a picture of it when the manufacturer's photo shows the same thing?

NOTE
Copyright laws are continually changing. Before you post a stock photo of a manufacturer's item—particularly if it's a brand-new model—double-check the statutes of the state you live in.

If your item is used and has some flaws, however, a picture will help ease the buyer's mind as to what they ultimately receive. By using techniques such as close-up shots on any affected areas, pictures taken from different angles, well-lighted pictures, and the inclusion of other objects in the picture to demonstrate the item's relative size, you give your buyers a much better idea of the condition of the product—much better than words can say. If you're unable to provide pictures, an accurate stock photo will at least convey the edition or version of the item, as long as it's accompanied by an accurate description and disclosure that the manufacturer's photo is provided for reference only and is not intended to represent the actual item for sale. Remember, you want to automate your business and have it grow, which means reducing the number of complaints and returned items, as well as the amount of lackluster feedback.

Third, if there have been any changes from the original configuration, be sure to note that clearly and boldly. For example, let's say you're selling a laptop computer but you've added more RAM to the system to boost the performance. You should definitely highlight that fact since people searching for laptops may assume yours has the default amount installed.

Lastly, don't be afraid to learn from your competition on Amazon. Take a look at other auctions similar to yours. See how fellow sellers are presenting their auctions. Sometimes, it may entail learning the specific HTML coding language they use to make their listings stand out; other times, it'll be the quality of their description or the way they compare and contrast their auctions that will be significant. Remember, don't outright steal a picture or a word-for-word custom description, simply observe the best techniques out there and incorporate them into your auction.

Price Your Product Accordingly

If there are any two words from the English language that are recognized around the world, they'd be "How much?" Especially in bazaars and tourist locations, where eager shoppers are haggling with the merchant, the matter of price is a very important one. In online commerce, it's no different. Now that we've discussed how to present your item, the next key is to determine how much to charge for it. In some cases, particularly Amazon Auctions, the marketplace will determine your ultimate price. But even in that situation, you need to think about your starting price, the reserve price, and your "Take It Now" price for an item (see Chapter 5).

Since you're not selling your items alone in a vacuum, it's always important to be aware of what other merchants are selling the item for, and how many sellers with the same product you're competing against. Thankfully, Amazon is very aware of this, and constantly presents you with that key information as you're selling your products.

The first thing to be aware of is the Amazon price for a given item. Remember, this does NOT have to be the Manufacturer's Suggested Retail Price (MSRP), or a given list price. Amazon routinely creates discounts in several categories, including Books, and can offer low prices due to their immense buying power and constant promotions. As an example, let's take a look at a very popular software program called QuickBooks Pro from Intuit, as shown in Figure 3-6. While Intuit's MSRP is $299.95, Amazon's price for the same new, off-the-shelf software program (as of this writing) is $239.99, which is a 20-percent savings. In most cases, you'll only be able to charge a price that's the same or below that (according to Amazon's general pricing rule). If your product is unique and/or collectible, you *can* ask for more money. If it isn't, make sure you can afford to sell your products at or near Amazon's price.

The next point to be aware of is the lowest price offered by another seller. If you look at Figure 3-6, you'll notice a link near the bottom of the page that says **"29 used and new** from $129.99." If you click that link, you'll be taken to the *Used and New* page for that item, which organizes all the featured merchants and new-and-used sellers of that particular item onto one page, as you can see

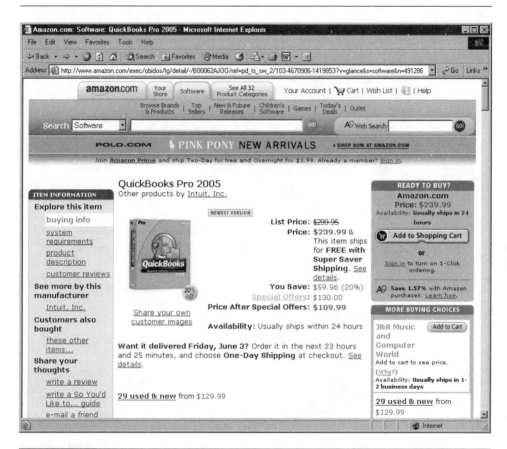

FIGURE 3-6   QuickBooks Pro on sale at Amazon for 20 percent off the list price!

in Figure 3-7. One consistent feature of all these Used and New pages is the Price At A Glance box. You'll be using this very helpful feature a lot in your research and sales activities. Its box will tell you the lowest price for a New, Used, and (if applicable) a Refurbished or Collectible version of the item in question. Right now, the lowest price for a new copy of QuickBooks Pro is $179.99, while the lowest price for a used copy is $129.99.

You've probably noticed the colorful "Low Price" burst graphic next to the price of the Used item. This is a key marker that Amazon uses to help guide the buyer to the absolute lowest price offered for a given product. This indication

FIGURE 3-7   Used and new prices of QuickBooks are listed in the Price At
A Glance box.

automatically shows up next to the lowest price *no matter what the product's
condition*! There are no special tricks or programming code that will help you get
this indication. It's simply part of Amazon's back end, and it dynamically changes
as sellers update their prices. As buyers peruse the listings, they'll also see the Low
Price indicator next to the individual listing with the lowest price.

From this Used and New page, scan the list presented to see the different
sellers and how they've priced their items. In some cases, like the QuickBooks
example shown in this section, Featured Merchants will be listed first. Part of

their benefit for joining up with Amazon is premier placement on these pages. If your company is big enough and specialized enough to become a featured merchant, you should consider talking with Amazon to make that happen. We'll touch on those specifics in Part IV of the book.

Rules of Thumb for Pricing

Several key points should be remembered when determining an appropriate price for your product:

- A penny can make all the difference.

- It pays to be in the Top 5.

- Location is a factor!

- Be in more than one place at the same time.

Specifically, you should keep in mind what these points mean to you:

- *A penny makes all the difference.* Amazon sorts their listings for these sellers by price only. To make things attractive to the buyer, they sort these listings low to high, meaning the lowest prices get the highest listings. Take a look at the listings. If most of them hover around the same exact price, consider lowering your price by a penny or two. You may vault past 50 sellers in the list this way. It doesn't remember where the person is located or how much feedback they have, the price you enter is what determines where in the list you fall.

- *It pays to be in the Top 5.* When you did your research, you should have noticed that Amazon shows you the Top 5 listings for each category of New, Used, Refurbished, Collectible, and Featured Merchants. That doesn't mean that only five sellers can list in that category. It just means that Amazon gives the buyer a snapshot of all potential sales by listing the top five. Now, while some buyers may delve deeper by clicking the links to see all the listings for a given category, most people want to buy and leave. This makes the Top 5 listings *prime real estate*. You may not have the lowest price overall, but if you can do it, try to position yourself so you fall in the Top 5.

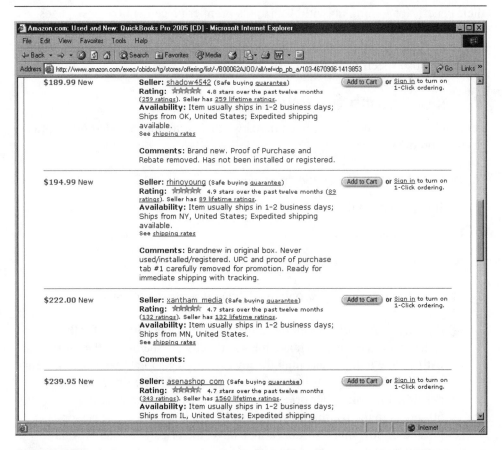

FIGURE 3-8 Pay attention to the location of each item for sale!

■ *Location is a factor.* While price, condition, and reputation are the primary drivers for determining a sale on Amazon, there is a fourth, less-talked-about criteria: location. Let's go back to the QuickBooks Pro example. If we look at some of the top listings for New copies, as shown in Figure 3-8, we can see where the item is shipping from—specifically, the U.S. state the item is shipping from. In this case, we have four copies offered from Oklahoma, New York, Minnesota, and Illinois. As a buyer, if the price is very similar, sometimes you'll look at the location of the item, hoping to get it quicker by picking a seller close to them. Be accurate when listing the location and specifically cite where the physical item is going out from, not from where you're located. Plus, if you live in a part of the country not well represented in the list, you should get some extra sales from that area if your item is well positioned on the list.

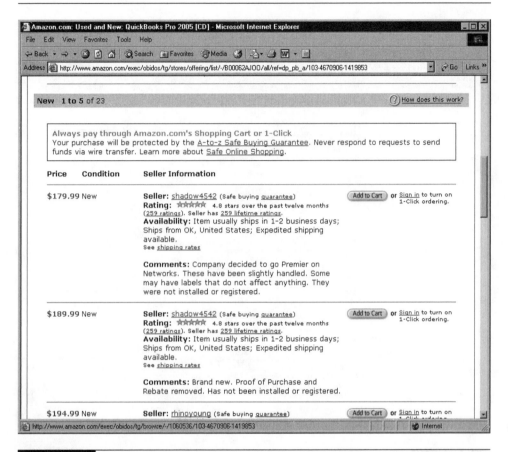

FIGURE 3-9   The same seller from Oklahoma is selling two different new items.

■ *Be in more than one place at one time.* Often, you'll be selling several copies of the same item, but they won't all be in the same condition. With Amazon, you can sell the same item, in different conditions, by creating multiple listings based on condition. Even within a category, such as Used, you can create a separate listing for each item with a distinct condition. Going back to the QuickBooks Pro listing, for example, notice the seller who has two different new listings (as seen in Figure 3-9), and two different used listings of the same software (as shown in Figure 3-10). He describes the exact condition of each listing in his Comments field. This allows the seller to price each condition appropriately without short-changing the buyer or forcing the seller to offer his product at the lowest price.

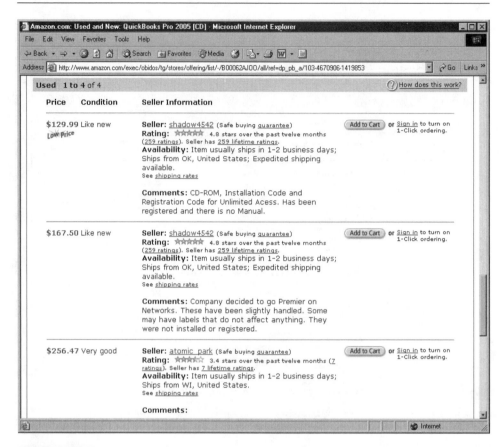

FIGURE 3-10   The seller is also selling two different used items of the same type of software!

Dynamic Pricing on Amazon—Nothing Is Static!

On top of every rule we could present here, there's one that supercedes it—nothing lasts forever. In the ever-changing environment that is Amazon, a decision that's been carefully made and analyzed may have to be reexamined in a day, week, or month, depending on other sellers' activities. It's important to do the research up-front, but don't forget to check on your products after they've been posted for sale. Take a look at the newest prices for different conditions of the item, and update your price accordingly. Keep your research handy from your initial listing, since you should use it when updating your price for the listing.

Conversely, if your products are selling out too quickly (we know, we know, if your products are selling very quickly, how can that be a problem?), you may want to see if you're pricing your items too low. After all, why "leave money on the table" if your customers are willing to pay a little more?

The key is to come up with a comfortable balance. Amazon sellers have observed that, after the initial listing of inventory, you should begin to keep track of certain ratios, like the percentage of items that have sold or the average amount of a sale. While you may experience periods of higher or slower velocity, your monthly or quarterly ratios should settle on a particular figure and your strategy should be to either improve the percentage of sold items or raise the average amount of a sold item. We'll talk more in Parts III and IV about tracking and improving your sales over time.

As you list your products and go back to update the prices when needed, Amazon has a feature to help you along the way. They call it Recommended Price. It's not overtly stated for each listing you create, but you'll see it on certain items. Basically, this feature tells you, based on the item and condition you specify, what Amazon thinks is an appropriate price for your product. The feature takes into account the current amount of sellers and sales prices that exist for the item, also factoring in previous sales for that item and at what price those sales occurred. Most of the time, the Recommended Price will be similar to the lowest price currently offered in your listed condition, but not always. Always take a look at the Recommended Price, and compare it to the current list of sellers for that item. Perhaps you'll find situations where sellers have abnormally lowered their price (for the moment), even when the item typically sells for more. It's up to you to consider whether to match this new low price or stay at the higher price, hoping that prices will return to their previous level.

Sell Your Collection on Amazon

If you're itching for a way to get started and list some items for sale on Amazon, a feature exists to help you do that. It's called Sell Your Collection, and it draws on inventory that Amazon knows you probably have—all your past purchases with them! If you're already an Amazon user and you've used it to buy books, DVDs, and other items, Amazon figures that you may be finished with these items or want to upgrade or swap them for something else, so it helps you re-post that merchandise so you can sell it to someone else. The best part is, they already have all the product information and details, so they can help you sell these past items with a minimum of fuss.

If you're interested in trying out this feature, you can access your past purchases by doing one of the following:

■ Click the Sell Your Stuff icon on the Amazon home page. In the right-hand bar, you should see a feature called Make $*XX.XX*, like the one shown in Figure 3-11. Click the link titled "your past purchases."

■ Go to this web page:
http://www.amazon.com/exec/obidos/tg/browse/-/886514/.
Click the link to access your past purchases.

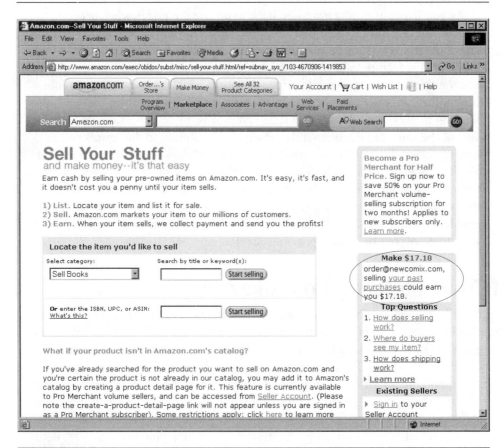

FIGURE 3-11 Start selling by putting your old purchases back on Amazon.

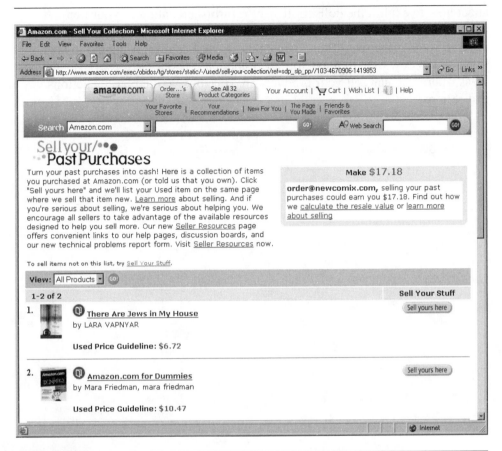

FIGURE 3-12   To start selling quickly, you can pick from a past purchase!

Once you've logged in, Amazon will present you with a list of items you've previously purchased, like that shown in Figure 3-12. Pick an item you'd like to try reselling, and click the orange Sell Yours Here button. From there, just enter the condition, comments on, and price of your item and it will be posted for sale! We'll go into more detail about the individual fields in the next chapter.

To Sum Up

In this chapter, we've talked about the necessary steps you should take when preparing to sell your items. Basically, you need to understand the details of the product you want to sell, including the condition of the item. We then talked about how to exploit the collectibility or refurbished nature of your item, and look for the hottest products to get the most attention. After having covered some important pricing strategies, as well as rules of thumb to keep in mind, it's now time to move to Part II and learn about the three basic areas where you can sell your products on Amazon: Marketplace, Auctions, and zShops!

Part II

Make Money with Amazon

Chapter 4

Use the Amazon Marketplace to Sell Goods

We see our customers as invited guests to a party, and we are the hosts.

—Jeff Bezos, founder of Amazon.com

In Part I of this book, you saw some of the amazing opportunities Amazon offers you, the seller. You received a detailed overview of their various categories, pointing out which ones are open for sellers to sell alongside Amazon's extensive catalog and which bear certain competitive restrictions. Most importantly, you learned about important listing and pricing techniques to keep in mind when selling anything on Amazon.

Now, we delve into the three specific areas that allow you to list merchandise online. The first of which is the Amazon Marketplace. This system is rather simple—in many categories, when Amazon lists a product for sale, like a book, DVD, or music CD, they allow the buyer to browse "Used and New" listings from other sellers who have the same item for sale. Buyers look through the list, and decide, based on price, condition, seller reputation, and in some cases, location, which sellers' item they want to buy, be it Amazon's own offering or that of another merchant. It's incredibly quick to list an item, Amazon handles a number of the after-sale processes, and they take a commission on each sale. So, since we've talked about *what* to do, let's dive in and learn how to list items in the Amazon Marketplace.

Ready to Sell?

You can start the process of listing your items in the Amazon Marketplace in several ways:

- From Amazon's home page, click the Sell Your Stuff link in the top subnavigation bar, as shown in Figure 4-1.

- From any individual product detail page, look for a button on the right-hand side of the page in the More Buying Choices box that says Sell Yours Here, as in the example of the DVD box set of *24 - Season One*, shown in Figure 4-2.

- From the Store Directory page (or the See All 32 Product Categories page) look for the Sell Your Stuff link on the right-hand side of the page. See Figure 4-3.

Click this link.

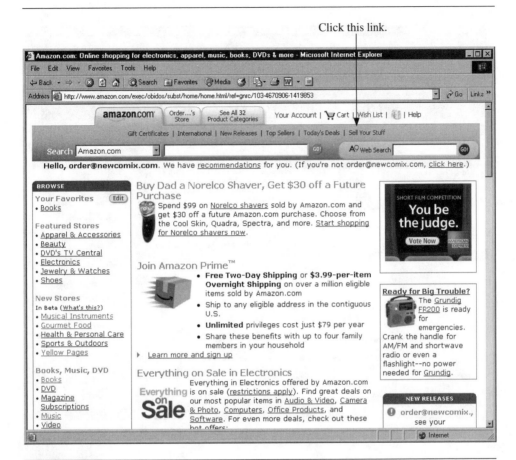

| FIGURE 4-1 | The first way to start selling is by using the Amazon home page. |

Those easy-to-navigate site pages will take you through the process that Amazon likes to refer to as "List, Sell, Earn." You'll be prompted to provide all of the important information about the item you have for sale and enter it as a listing in their catalog! And away you go!

How to List an Item in the Amazon Marketplace

Having started the process, you should now be looking at the first screen in the listing procedure, as shown in Figure 4-4. Remember, Amazon organizes all their items around a unique identifier. In this case, Amazon calls it their Amazon

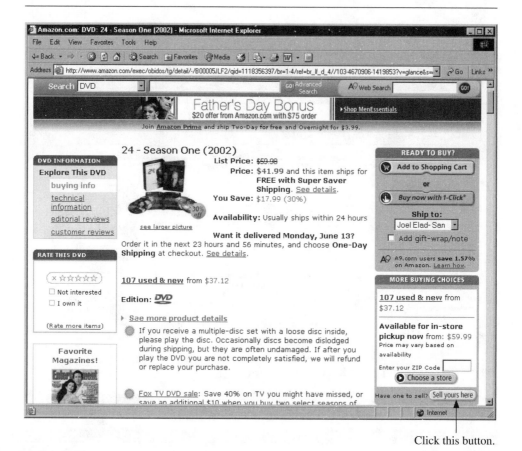

Click this button.

FIGURE 4-2 Once you find an item that you have, you can also click the button to sell yours.

Standard Identification Number, or ASIN for short. In most cases, this number will be physically located on your item. For books, it's the ISBN number. Regarding products such as DVDs, CDs, and some electronics items, this number is the UPC (or Universal Product Code) listed on the package. In some cases, Amazon has to create their own ASIN, and in those instances, you'll need to search for the product based on the title or keywords to help you identify it.

From this screen, pick the category in which you want to sell your product. You can then either enter the ISBN, the UPC, or another identification number,

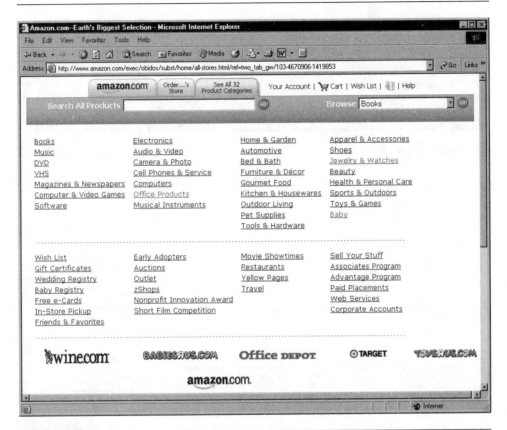

FIGURE 4-3   Another way to start selling is by simply looking around Amazon's categories, and then choosing what to sell.

or search for the product based on the title or keywords. For our example here, we'll use the listing for our previous book, *eBay Your Business*. It's published by McGraw-Hill/Osborne (as is this book) and the ISBN number is 0072257113. For demonstration's sake, let's input the keywords **eBay Your Business** into the Search box, and then click Start Selling to move to the next step.

When you do a search based on the title or keywords, you'll be presented with a list of matching titles. Find the product you have for sale, and click the Sell Yours Here button to start the process. You'll navigate through the three screens previously discussed where you'll enter all the pertinent information, proofread your listing, and then post your item for sale.

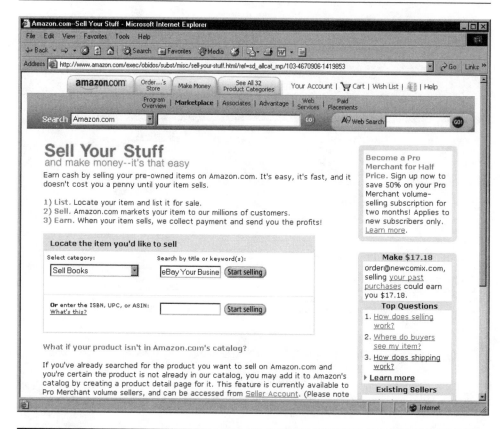

FIGURE 4-4   Your entry point for selling in the Amazon Marketplace!

The first screen catalogs the condition of the item, as shown in Figure 4-5. The only information fields you need to worry about are Condition and Comments. The main condition definitions you need to be aware of are these:

- **New** This means the item is brand new, unused, and if applicable, still in its shrinkwrapped or original container.

- **Like New** The item has no major defects, flaws, or missing items, and has hardly been used. Items in this condition typically aren't shrinkwrapped, but they also don't appear to have been used heavily.

- **Very Good Condition** The item has clearly been used, but only contains minor flaws, defects, or blemishes. Though not shrinkwrapped, the item is still expected to come with all its accessories, when applicable.

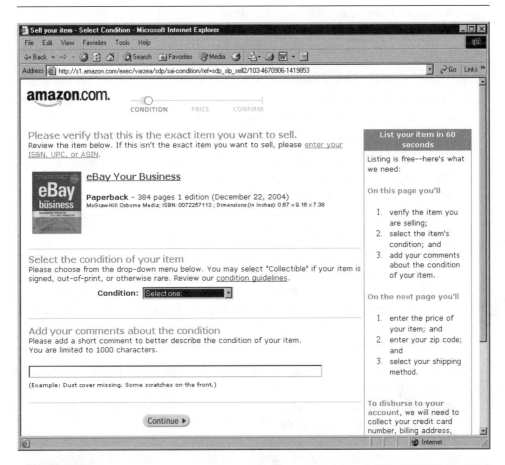

You can post your item for selling after filling in its Condition and Comments fields.

■ **Good Condition**   The item has been used, and has definite wear, defects, or blemishes on the outside of the product. It also may not have all its accessories, but any missing parts should be clearly noted in the Description.

Evaluate your copy of the product, and select the appropriate condition. Inspect your item thoroughly, and take note of any scratches, dings, stains, marks, or other problems that were not on the item when it was purchased brand new. The best practice when grading your item to be listed is to hold the item, physically inspect it, and "demote" the condition from New every time you find a problem with the item. Once you're done inspecting the item, you should have determined the condition from the number of flaws you found.

Next, use the Comments field to bring attention to your listing. Highlight all the positives of your item, and based on its condition, focus on the following things:

- **New**   As silly as the question sounds, be sure your comments answer the question: "How new is it?" Is it new in the package, shrinkwrapped, in mint condition, or unread? If so, mention it. Don't assume that simply assigning the item a condition of New tells the user it's brand new.

- **Used**   Describe any specific flaws that make the item look used. Are there creases, folds, dings, scratches, marks, discoloration, water damage, or anything similar? The better you describe the item, the fewer problems you'll have post-sale, and the more confidence you'll generate in your buyers when they're ready to buy.

- **Collectible**   If you want to use this category, be sure to mention first why your product is collectible. Is this a first-edition book/CD? Is it signed by the author, artist, writer, or someone involved with the production? Does it have a different cover, print run, or other unique quality? Describe it as much as possible (within your limit of 1000 characters) and don't forget to address the actual condition of this collectible item.

- **Refurbished**   Describe what work had to be done to the product when it was refurbished. Were specific parts swapped out? Was the item simply cleaned and tested? How long has the item been used? After that, describe any obvious flaws and, if applicable, any warranty information.

Once you've entered the condition and comments, click the Continue button to move to the second part of the process. On this screen, as shown in Figure 4-6, you'll be asked to enter the Price, Quantity, Location, and Shipping Information about your item. As discussed in Chapter 3, you'll see a Pricing Information box that'll give you the current information for the lowest price of a Used, New, and, if applicable, a Collectible or Refurbished Item. Use that information plus your previous market research of potentially competing goods to determine the appropriate price for your item. Next, pick the quantity you want to sell for this listing. Remember, if you have more than one of the same item, each with a different condition, you should create separate listings, but if you've got a pallet of the same item in the same condition, feel free to list the quantity here. Incidentally, your quantity information is *not* displayed to the buying public when they're going through your listings.

Next, list your ZIP or postal code where the item will be shipping from, which may or may not be the same as where you're physically located (in the case of

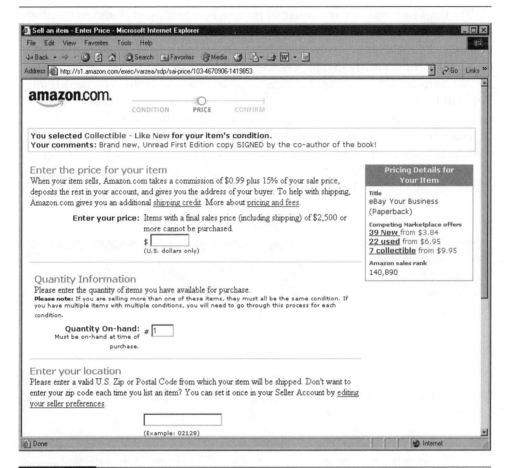

FIGURE 4-6 On this screen, pick your price, set your quantity, and then cite the location and shipping details!

shipping from a remote warehouse or third-party supplier). Finally, at the bottom of the screen, you'll be asked whether you want to offer International and/or Expedited shipping. By clicking these checkboxes, you'll receive an extra reimbursement amount from Amazon, equivalent to the expected carrier cost of shipping the product if your item is sold to either an international buyer or a domestic buyer who wants expedited shipping.

However, you will have to send the item express or by global air mail. We'll talk more in Part IV about the advantages of going global with your sales. Once this step is complete, click Continue.

The third and final step in the listing process is to proofread all the information you've entered in Steps 1 and 2 to make sure your listing appears the way you want it to. You'll be presented with a screen similar to Figure 4-7, where you'll see the summary of your item details. Look over all the fields, make sure everything is spelled correctly and priced appropriately. Pay attention to the field marked Total You Will Receive (If Sold), which will tell you exactly how much money you'll receive if your item is sold with standard, expedited, or international shipping, depending on which options you picked in Step 2. This takes into account the commission and shipping credit that Amazon administers. If you see a problem, use the Edit button on the web page to go back and fix something. Otherwise, click the orange Submit Your Listing button to post your item.

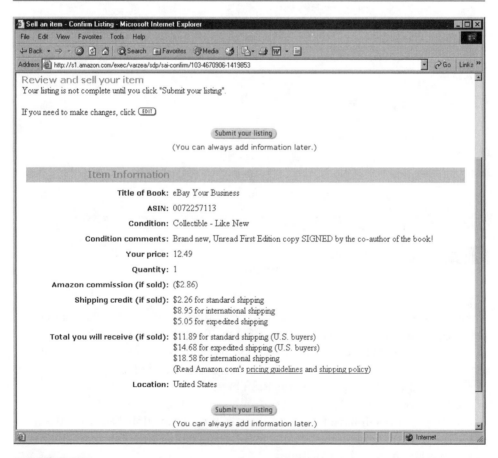

FIGURE 4-7   Now look over all your information and click Submit Your Listing to start selling!

That's it. You'll receive an e-mail confirmation from Amazon indicating the success of your listing. (Remember, this e-mail will go to the e-mail address on file for your seller account.) It will take up to one day for your listing to show in the Marketplace since Amazon must verify your listing and update their computer systems. Now, of course, this listing isn't fixed in stone, you are free to edit or even withdraw your listing if you need to, which we'll discuss later in this chapter in the section "How to Change an Item Listing."

Fees/Costs of Using the Marketplace

Having talked about listing your item, now comes the important part: what it will cost you to sell the item. The key point to remember for sales in the Amazon Marketplace is that Amazon.com only collects a commission fee when an item actually sells. There is no listing fee (as at eBay) and there is no payment fee deducted for collecting your money (as at PayPal). At the time of sale, Amazon .com will deduct a commission of $0.99 plus 6 to 15 percent of the sales price, depending on the item type. The commission fees are listed in Table 4-1.

NOTE   *There is no official explanation as to why you are charged different percentages for different categories. It's assumed that the categories with lower percentages typically have a higher dollar amount for an average closing price, so Amazon still makes their money and stays competitive in the process.*

TIP   *Pro Merchant subscribers have the $0.99 fee waived, and Amazon even offers an additional credit to help cover shipping costs. Also, if you're a Pro Merchant seller, your listings will remain on the site indefinitely until they sell, you remove them, or you cancel your Pro Merchant Subscription. We'll talk more about the Pro Merchant Subscription in Chapters 6 and 10.*

Items by Category	Commission Fee Percentage
Computers	6 percent
Camera & Photo, Cell Phones & Service, and Electronics items	8 percent
Items in the Everything Else Store	10 percent
Musical Instruments	12 percent
All other product lines	15 percent

TABLE 4-1   Commission Fees Based on Merchandise

Merchants in the Amazon Marketplace may price their items as they see fit, provided those prices adhere to the stipulations of the Amazon General Pricing rule: the item price and total price of an item listed on Amazon.com are at or below the item price and total price at which the vendor will offer or sell the item via any other online sales channel. This rule is designed to help Amazon direct price-sensitive traffic to its sales portal. The item price is the amount payable by a customer, excluding shipping and handling. This price should not include discounts, sales, rebates, or other promotional offers that Amazon does not honor or support. Your commission comes from this item price, and remember that you get an additional credit to cover your shipping costs.

Prohibited Items in the Amazon Marketplace

Merchants selling via Amazon.com are expected to conduct proper research to ensure that the items posted are in compliance with all local, state, national, and international laws. Sellers are also encouraged to review the Amazon.com merchant guidelines should they have the slightest question whether an item can be sold. If Amazon determines that the content of a listing is prohibited, they can summarily remove or alter the listing without returning any fees the listing has incurred. As of this writing, the following is a list of the items that are prohibited from being sold on Amazon:

- Pornography and "adult-only" novelty items that are primarily sold through adult-only novelty stores

- Offensive material such as crime-scene photos or human organs and body parts (Amazon.com reserves the right to determine the appropriateness of listings.)

- Illegal items, such as illicit drugs

- Stolen goods

- Items that infringe upon an individual's privacy. Bulk e-mail lists, direct-mail marketing lists, and so on are also prohibited.

- Solutions manuals

- Recopied media

- Promotional media

- Recopied and transferred video games

- Software that has been copied or duplicated in any format is prohibited

- Copies of movies (VHS, DVD, and so forth)

- Copies of television programs, including pay-per-view events

- Recopied music in any format

- Replicas of trademarked items

- Rights of publicity

- Domain names

- Firearms, ammunition, and weapons

- Advertisements

- Products that have been recalled by the Consumer Product Safety Commission (CPSC)

- Living creatures and unauthorized/illegal wildlife products

- Real estate

- Wine and other alcoholic beverages

You're Selling... Now What?

By now, you've hopefully created several listings in the Amazon Marketplace and are scouting around, looking to post more items for sale. Since your products can be made available for a potentially infinite amount of time, it's important to monitor your sales activities and gauge your product prices accordingly in order to effectively balance sales volume with maximum profit potential. Remember, your competition is out there researching and re-pricing their goods to respond to others. You need to be responsive and flexible as well in order to compete effectively. In general, your listings are good for up to 60 days, at which time you can relist your item, free of charge, in exactly the same manner, or with some modifications. As previously mentioned, when you move up to a Pro Merchant Subscription, your listing remains on the site until the item is sold or you remove the listing.

In the meantime, Amazon has organized your selling activities into a helpful set of features that you can log into and monitor under the heading Your Seller Account. You can also expect to get e-mails notifying you of certain events, such as when an item sells, when an item listing expires, or when you're about to get a deposit of money from Amazon Payments. It's important to know what this looks like, and how best to use it, so let's dive right in … again.

Overview of Your Seller Account

There are several ways to get into Your Seller Account. The easiest way is to first log into your Amazon account, by clicking the Your Account link at the top of most Amazon screens. This will bring you to your Amazon account screen, as shown in Figure 4-8. If you've been buying on Amazon, you should be very familiar with this screen. At this point, notice the important box on the right-hand side of the page titled Auctions, zShops, and Marketplace. In that box, you'll see a link titled Your Seller Account. Click that link to go to the screen shown in Figure 4-9: your Seller Account home page.

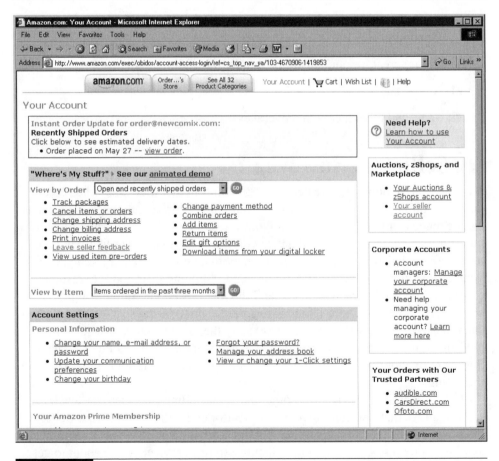

FIGURE 4-8   First, go to your Amazon account screen.

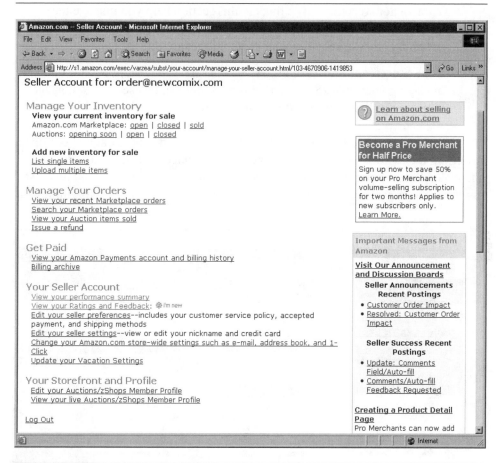

FIGURE 4-9   Your Amazon Seller Account home page

On your Seller Account home page, you should notice five very distinctive and important headers:

■ **Manage Your Inventory**   This section helps you manage and organize all the sale items you have that haven't been sold yet.

■ **Manage Your Orders**   Once an item of yours is sold, an order is generated. The links in this section help you view and update the status of these orders.

■ **Get Paid**   The links in this section help you view your Payments activity and change any important settings.

■ **Your Seller Account**   The links in this section help you manage the specific details of your seller account, from your Performance Summary (when it comes to sales) to your preferences and settings.

■ **Your Storefront and Profile**   As you progress to hosting auctions and managing your own zShop, you'll use the links in this section to manage both your online profile and virtual storefront.

One of the more routine things you'll want to do is take a look at all your open listings in the Marketplace. To do that, go to the Manage Your Inventory header, and under Amazon.com Marketplace, click the link marked Open to pull up a list of your items for sale, which should look like Figure 4-10. The beautiful thing

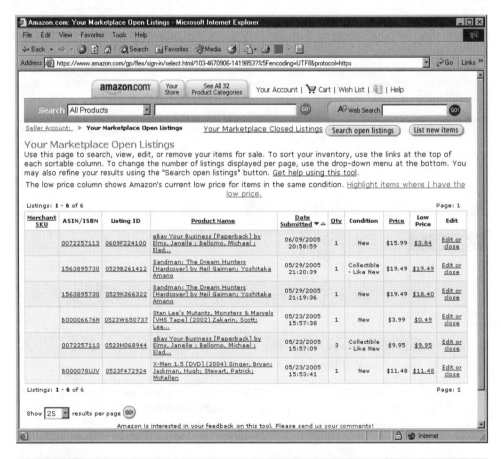

FIGURE 4-10   Take a look at all your Marketplace listings!

about this screen is that, next to each price you've set for your items, you'll see the lowest price available for that item. It's important to remember that this Low Price may be for a Used, New, Collectible, or Refurbished listing. It won't necessarily be the Low Price for the category of your item for sale.

There are two important functions on this page we want to bring to your attention. The first is cosmetic. At the bottom left of the page, you'll see a line that reads Show 25 Per Page. By changing the value in that box (just click the down arrow next to the number 25), you can set it so as many as 350 listings show up on one page. If you're managing a lot of listings, you might want to look at more than just 25 at a time.

Speaking of multiple listings, the more powerful feature available to you can be found at the upper right of the page. In order to help active sellers manage large numbers of listings, Amazon has built a search function to help you find that particular listing without a lot of scanning and reading. Look for the Search Open Listings button in the upper-right part of the page, and click it to bring up a search page like the one in Figure 4-11. You can search based on five different criteria:

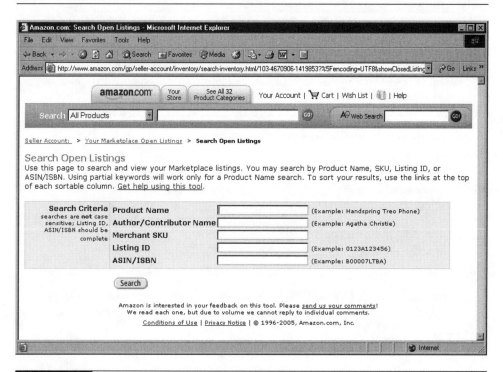

FIGURE 4-11   Can't find that one particular listing you made? Use the Search function!

Product Name, the Author or Contributor's Name, the specific Merchant SKU, the Listing ID created when you posted the item for sale, or the Amazon ASIN or book ISBN number. Like most search functions, multiple results will be shown to you in a list, and if one and only one listing meets the search criteria, you'll be taken to that specific listing.

Of course, if you want to sort or organize the listings in front of you, then you don't necessarily need the search function. If you go to your listing of your open items, you can change the sorted order by clicking a column heading. So far, the columns you can sort by include SKU, Product Name, Date Submitted, Quantity, and Price. In Figure 4-10, the listings are sorted by Date Submitted, where the newest submission is on top. In Figure 4-12, by clicking the Price heading, the products are now sorted from lowest to highest price.

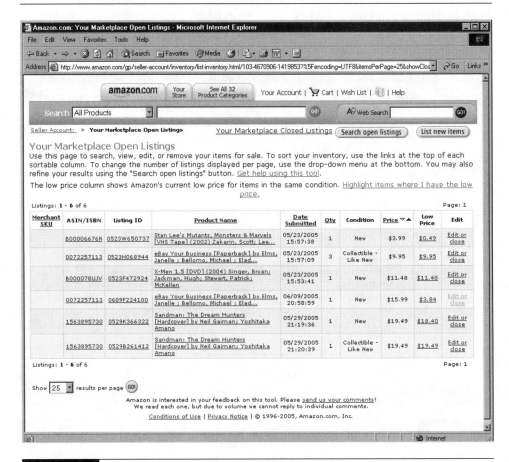

FIGURE 4-12   Here, your products for sale are sorted by price, from low to high.

How to Change an Item Listing

It's very common to realize something about your item after you've put it up
for sale on Amazon. Sometimes, additional research done after your listing will
determine that you've incorrectly identified your item. In either case, Amazon
allows their sellers to make updates and changes to their listings. From this listing
page, changing one of your product listings is as easy as a mouse click. Just click
the Edit Or Close link next to the item listing you want to change, and you'll be
taken to a new screen containing all the information you initially entered about the
item, like the screen in Figure 4-13 we created for editing the *eBay Your Business*

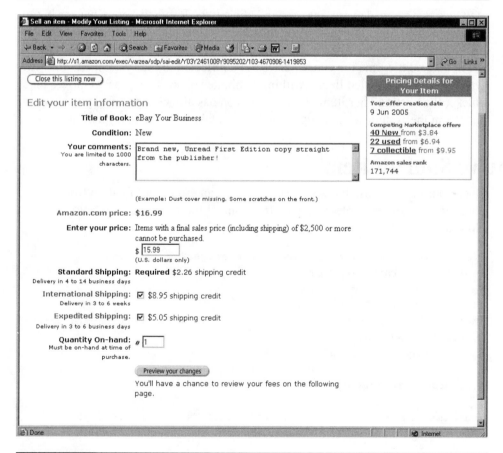

FIGURE 4-13   Change the price, quantity, shipping details, or comments simultaneously!

book we listed in the previous section. From here, you can edit the comments, change the price and/or quantity, and decide whether to add or remove additional shipping options. You can also close (or end) your listing by clicking the Close This Listing Now button in the upper-left corner of the page.

> NOTE
>
> *You cannot change the condition of your item in the listing. If your item's condition has changed (for example, you listed it as New but upon closer inspection, you see that it's Used), then you need to Close Your Listing and create a brand-new listing with the correct condition. The last thing you want to do is sell something that's been misrepresented and risk earning a negative selling reputation on Amazon.*

Once you've made your changes and clicked the Preview Your Changes button, you'll be asked to review your information a last time, and then click the Submit Your Listing button, just like when you initially created your listing. Remember, it will take a little time for your updates to be reflected in the system, but you will typically see the updated listing within 15 minutes or so. This process moves much quicker than listing your item because Amazon has already approved your listing and it's in the system, so sending an update can take minutes instead of hours.

You've Sold an Item!

Once your merchandise has sold, you'll receive an e-mail notification from Amazon.com. An example excerpted from one of these e-mails (the Sold/Ship Now notice) is shown here:

```
From: Amazon.com Payments <payments-messages@amazon.com>
Reply To: yourname@isp.com
To: order@newcomix.com
Cc: payments-mail@amazon.com
Subject: Sold, ship now. Empire's End (Star Wars: Dark Empire Series)
by Veitch, Tom; Baikie, Jim
Sent: Monday, May 9, 2005 3:32 AM

Dear order@newcomix.com,

Your Amazon Marketplace sale is official! We've deposited your
earnings from the sale of this item into your Amazon Payments
account.
```

```
Please ship item immediately via standard shipping speed.

1 of Empire's End (Star Wars: Dark Empire Series)  by Veitch, Tom;
Baikie, Jim


You have agreed to ship no later than two business days after the
buyer's purchase on 09-May-2005.
```

How to React to Sold/Ship Now E-mails

By the time you receive e-mail notification of a sale, the buyer's credit card has already been charged for the item and you can begin the shipping process right away (assuming that all of the information about the order is verified by you or whomever handles the shipment of your products).

Amazon's e-mail will be especially helpful in that it includes all of the information needed for you to fulfill the order, such as the title, SKU, and price.

Using this e-mail as your starting point, Amazon.com encourages all sellers to use a two-step process in order to fulfill an order:

- First, review your Sold—Ship Now e-mail and identify the inventory that needs to be shipped to the buyer.

- Second, visit your Payments Account page to verify order information, including transaction status and shipping address. The transaction status should read "Completed" before you commence shipment.

Getting Paid

Amazon.com automatically processes a payment from the buyer and deposits it in the seller's Payments Account. An e-mail, similar to the one shown here, is generated and sent to you so that you're aware of the amount and the source of the funds.

```
From: Amazon.com Payments <payments-messages@amazon.com>
Reply To: "Amazon.com Payments Customer Service" <payments-
messages@amazon.com>
To: yourname@isp.com
Cc: payments-mail@amazon.com
Subject: Your Amazon.com Payments deposit is on its way
Sent: Friday, April 1, 2005 10:50 PM
```

```
Dear yourname@isp.com,

We've initiated a transfer to your checking account (last
five digits 11111) of the following amount:

$16.36

Funds should appear in your account in approximately five banking
days.

Here's your statement.

-----------------------------------------------------------------

                            STATEMENT

Account Summary

Closing Balance as of 01-Apr-2005: $16.36

      Marketplace
            Payments Received        $20.74
            Fees                     -$4.38
            Seller Fees              $0.00
            Buyer Refunds            $0.00
            -----------------------------------------
            Subtotal for Marketplace $16.36


                                     -----------
      Closing Balance:               $16.36
-----------------------------------------------------------------
```

Keep in mind that having funds in the Payments Account does not yet mean that the money is immediately accessible. Amazon does not automatically disburse the money into your account immediately. Instead, it sends out your accumulated sales total to your checking account every 14 days.

When you first become an Amazon seller, there's an initial 14-day holding period after your checking account information has been provided. This holding period is part of Amazon's security requirement. Funds cannot be disbursed to your checking account during this time for any reason. While most authorizations happen in less than 14 days, Amazon has made this a special procedure to prevent get-rich-quick con artists from jumping onto their system and making off with customers' money before they can be shut down.

 *Sellers* must *ship within two business days of the purchase, even during the initial payments holding period.*

Guarantee Claims and Chargebacks

A guarantee claim is very much what it sounds like—a program which guarantees that when a buyer has a claim, Amazon will act quickly and responsively to settle the issue. A chargeback is similar. When a customer contacts their credit card company outside of Amazon.com over a transaction problem, the customer submits a chargeback request.

The A to Z Guarantee Protection Plan

Amazon's A to Z Guarantee Protection plan is a program in which Amazon strives to settle customer claims quickly, usually through reimbursement. The A to Z program differs from a chargeback request in that the customer is dealing directly with Amazon.com instead of their credit card company. Amazon.com has been able to extend this program to sellers in the Amazon Marketplace as well. Although infrequently used, the guarantee claim provided by the A to Z program gives customers a greater feeling of trust and confidence when purchasing from sellers at Amazon.com.

The A to Z Guarantee Protection plan covers two primary areas of customer dissatisfaction:

- Items *never arriving* to the customer
- Items being *materially different* than expected

Handling A to Z Guarantee Claims

When a customer has a problem with a transaction, Amazon.com directs the buyer to contact the seller so that the seller has an opportunity to address the problem. According to Amazon.com, the guarantee claim eligibility window is limited. The window of time where customers may file a guarantee claim is up to 90 days from the order date. The clock starts running three calendar days after the maximum estimated delivery date for the applicable order, or 30 days from the order date.

In order to limit the abuse of guarantee claims, Amazon Marketplace customers may only file a lifetime total of five A to Z Guarantee claims. Furthermore, Amazon Auctions and zShops buyers may only file a total of three claims.

The Amazon Marketplace customer must choose one of the following options to proceed with their claim if they state that they received an item that was materially different from the item they ordered.

- Wrong version/edition

- Item condition/details not as described

- Wrong item

- Missing parts/components

- Defective item

- Damaged item

The customer must also explain why the item they received was materially different than the item ordered. This is different from the requirements of buyers filing a claim in the Auctions and zShops. These buyers do not have to select a reason for a "materially different" claim, or to provide any explanations.

> **NOTE** *An item is not "materially different" if the buyer is simply disappointed with it or has otherwise had a change of heart regarding the purchase. Amazon.com is the ultimate authority when determining material difference.*

Once the buyer has submitted the claim, Amazon will automatically generate an e-mail presenting the details of the claim and requesting a response from the seller. At the same time, Amazon.com investigates the situation by asking the seller for further information about the transaction. There are two ways to provide information to Amazon.com.

First, the seller can simply reply to the e-mail message sent by Amazon, providing the information requested within the timeframe specified in the e-mail message. Amazon's message to the seller will identify the transaction in question and the reason the buyer filed the A to Z Guarantee claim. In return, Amazon normally asks for verifiable shipping details and other transaction information.

Second, sellers can also manage their A to Z Guarantee claims through their Performance Summary. To do so, they should go to their Seller Account page and click the View Your Performance Summary Page link. Once there (like the one shown in Figure 4-14), the seller must click the View Details button to manage any open A to Z Guarantee claims.

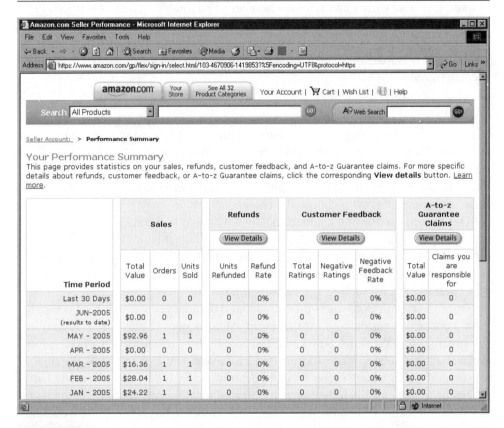

| | Sales | | | Refunds | | Customer Feedback | | | A-to-z Guarantee Claims | |
| | | | | View Details | | View Details | | | View Details | |
Time Period	Total Value	Orders	Units Sold	Units Refunded	Refund Rate	Total Ratings	Negative Ratings	Negative Feedback Rate	Total Value	Claims you are responsible for
Last 30 Days	$0.00	0	0	0	0%	0	0	0%	$0.00	0
JUN-2005 (results to date)	$0.00	0	0	0	0%	0	0	0%	$0.00	0
MAY - 2005	$92.96	1	1	0	0%	0	0	0%	$0.00	0
APR - 2005	$0.00	0	0	0	0%	0	0	0%	$0.00	0
MAR - 2005	$16.36	1	1	0	0%	0	0	0%	$0.00	0
FEB - 2005	$28.04	1	1	0	0%	0	0	0%	$0.00	0
JAN - 2005	$24.22	1	1	0	0%	0	0	0%	$0.00	0

FIGURE 4-14   The seller's Performance Summary page allows them to check on Guarantee claims.

In either case, the seller has a required number of days to respond to Amazon .com via e-mail or via their performance summary, but the sooner the better. It is very important for sellers to tell what happened with the order since part of this process involves assessing who is responsible for the problem should the claim be granted.

TIP   *If a claim is submitted for orders that were not fulfilled, the seller should immediately issue a refund once they can prove the order wasn't sent.*

Of course, Amazon advises all sellers to minimize their number of granted claims. Responsible and responsive sellers should have very low incidences of these claims. Furthermore, Amazon cautions that merchants in the Amazon

Marketplace who garner an excessive number of guarantee claims or service chargebacks are subject to warnings, suspensions, and eventually account closure. Amazon measures your percentage of guarantee claims compared to other users and uses that comparison to decide when to issue their warnings, suspensions, or account closures.

Chargebacks

Chargebacks differ from guarantee claims in that they result from a customer contacting their credit card company. Amazon.com encourages customers to resolve problems by contacting their sellers, and then filing an A to Z Guarantee claim. However, it is ultimately the customer's decision as to how to resolve their issue, and some invariably choose the chargeback route.

One reason may be that chargebacks do not adhere to the A to Z Guarantee timeframe guidelines. Essentially, customers may contact their credit card company to request a chargeback at any time from one day after the transaction date until many months later. This is particularly true if the purchase was made on a "preferred" card such as a gold or platinum card.

Once the customer contacts their credit card company, the credit card company in turn contacts Amazon.com. At that point, Amazon.com requests transaction information from the seller. The key difference in this process is that while Amazon.com requests information in order to investigate a chargeback, the final outcome of a chargeback request will be determined by the customer's credit card company. In any case, as long as you have proof that you sent the item to the buyer and there's a record of that package being delivered, the buyer will have a difficult time benefiting from a bogus claim.

Relisting Items on Marketplace

If one of your items for sale has been listed for 60 days without being bought, you'll get an e-mail from Amazon stating that the listing has been closed. However, relisting the item in the Amazon Marketplace is very simple. In the e-mail, look for a section that reads

```
If you would like to relist this item now, follow this link:
http://s1.amazon.com/exec/varzea/sdp/sai-relist/Y04Y5392437Y4305980
```

Simply click the link within that e-mail and you'll be taken back to Amazon where you'll be presented with one screen containing all the information about your listing. In the same way that you edit an open listing, you can adjust the price, quantity, comments, and shipping options before relisting your item. Simply check

Good Merchant Practices When Selling "On The River"

Amazon offers some recommendations on protecting oneself from claims and chargebacks:

- Keep your proof of shipping for every order sent.

- Consider getting a tracking number when shipping orders.

- Answer customer e-mail messages.

- Refund proactively in the case of a claim or chargeback request.

- Keep accurate product descriptions and images to eliminate misunderstandings over what the customer is actually expecting to receive.

- Institute a conscientious shipping policy.

- Keep the customer informed.

- Promptly cancel any out-of-stock orders.

that everything you want is correct. Consult the Pricing Details For Your Item box to decide if you want to update your price accordingly. If you do make any changes, click Preview Your Changes, proofread your listing one more time, and then click Submit Your Listing.

That's it. Your listing will be re-posted on Amazon for another 60 days, or until the entire quantity has sold.

To Sum Up

In Chapter 4, we walked through the main activities involved in selling through the Amazon Marketplace, from start to finish. We discussed the process of listing an item in the Marketplace, the costs involved in doing so, covered how to edit an active listing, and monitor your items for sale. We talked about which items are prohibited from the Marketplace, and what to expect (and do) after one of your Marketplace items has been sold. In the next chapter, we'll go through all the key processes for selling when using Amazon Auctions.

Chapter 5

Create Amazon Auctions for Special Items

The competition is not so much eBay or another online company as it is the physical world, because that's where all the sales are.

—Jeff Bezos, founder of Amazon.com

While Amazon's product offerings became very extensive throughout their growth period, they were looking for more ways to service their customers and create a one-stop shop where their customers could find everything they needed, from books to electronics. Given the success that eBay was enjoying with their auction site, the concept of person-to-person commerce became a very real way to do business, not to mention the "excitement" and high prices that an auction-style shopping experience creates for their buyers and sellers.

Therefore, on March 3, 1999, Amazon decided to add auctions and offer additional product categories, particularly those too varied or specialized to be serviced by their normal catalog. Collectibles, once eBay's bread and butter, was a perfect core, but Amazon expanded their categories, as eBay has, and provided the appropriate linkage and traffic from their core business to create one of the top three auction sites on the Internet. In order to launch the effort successfully, Amazon partnered with a set of "charter merchants" to help ensure a reasonable selection of items on this new section of their web site.

The Best Uses of the Auction Format

The main question you, as a seller, need to ask is, "What is appropriate to sell in an auction?" While there's no one right answer, there are some guidelines and factors to take into consideration. Mainly, you need to determine if your product for sale is more of a regular commodity item or something more specialized or unique. Typically, the unique items do much better in an auction, especially if you have low quantities. Auctions let the buyers compete so they each have a valid chance to acquire the item, but they compete on price so the seller can get a higher price than setting some arbitrary number and hoping for the first customer to buy it outright.

Conversely, if your item is more of a "commodity," where your actual item is exactly like what others are selling, and there are high quantities available of this item, your buyers may not instinctively go to the auctions page first, though some savvy shoppers will always check the auctions page for a deal initially.

Amazon has pioneered online retailing by becoming focused on bringing the customer to the exact page they need to buy the product they're looking for. The Marketplace allows you to compete more effectively for that traffic, and if your item is a commodity and allowed on Marketplace, that should be your first consideration. If you open your own zShop (which we'll discuss in the next chapter), you will probably want to add this commodity item as an inventory item in your zShop. If there's a lot of that item available, very few buyers (in most cases, none) will fight over the price to get it.

Remember, there are exceptions. One such exception has to do with timeliness. In Spring 2005, Sony launched a portable game system called the PSP. While hundreds of thousands of units were released in the United States, demand far outstripped supply and they were initially hard to find in any store. As you can see from Figure 5-1, one Amazon seller put his game pack up on Amazon Auctions.

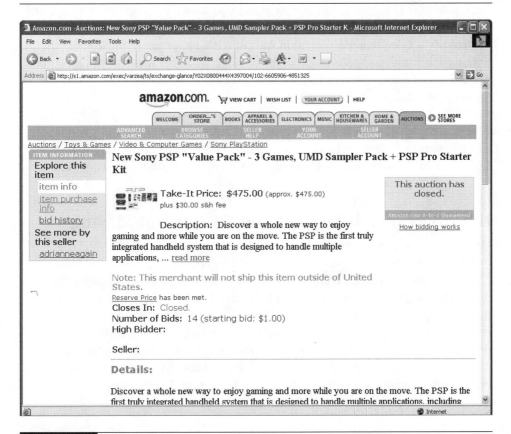

FIGURE 5-1   Buyers competed to get their hands on the new Sony PSP.

He got $475 after 14 bids were received for the item, much higher than the retail price for the PSP in stores.

Researching First

The best way to succeed in Amazon Auctions, or any auction site, is through research. Use the volumes of buying data generated by other buyers and sellers to give you a real-time, current view of the trading area so you know how your item might fare. While the same prices are not reached consistently, week after week, you can get an idea of the price range to expect, as well as the number of competing units simultaneously up for sale.

When you list something in the Amazon Marketplace, all the pricing data is presented to you in real time, so you can see the current low price for different condition items. In Amazon Auctions, you need to use the search engine and do the work yourself. Thankfully, Amazon now lets you search both open and completed auctions so you can see sales data for the past few months. Because of the large volume of auctions that are posted on Amazon, it's important to think about the right search words and perhaps do multiple searches to get the data you need. You can also reorder your data based on different criteria, which will help you cut to the heart of the data.

NOTE   *One of the most important aspects of research may be in discovering that your item won't succeed in Amazon Auctions. So, be sure to look at similar markets as well to see if buyers are responding to Auctions of this type of item.*

How to Research Current and Past Auction Listings

On the Amazon home page, click the See All 32 Product Categories tab, and then look in the Bargains section of the page that appears for the Auctions link. Click this link and you'll be taken to the home page for Amazon Auctions. Near the bottom of the page, look for the link Auction Search, which will take you to the Search page shown in Figure 5-2. This will be your "home page" for doing research on Amazon Auctions. First and foremost, enter the keywords that best describe your item. Remember, you may not get any hits on the first try, so use different combinations to see if your item has been listed in Auctions. If possible, omit words that are easy to misspell or include relevant keywords like an author's name, the subject matter, and so on.

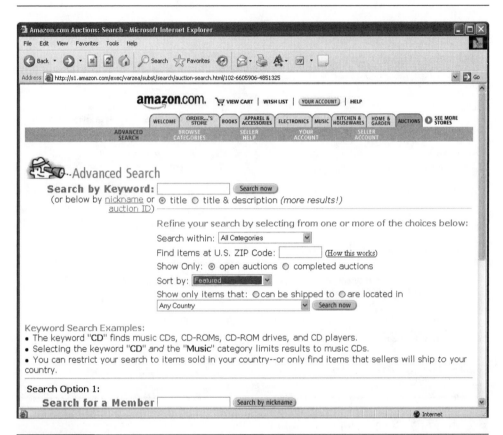

FIGURE 5-2 Your Amazon Auctions searches start here.

Once you've entered your keywords, you should then add "qualifications" to your search. To do so, you must decide whether you want to look at open listings, which are current auctions that haven't ended yet, or completed listings. You should also select how you want your data to be sorted.

For example, let's say you have a Sony laptop computer that you want to put up for auction. It's a slightly used laptop, and since you can't list computers in the Marketplace, your next avenue is auctions.

Your research should involve two steps. First, go to the Search engine page and search Open Listings with the keywords Sony Laptop. You'll get a search results page that looks like the one in Figure 5-3 where you can see how many other people are selling Sony laptops. Take a look at whether these open listings

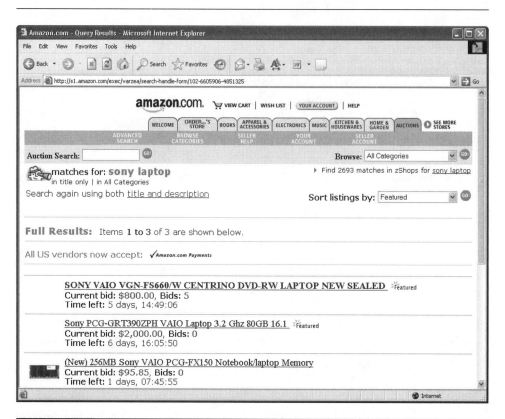

FIGURE 5-3   Sony laptops for sale in the Amazon Auctions

have bids, how they're described, what opening price they have, and the types of policies these sellers have. You're looking for a vibrant listing that will attract more buyers. After all, if Sony laptops sell frequently, that means buyers know to look on Auctions for them and find good prices. If no one is selling your item, then buyers may not be used to going to Auctions to shop for that specific item, or nobody wants to buy that item through an auction. Understand, though, that this means you could own the market if you're the only one to sell an item, and that will help you control a favorable price . . . for you!

Secondly, you'll want to change the Search so you get a listing of completed auctions. Here, you want to study the success rate of sales, what the highest bids are for your item, and how many of them have sold in the last few months.

You'll also want to select the Price High To Low option to sort your data. This way, you'll have the highest-priced auctions coming up first, like in Figure 5-4. While this example may be harder to compare, since different Sony laptops may have different features that affect the price, you can typically compare the same model and identify the more successful sellers of your item. When you do this, take a look at their auction listing to, in a sense, see what they did right. Look at their description, make sure it's the same item you're selling, observe the words they use to describe the item and what policies they offer, like maybe different shipping options or a generous return policy. This research allows you to learn from "the pros" and use that knowledge to make your auction more successful!

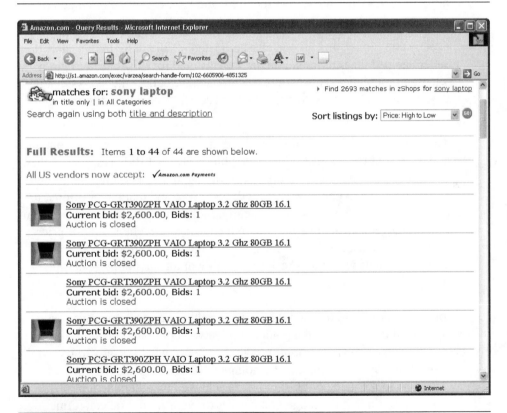

FIGURE 5-4   Sony laptops that have already sold in Auctions

How to Price an Auction Listing

The other part of your research involves finding out how to price your auction. You can do so by taking a look at the auctions that have ended at the highest price, as well as auctions that have attracted the most bids. Be sure to note both the starting price and ending price of each auction. You'll most likely note one of three possible scenarios:

- The item started at $0.99 or $1 and was bid up to $100. This means that there's enough bidding action that the starting bid is not that crucial to the final price. Since the listing fee is the same regardless of what the starting price is, sellers will put a low starting price to encourage bidding, get the buyers emotionally invested in the item, and then watch the price go up.

- The starting bid and the ending bid were the same amount, there was exactly one bidder, and no one else competed for the item. In this case, the seller decided the minimum amount they wanted for this item, and got it with the first bidder. This case better protects the seller, and shows that this item has enough interest to generate a successful sale without the need for frenzied bidding.

- The starting bid and the ending price are different, *but* you only see one bid, and instead of the words Ending Bid, you see Take-It Bid. This means that, while there may have been bidding activity from the beginning, the seller has set a price that one buyer was willing to pay, and that buyer offered to pay that amount to end the auction early. In this situation, it means you can pick whatever starting bid you like, but choose an excellent Take-It price as well. We'll discuss Take-It bids more in the next section, but if you see several auctions where a Take-It price will win the auction, you definitely want to include that in your auction.

Of course, other factors that should go into pricing your item are your cost, the retail value of the item, and the potential price you could get for selling it elsewhere. Your research should point you in the area of what strategy to try, while other factors will help define the exact amounts you want to enter.

Pay attention to the range of closing prices achieved by other auctions. That's a great first step in finding the range you can set for your item. You can refine that range to a particular amount based on the quality of your item, the number of others like it in the Auctions, and your ability to encourage more bidding through a creative, well-thought-out, organized description, matched with clear photos of the item. The key is to study your competitors and emulate the best aspects of the highest-selling auction listings you find for that product.

The Reserve Price

You can implement an option that allows you to start the bidding low and encourage action, while protecting you, as a seller, from taking a huge loss on a given auction. It's called the reserve price. In essence, the reserve price is the lowest price you'll accept for that item. You must set some sort of minimum bid, but it will operate independently of the reserve price at first.

When you use the reserve price, your bidders will see that you're using a reserve, and the auction system will tell the bidder whether the reserve has been met or not. Bidders can thus still bid normally on the auction, and the price will go up as people compete. The system doesn't specify what the reserve price is to the bidder, but as long as the current high bid is below the reserve price, the system will say that the reserve hasn't yet been met, and it's not a qualifying winning bid. Also, Amazon hides the identity of the bidders while the reserve remains unmet.

Once the bidding has reached the reserve price, bidder identities are revealed, the auction reverts to a standard auction, and whatever the highest bid happens to be at the end becomes the legal sale from seller to buyer. However, if the bidding ends without reaching the reserve price, you as the seller aren't obligated to sell the item at the high bid.

CAUTION | *You can't change the reserve price once the auction item receives a bid. At that point, you're obligated to sell the item if the reserve price is met.*

The one thing to keep in mind is buyer sentiment. Many people pick a reserve price that's far above the retail price in order to gauge what buyers will spend without having to sell the item. Because of this, many buyers are leery to participate in a reserve price auction for fear they'll never win. Therefore, when using a reserve price, pick a fair or reasonable price, and state in your description that the reserve is a price appropriate to your costs and the worth of the item. You have the right to protect your assets, but just be aware of a buyer's concerns and address them so you can encourage more bidding on your item.

Ready to Sell?

Now that you've done some research, it's time to jump in and list your product in an auction. As outlined earlier, the easiest way to access Amazon Auctions is to go to the See All 32 Product Categories page, find the Bargains section, and click Auctions. You can also check the Browse box on the left-hand side of the page. Near the bottom of that box, you should see the link to the Auctions home page. For some, the easiest option is to simply type in the URL **http://www.amazon .com/auctions/**.

How to List an Auction Item

When you're ready to start listing auctions, the first thing to do is go to Your Seller Account by clicking Seller Account on the orange subnavigation bar near the top of the screen. You'll then be taken to your Seller Account home page (more on that in the next section) where you should see the header Manage Your Inventory and a subheader Add New Inventory For Sale underneath that. Simply click the List New Items For Sale link to get started! See Figure 5-5.

You'll be taken to a (long) one-page form titled List Your Auction, which includes the following five key areas of information:

- Item Information

- Location

- Listing Information

- Selling Preferences

- Optional Features

These five areas cover everything Amazon needs to know to make your auction a viable listing. In later chapters, we'll talk about a method called Auction Bulk Loader, where you can specify all of this information in one file and upload multiple auction listings in one shot. But for now, on with the auction listing form . . .

Item Information

The first section in the form concerns the basic information about your item for auction, as shown in Figure 5-6. At this step in the game, it's helpful to have the

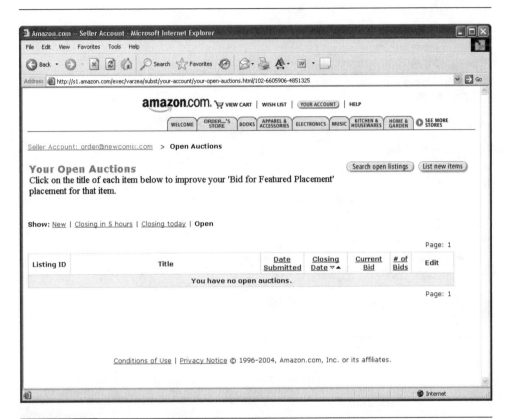

FIGURE 5-5   Your list of open auctions. Simply list any new items to get started.

item close by so you can inspect it while writing. Also, make sure you've taken at least one digital picture or scan of the item, or have a digital picture available.

First up is your Auction Title, item A in Figure 5-6. We like to call this the "most important real estate" you own for your auction. You're allowed up to 80 characters in your title, and we advise you to use as many as possible. The title is what buyers first see when they're searching auctions and going through long lists trying to decide which to view. Use a title that will show up in many search results and be compelling enough that users want to click it to read more. Make sure any and all valid keywords about your item are also in the title. Your research (discussed earlier) should indicate what keywords other sellers are using, so don't be afraid to use the same keywords. Do make sure they're in some logical order, however, so that when people read the title, they get a sense of what's for sale.

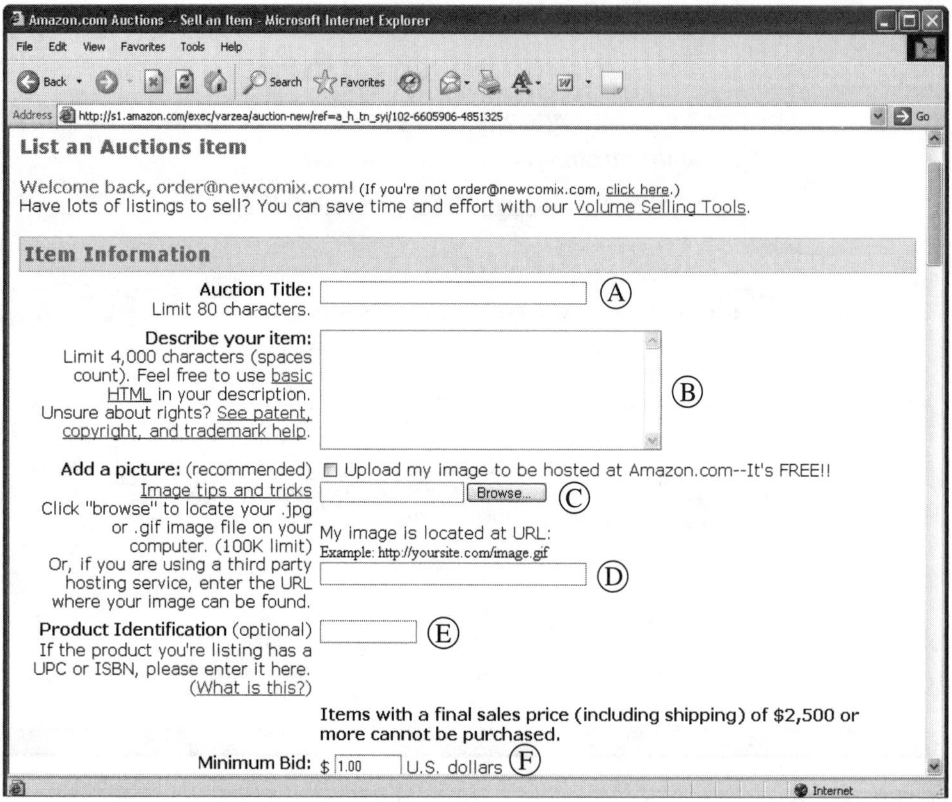

FIGURE 5-6 The Item Information section of the Auction form

For example, let's say you're selling a new Panasonic DVD recorder and you're trying to come up with a title:

> BAD: New Panasonic DVD Recorder
> GOOD: NEW Panasonic DMR-E500HS DVD Video Recorder Mint In Box

TIP

If you've got room, consider adding keywords that are slightly misspelled in order to help catch buyers who misspell their search terms when looking for your product!

Next up is the Describe Your Item field, item B in Figure 5-6. This is where you can really make the item stand out. Use a full description, but try to present information in a clear and compelling manner. Employ things like bulleted lists, vivid examples, and talk about the use of the product. Also, use different paragraphs and subheadings whenever possible so people can read through the page quickly, find the information they need, and be interested enough to enter a bid. The way Amazon presents their auctions is to put all the valuable information at the top of the screen, and then show the full description below, so most people will have to scroll down or click a link marked More to see everything. Because of this, make sure the first two sentences give the core details of the item. Don't spend the first two lines in an anecdote or story trying to get an emotional hook. Relate all the key information and facts first, and then elaborate later. You want that "snippet" of the description to make sense on its own and act as a logical hook so viewers consider bidding on the item.

Third is the picture. Amazon allows you to upload one picture to use in your auction. In some cases, you can actually use your description to add HTML tags that include more pictures. However, since Amazon will put a thumbnail of your first picture next to your title, you should use a strong representative image to catch the eye of anyone searching the listings. Some great books go into a lot of detail about digital photography, so if you want to know more about how to take your picture, we recommend picking one of them up, like *How to Do Everything with Digital Photography* by David Huss (McGraw-Hill, 2004).

If your item is flat, like a book, CD/DVD, or piece of paper, we suggest using a scanner to take a crisp picture. Scanners are available at your local electronics store starting at $50, while digital cameras begin around $100. You can also find tools like these in print shops like FedEx Kinkos. If you're building an Amazon strategy for your own business, see if your IT department can help out in these areas.

If you can't take a digital picture of the item, one option is to use a photo from the manufacturer's web site. A stock photo will at least show the buyers what they're bidding on. We strongly recommend you make a note in the description that says this is a stock photo and not the actual item, since these images still enjoy copyright protection even though they're on the Internet.

You have two choices about how your picture is stored. You can click the Browse button (part of item C in Figure 5-6) to locate the picture on your computer, and then click the check box next to the option Upload My Image . . . This sends your picture to Amazon, where your picture is then kept on the server. If your image is already stored and accessible on the Internet, you can enter the full URL web address of your picture in the box underneath the My Image Is Located At URL header, window D in Figure 5-6.

If your item has any kind of UPC code or ISBN number, you can enter it in the Product Identification box, item E in Figure 5-6. This is an optional field, but if the item has an identifying number, entering it will allow the buyer to get more details about the product, which will hopefully lead to a sale. For example, if this number matches an item in Amazon's catalog, Amazon will present key product information on the auction page. Additionally, if someone wants to research a product on a manufacturer's site, the UPC number could help the buyer isolate the correct model.

The next three fields have to do with the pricing information for your item. You must enter a decimal or whole number to indicate your minimum bid, field F in Figure 5-6. If you'd like to use a reserve price for your auction, then click the Yes radio button next to Reserve Price, and indicate your reserve price in the box provided. Finally, if you'd like to set a special price called the Take-It price, click the Yes radio button and enter your Take-It price in the box provided. (For more information on this feature, see the sidebar.)

The Take-It Price

One unique pricing feature that Amazon offers for their auction sellers is the Take-It price. When auction sellers list their item, they can set a price that says, "Ok, if someone pays me $X amount, I'm willing to stop the auction right there and sell the item to that bidder for that price." Usually, people pick the high limit of what they think their item will go for, or an attractive price meant to encourage a buyer to take advantage of this price to end the auction early.

What makes this feature unique from other sites, such as eBay and their "Buy-It-Now" price, is that the Take-It price does *not* disappear after the first bid has been made. As long as bidding remains below the Take-It price, that option remains. So, let's say you're auctioning a digital camera with a $1 starting bid and a $200 Take-It price. As bidding approaches $200, the option remains for anyone to come along, bid $200, and end the auction, guaranteeing that they'll win the item. Once that amount is bid, the auction is over and you, as the seller, would contact the bidder to seal the deal.

You have the option to change the Take-It price until at least one person bids on the item. You cannot use the Take-It price if you're doing a Dutch auction for multiple items. If you do use the Take-It price and nobody takes advantage of it, your auction will close normally with the high bidder winning the item.

The key to a good Take-It price is to find a healthy balance between presenting an attractive deal/bargain to your buyer and achieving a satisfactory profit margin for your sale. By studying completed auctions, you should see a range of sale prices. Aim for something above the average but below the highest price bid since that can help you achieve that balance.

The last piece of information to enter in this section is your Shipping and Handling fee. This is an optional field, so you can leave it blank and negotiate your shipping and handling fee with the buyer once you know their location. But if you have a flat price you'll charge all U.S. customers, go ahead and fill out the shipping and handling fee here. This way, your buyer will know their full amount before they buy, and are less likely to be surprised by the shipping and handling fee later. Buyers have been burned by people who make their true profit with an overinflated shipping charge for a small or light item. We'll cover the ins and outs of managing your shipping costs in Chapter 11.

Category: Location, Location, Location

The next section simply asks you to assign a category to your auction. Since Amazon hosts so many auctions, they've established over 20 main categories, and several levels of subcategories in each category, everything from Art & Antiques to Travel and Real Estate. Simply peruse the different category listings in the form, and when you spot the category that best represents your item, click the drop-down arrow to pick the best subcategory for your product. Remember, when doing your research, note which categories were used by other sellers when they auctioned off a similar item.

Listing Information

The third section of the form deals with the characteristics of your auction listing itself, not the item, as you can see in Figure 5-7. First, you need to pick the duration of your auction, and how long you want it to be open for bids. You can pick any amount of days from the drop-down box, from 2 to 14. The rule of thumb here is that you want your listing to be active long enough for a group of people to find it, but not too long so people aren't waiting forever. A seven-day listing ensures that it's visible for a full workweek and one weekend, but a well-timed three- or five-day listing can give you visibility over a weekend and a quicker turnover on your inventory.

Higher-priced items may need a 10- or 14-day auction so the greatest amount of people will have the opportunity to log in and bid for it. While this means the buyers will have to wait longer, saving money on a high-priced item is usually worth their wait.

Next is the type of auction. If you're just auctioning off one item, or one specific lot, stay with the Standard auction, which has the traditional "ascending-bid" auction format you're used to seeing in live auctions.

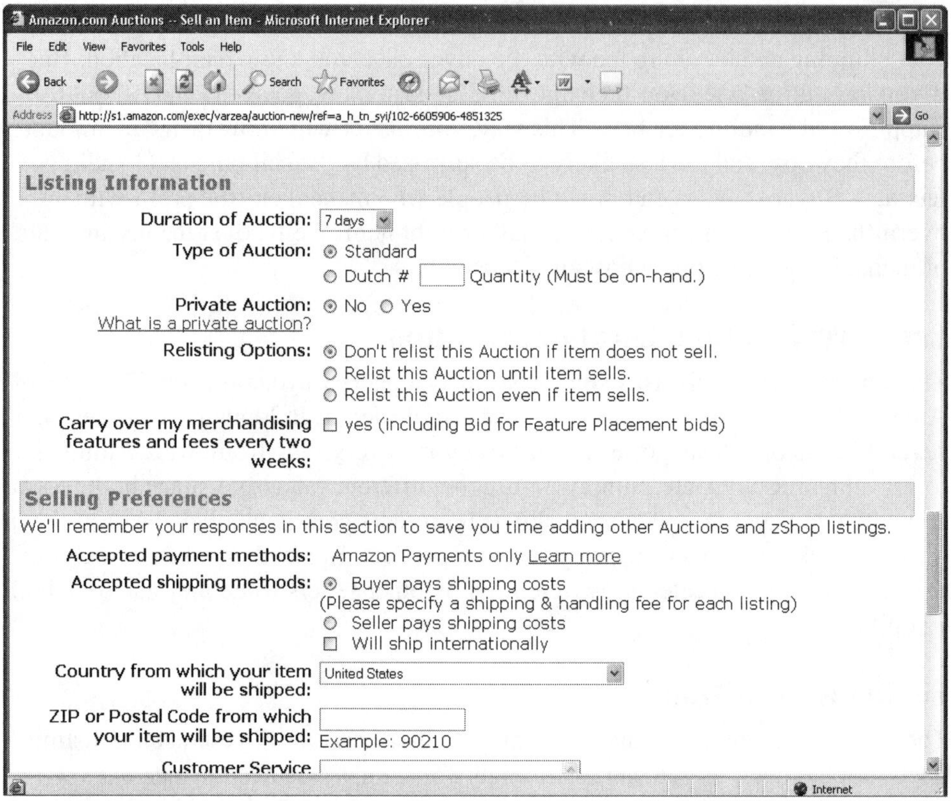

FIGURE 5-7   Information about how your listing will operate on Amazon

However, if you'd like to sell multiples of the same item, click the radio button marked Dutch and enter the quantity you're selling. For example, if you've got ten identical watches that you'd like to sell at once, enter ten and the ten highest bids for your item will be the winning bids.

If you want to restrict the type of people who can participate in your auction, click the Yes radio button next to the Private Auction header. This allows you to limit your auction so only a predetermined, pre-approved list of people can bid on your item.

Finally, you can set an option that tells Amazon to automatically relist your auction one time if there is no successful bid the first time. Later on in the chapter, we'll talk about how you can relist your auction yourself, but this can be a good option to set if you know you want to sell it in the Amazon Auctions. Along with that option, if you want the same features to be continued in the relisted auction, click the Yes check box in the appropriate field.

Selling Preferences

The fourth section of the List Your Auction form has to do with your Selling Preferences, as shown in Figure 5-8. The nice thing about this section is that Amazon will remember your Selling Preferences and carry them through to all your other auctions. Thus, having filled it out once, you won't have to fill it out for the next auction; Amazon will keep all the same settings.

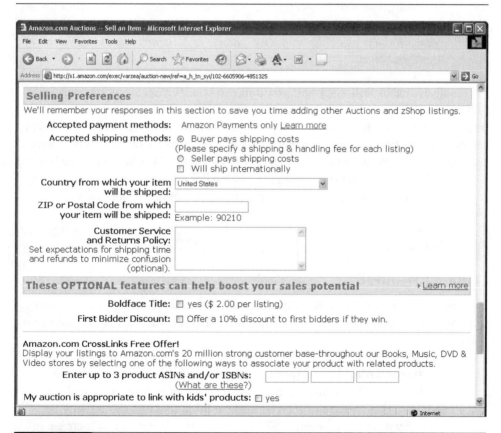

FIGURE 5-8   Your Selling Preferences in the Amazon Auctions

As far as payments go, Amazon Payments will coordinate collecting the money from your buyer and will disburse accumulated funds to you every two weeks, as we discussed in Chapter 4. As for shipping costs, you must decide whether the buyer or the seller will pay for shipping. (Typically, the buyer pays for the shipping. In fact, for online auctions, the buyer expects to pay for the shipping.) You also have to decide whether you're willing to ship the product internationally. We'll spend all of Chapter 13 talking about the global potential that Amazon can bring you.

Next, Amazon wants to know where your item will be shipping from, so it can help calculate shipping costs for your buyer. You need to specify the country in the drop-down box, and then enter the ZIP or postal code where your item is currently located. Amazon will compute costs based on standard (or Media Mail) and Express Mail from the U.S. Postal Service.

> NOTE *Typically, you should specify where the item will actually be shipping from, not where you're doing business from. If you're located in California, but your products will ship from a warehouse in Missouri, use the ZIP code of the warehouse.*

Finally, Amazon will ask you if you'd like to specify your "customer service policies." This field is optional. Basically, this is the area where you can describe how and when your items will be shipped out, and how you'll respond to refund or return requests. For example, you can put "Next day delivery on all orders received by 5 p.m. All returns accepted with a 10% restocking fee." It's helpful to the buyer to know what to expect before they place a bid. After all, Amazon is tracking your results and can penalize you if buyers report too many troubles working with you.

> NOTE *Details about creating other sales policy will be covered in more detail in Chapter 10.*

Optional Features

The last section of the Auction form deals with optional features you can include to bring more attention to your item. Currently, there are four optional features you can consider:

- ■ **Boldfaced Title** For $2 more, Amazon will put your auction title in **boldface** to help it stand out from the long list of items buyers will see when they browse or search. Keep in mind that this should only be considered for items where a $2 investment will bring a great increase in bids. Don't use it for your $1 set of books, for example, but a $450 set of golf clubs might warrant this usage.

- **First Bidder Discount**   As we'll explore more in the next section, this feature, unique to Amazon, gives the first bidder to your auction a ten-percent discount on the final price of that auction, if that first bidder wins it. This encourages bidders to bid early so they won't leave and forget to come back, but you as the seller will have to "pay" for this function by allowing the discount to occur.

- **CrossLinks**   Amazon allows you to crosslink your auction to any relevant books, music albums, movies, or DVDs in order to draw people to your auction. This free option can be very useful for the right kind of material; thus, we'll explore it further in the next section.

- **Bid for Featured Placement**   Similar to bidding on keywords on search sites such as Google, this feature allows you to place bids on specific keywords used when people search Amazon. By placing these bids, you're paying for your auction item to show up early in the results when particular keywords are used by a buyer. We'll explore this compelling, fortune-fetching feature again later in the chapter.

Previewing Your Auction and Choosing Submit!

Once you've entered all the relevant information and selected the various options available, click the Preview Your Listing button to proofread your entry and go over the information. Make sure everything is spelled out as clearly as possible and that you've picked everything you want to use for your auction. If you need to make any changes, click the Edit button near the top of the page instead of clicking the Back button on your browser. Clicking the Back button could confuse the system and prevent certain newer changes from appearing in your listing.

After reviewing the information for your listing, you'll be presented with a summary of fees so you'll know what your listing and merchandising fees will look like once you submit your listing. If you've signed up for a feature you don't want to use, now's the time to go back and edit your listing. This is a handy check to make sure you've implemented everything properly. When you're ready, click the orange Submit Your Listing button and your auction will go out live on the site, ready for bidding.

Costs Involved with Using Auctions

There are three kinds of fees involved in Amazon's auction system: listing fees, merchandising fees, and closing fees. The burden of fees for using Amazon. com auctions is borne, sensibly enough, by the seller and not the bidder or buyer.

While Amazon won't refund an item's listing fees if it doesn't sell, you still retain the option of relisting the item again without being charged a second listing fee.

> *There's one exception where the seller doesn't bear the fee: Special-event auctions. In this kind of auction, such as one for a highly desirable piece of memorabilia, the seller can charge a special fee for the winning bidder. Special-event auctions must be coordinated with Amazon staff first, so contact your Amazon customer support representative if you want to create a Special Event auction.*

Listing Fees (Required)

A listing fee is mandatory when selling on Amazon.com, and constitutes a straightforward $0.10 per listing, regardless of your minimum bid. The Pro Merchant subscription, available for $39.99 as of this writing, allows you to waive the fee. Therefore, part of your decision to purchase the Pro Merchant account should be based on whether the fee will be worth the money spent in the long run. For example, if you know you're planning to auction 100 items per week, your listing fees would be $40 a month, so you should definitely sign up for the Pro Merchant subscription as it would pay for itself just in auction listing fees alone. We'll walk through how to add this subscription in the next chapter.

Merchandising Fees (Optional)

Merchandising fees are optional on Amazon, allowing you to pay only if you wish to draw additional attention to your auction listings. Two of the merchandising services (CrossLinks and First Bidder Discounts) are free, while two others are fee-based. These are

- **Bid for Featured Placement**   With this service, your listing will show up towards the top of its category. The charge is five cents per category, per day.
- **Bold Listings**   The title of your item is listed in **boldface** via the search and browse results when this service is used. The charge is $2 per listing.

> *Merchandising fees are nonrefundable. Furthermore, unlike the listing fees, they are charged again if automatic relisting is selected.*

Closing Fees (Required)

Closing fees are mandatory, but they're only charged when an auction results in a sale. On Amazon, auction fees are calculated on a graduated scale of percentages,

Item Sales Price	Closing Fee
$0.01–$25	5 percent
$25.01 to $1,000	$1.25, plus 2.5 percent of any amount greater than $25.
$1,000.01 or more	$25.63, plus 1.25 percent of any amount greater than $1,000.

TABLE 5-1   Amazon's Sliding Scale for Closing Fees

based upon the amount of the final winning bid. Table 5-1 shows the current closing fee calculation rates.

Paying Amazon.com Auction Fees

You can pay your Amazon fees using any major credit card, ranging from Visa to Diners Club. However, you cannot use checks (even from a business checking account) or a gift certificate. If you have a Pro Merchant subscription, note that the service's sign-up fees are charged immediately upon subscription. From then on, the fees are charged on a monthly cycle to your Amazon Payments balance.

You're Auctioning—Now What?

Now that you've decided what to sell on Amazon and you're busy placing auctions on their site, what next? Well, the most successful merchants on Amazon have tended to be the ones who are most aggressive in promoting their product. Unless you have a product niche entirely to yourself (which is unlikely in today's ultra-competitive environment), you'll want to use the available methods to draw more attention to your offerings.

Bringing Attention to Your Listings

When you add an auction to your listings on Amazon, you can increase its exposure via two main methods. These are listed in Table 5-2, along with the percent increase in the sell-through of items using these methods, according to Amazon.com.

Listing Technique	Amazon's Claimed Increase in Sell-Through
CrossLinks	20 percent
First Bidder Discount	15 percent

TABLE 5-2   Amazon's Merchandising Methods

The CrossLink Function

The CrossLink function allows you to associate your items with others that complement what you're selling. To use this feature, find the ten-digit ASIN or ISBN number for an item listing and insert it in one of the CrossLink fields. So long as the link is to a book, music album, video, or DVD that isn't already in the top 500, you can CrossLink it for free!

The beauty of the CrossLink function is that it allows you to take advantage of the Amazon.com customer base and the site's strength in understanding customer demands. In essence, if a potential customer is interested in a specific product, it's likely he or she will be interested in a product that's of the same genre or category.

For example, let's say one of your auctions is for a DVD of *Tomb Raider*. Before you list the auction, you run an All Products search for *Tomb Raider* on the Amazon.com home page. Perhaps the top result is the *Tomb Raider Video Game Guide*. Simply click the result to get the ASIN (Amazon Standard Identification Number) or ISBN (International Standard Book Number) and you can CrossLink your DVD to the game, encouraging those auction bidders who are interested in the game to also check out the DVD you have for sale.

Using the First Bidder Discount

First Bidder Discount is a new feature on Amazon which you can use to entice bidders to bid early. This option gives the first bidder ten percent off if they win the auction, encouraging people who visit your auction to bid at the first opportunity in order to get the discount.

Amazon.com claims that items using the First Bidder Discount sell at a rate that's 15 percent higher than average. This is likely an accurate estimate given the psychological nature of an auction—once a bid is placed, the bidder feels psychologically invested in the item and will continue to bid to win it.

An additional advantage to this option is that it's very easy. Amazon.com handles the accounting by calculating the final amount due to you (the final bid less ten percent) automatically.

An Overview of Your Auction Seller Account

While your auctions are underway, you'll want to check and see how they're doing. The way to monitor your auctions is by accessing your Auctions/zShops Seller Account. From the Auctions home page, just click Seller Account. If you're looking at your Marketplace seller account, just look for a box along the right side of the page titled Auctions/zShops Seller Account and click the link. Either way, you'll get to your auctions home page, as shown in Figure 5-9. This is your central hub to access any of the functionality related to Amazon Auctions.

Several functions on this page will be used as often as you use Amazon Auctions:

■ **Manage Your Inventory**   Beside the word Auctions in this section, you'll see links to monitor auctions that are opening soon, are already open, and those that are closed. Click the links to see the status of your auctions. You should also use the links in the next section, Add New Inventory For Sale, to add one or multiple new auction listings to the site.

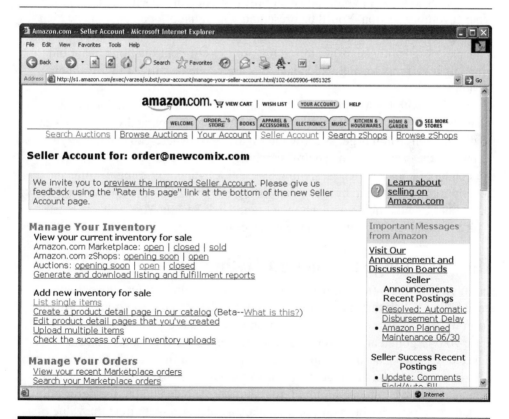

FIGURE 5-9   The Amazon Auctions Seller Account page

- **Manage Your Orders**   The third link in this section, View Your Auctions Sold, will give you a list of all your completed auctions where the buyer has paid for your item. This page is extremely useful for pulling up buyer information, such as their address, in order to mail the item. This page will also show all your Sold Auctions for the past 60 days.

- **Get Paid**   From here, you can view your Amazon Payments account and see which auctions you've been paid for, and when you were paid.

- **Your Storefront and Profile**   From here, you can update the profile that auction buyers see so you can tell them more about yourself and convince them to shop with you and your auctions.

In order to view all your open auctions, just click the Open link in the Manage Your Inventory section. You'll be presented with a list of open auctions, which you can sort by starting date, ending date, current bid level, and number of bids. This page is a handy snapshot to see the progress of your auctions, what bid amounts they're up to, and which auctions are active or still waiting for their first bid.

Just like with the Marketplace, Amazon offers you a search engine to search your auction listings. Click the Search Open Listings button and you'll be taken to the Auction search page, as shown in Figure 5-10, where you can use keywords to pull up the exact auctions you're searching for. You're given three options for conducting your search: searching by the title, searching using the title and description, or searching by using the Listing ID. Enter the appropriate keyword(s) or number into the field you want to use, and click Search. You'll be presented with a list of auctions that match the given criteria.

How to Change an Auction Listing

From your listing or search page, you should notice an Edit Or Close link next to each listing. Click that link and you'll be taken back to the Auction Information form where you can alter the information given. Please note, however, that once you've gotten at least one bid, you are very limited on what you can alter. The bid (or bids) placed were intended for the listing as it was originally described. Therefore, you cannot change the details of the auction to substitute a cheaper item once you've gotten a high bid, for example. You can add to the description, or add more pictures, but you cannot make any changes that affect the value of the item.

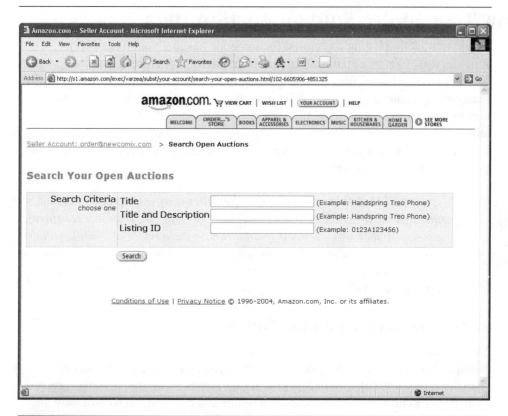

FIGURE 5-10   Search for the auction you need to see.

However, you might have good reasons for making a change. Perhaps you discovered after additional research that you forgot to mention a key fact about your item which will bring you more money for the product. Or maybe you found an important accessory after the main product was listed and you want to incorporate this newly found accessory into the lot. Perhaps you stated a benefit that you were later told wasn't true. In cases like these, and many others, you need the flexibility to make a change.

Therefore, it's recommended you make any changes early on before you receive any bids. Once you've made your changes, you'll be asked to preview your changes, just like you did when you first listed your item. Once you've finished previewing your changes, click Submit Changes to make the changes active. As always, allow Amazon some time for the changes to be reflected in your listing, something which should only take a few minutes after their submission.

Now That You've Sold an Auction Item

Once your auction listing has closed (or someone has met your Take-It price, if used), you'll get an e-mail stating that your auction has closed, with the information needed to contact your winning bidder. Once that bidder has used Amazon Payments to pay you for the item, Amazon will send you a payment confirmation e-mail containing the appropriate shipping information so you can ship out the auction item. Prompt shipping is always encouraged, and Amazon formally requests that you ship out the item within three business days of receiving the payment confirmation e-mail.

> TIP
>
> *It's usually helpful to e-mail your buyer after the item has been shipped, and include the tracking number of your package. Not only is it considered good customer service, but it'll cut down on the number of e-mails you get asking about the item. Plus, you now have a record of the tracking number you can access, in case the buyer never receives their item. For more on packing and shipping like a pro, see Chapter 11.*

Handling Returns and Refunds

Since Amazon has provided the means for you to reach your customer—via their well-trafficked online marketplace—it's up to you and your customer to reach a mutually agreeable solution in cases involving disputes over the product received. Whether you end up using a refund, or a return and a refund, do so promptly and courteously.

Returns

While not explicitly mandated, the merchant should cover the return expenses for an item if the incorrect one has been sent. If the buyer isn't satisfied even when the item has been properly represented and delivered, request that your buyer pack up the item and return it to you at their cost. (Of course, upon receipt of the item in saleable condition, you should issue a full refund to the customer.)

Refunds

Amazon.com provides a very thorough description on how to refund a payment. Simply perform the following steps in order to complete the task.

1. Click the Your Account link at the top of most pages at Amazon's web site.

2. Click the Your Seller Account link.

3. Click the View Your Amazon Payments Account And Billing History link.

4. Click the Search Your Payments Transactions link.

5. Sign in using your e-mail address and password.

6. Set the parameters for your search by entering the transaction number or date range (15 days is the default search).

7. Click the Search button to display your transactions.

8. From the resulting list, click the transaction ID that requires attention. At the bottom of the Transaction Details page, you'll find a link that allows you to create a refund. You may include a short memo explaining the reason in the Memo to Buyer message box.

9. Amazon.com sends the buyer an e-mail containing this information as soon as the refund is processed successfully. When the refund has been completed, Amazon automatically debits your merchant account for the refund amount.

What If the Buyer Doesn't Come Through?

When a buyer backs out of an Auctions transaction, or fails to submit payment, Amazon can automatically send an e-mail urging the buyer to complete the transaction so long as you submit your request for buyer contact assistance. If all efforts to resolve the transaction are unsuccessful, you should file your request to credit back your closing fee within 40 days and Amazon will do so.

CAUTION   *Remember, listing fees, Bid For Featured Placement fees, and other merchandising fees are* not *refundable!*

Unfortunately, there's always the chance that a buyer who doesn't come through will leave you negative feedback as well. Amazon's policy is to not remove negative feedback unless it lists your personal information (such as your phone number) or if it includes obscene language. If you can't convince the buyer to remove the feedback themselves, you have two options. First, you can leave feedback on the buyer. However, this isn't very useful as relatively few buyers read their feedback and Amazon does not use buyer feedback to evaluate buyers. Second, you can leave a comment on your own account. If you cannot work with the buyer to remove the feedback, at least with your comment you can present (in a few words) your side of the story.

To do the latter, go to your seller account and click the View Your Live Auctions/ zShops Member Profile link under the Your Storefront And Profile heading. Once there, use the Leave Feedback On Your Own Account link at the top of the page.

> **TIP** *Post your response as soon as possible so that the response will be displayed in close proximity to the negative comment on your feedback page.*

Relisting Auction Items

Of course, not all items sell—at least not the first time! Depending on whether you have a Pro Merchant subscription, your relisting options can be substantially different. For example, regular auction sellers can relist the auction listing one time for free. (Of course, you'll still have to pay for any optional merchandising features such as Boldface type or Bid For Featured Placement.) As a regular auctions seller, you relist items by simply clicking the Closed link for Auctions under the View Items heading on the Seller Account page.

If you're a Pro Merchant and you decide to relist, you have two choices. First, you can relist until your auction attracts a winning bidder. Second, you can relist indefinitely, even if an item attracts a winning bidder. Of course, incurring extra fees if you decide to relist indefinitely is only a smart thing to do if you have many more items to sell.

Finally, if your listing offers two or more identical items, this is called a Multiple Item Auction—a.k.a., a Dutch auction. For example, let's say you have a gross of television sets to sell. Unlike a regular auction, this type of auction can have multiple winners—in the example of the TVs, up to 144. Any Dutch auction, where relisted on Amazon as "until your auction attracts a winning bidder," will be relisted in the original quantity, less any items sold, until you retract the auction or the quantity drops to zero.

> **TIP** *Because auction listing fees are a dime, and Pro Merchant subscriptions are typically $39.95 per month, you should definitely consider getting a Pro Merchant subscription if you plan to list 100 items per week or more.*

To Sum Up

In Chapter 5, you explored the main activities involved when selling through Amazon Auctions. You saw the important part that research plays as you consider listing something on Amazon Auctions. You learned how to create an Auctions listing, the costs involved in doing so, and the different optional features available to promote your auctions listings. You also discovered how to monitor your Auction listings and how to edit any open auctions. In addition, you now have some idea of what to expect (and do) after one of your Auction listings has closed, and some of the situations you may have to handle, such as return or refund requests. In the next chapter, we'll go through all the key processes for setting up your own virtual storefront on Amazon, known as a zShop!

Chapter 6

Establish an Amazon zShop to Organize Sales

It's our job every day to make every important aspect of the selling experience a little bit better.

—Jeff Bezos, founder of Amazon.com

As Amazon's catalog began to grow beyond their first few categories, they realized that, among other things, they could never keep inventory and present every single item for sale. It was a heavy investment to carry stocks of inventory and pay to warehouse it. At the same time, companies such as eBay were proving that the market can establish itself through ambitious sellers who know their niche of merchandise better than most, and who just need a rich, steady, visible platform to set up and sell their wares. eBay grew without having to stock inventory. Therefore, Amazon decided to establish a program to become a leader in offering widely diverse product lines without having to invest in goods and warehouses. They accomplished this by having individual sellers bring their own wares to Amazon's platform and set up shop. They called the program *zShops*.

The Best Uses of a zShop

Amazon decided that a zShops seller would be a set of smaller merchants who could sell items already in the giant retailer's catalog. Since the launch of the zShop concept, many individuals and established businesses have signed on. These merchants included people who had been selling on other avenues, such as eBay, but who wanted a more stable platform without the outages and fraud concerns that eBay sellers were facing in 1999. These merchants saw that gaining a spot on Amazon would be an inexpensive and effective way to expand their online presence and utilize a multichannel strategy to give them other options if one of their channels started to falter.

As a very general rule of thumb, having an Amazon zShop makes the most sense for two kinds of sellers: those who deal with a great deal of "volume" when they sell (say, thousands of used books or DVDs versus the contents of a person's attic), and those who are committed to making a "brand presence" known on Amazon, even if they aren't a major retailer. The advantages to the first kind of seller are obvious. As a zShops proprietor, you can take advantage of a Pro Merchant account subscription rate to list an unlimited number of items, make use of fixed-price sales as well as auctions, and utilize your individual zShop storefront.

The second type of seller has been the one who's made the most of Amazon's culture. The advent of the zShop has encouraged sellers with niche specialties to make more of a home for themselves on Amazon.com and take advantage of the Amazon.com brand name to attract more clientele. These merchants were able to bring other items to Amazon's catalogs, whether it was autographed, vintage, or antique items, perishable or gourmet food, and products in categories Amazon hadn't even thought of yet for their catalog.

Amazon simply added the functionality to tie all their inventory items together and present them in a unified fashion. In addition, Amazon was able to direct buyers quickly to the right merchants by not listing zShops by storefront, allowing the buyers instead to search by category. This in turn allowed sellers to present their merchandise to prequalified buyers—those who were already looking for their specific products—and build their own brand . . . underneath the Amazon umbrella, of course.

In order to build your own zShops store, you must register for the Pro Merchant Subscription. As a Pro Merchant subscriber, you're charged $39.99 per month to maintain an unlimited number of items. Luckily, Amazon has made it easy to sign up for a Pro Merchant Subscription.

How to Set Up a Pro Merchant Subscription

The Pro Merchant Subscription is really for any seller who plans to do a lot of business on Amazon, meaning hundreds of transactions (or even thousands) per month. As a point of reference, this subscription pays for itself if a seller lists only 100 items per week. In the past, getting this subscription was optional for zShop sellers, but Amazon saw that most store owners were already achieving the sales levels that make the Pro Merchant Subscription necessary. Given the cost savings of using the subscription, and Amazon's desire to qualify their merchants to reduce fraud concerns with their buyers, the Pro Merchant Subscription is today a wise and necessary step in establishing your zShop. As we'll talk about later in the fees section, you'll save enough money through no listing fees in zShops, Auctions, and the Marketplace to pay for your subscription.

Once you're ready to get started, go to the Amazon home page, click Your Account at the top of the page, and then click the Auctions and zShops Seller Account link on the right-hand side of the page to get to your Seller Account overview screen. At this point, you should see a box asking you to start your Pro Merchant Subscription. Click that link, and you'll be taken to the first step, as shown in Figure 6-1. This screen gives you an overview of the program, covers

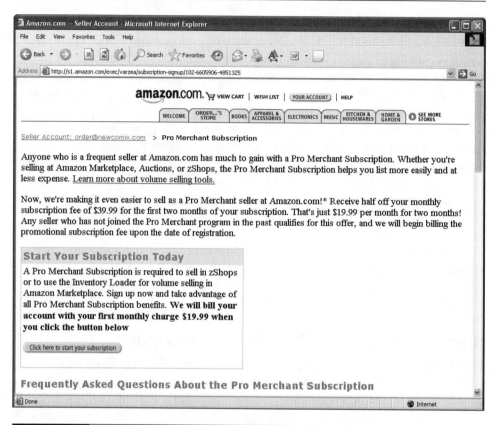

FIGURE 6-1   Ready to start your Pro Merchant Subscription?

Frequently Asked Questions, and offers you the chance to start your subscription. Click the orange Click Here To Start Your Subscription button.

If you're concerned about possibly starting a long and arduous process of entering information, deciding on attributes, and so on, you needn't worry! You're already done! Your subscription is created, and you'll see a screen announcing your success. Amazon now will go through your listings and update them so you won't have to pay any more listing fees. Remember, when it comes to your Marketplace items, for example, that 99-cent fee is only incurred when the item sells. After 15 to 30 minutes, all of your listings are automatically converted so any sales from that point will not incur the extra fees. You're now ready for the next step: establishing and customizing your very own store!

If you're still organizing your inventory and waiting for shipments to come in, you may want to wait to establish your subscription until you're ready to sell. You pay for the subscription whether you have one item or 10,000, so pick the right time to "start the clock" on it. If you plan to mainly utilize the Marketplace, for example, start your subscription when you can comfortably list at least ten items per week, since that action alone would pay for your subscription.

Ready to Sell?

Now that you've gotten your Pro Merchant Subscription, and you have your inventory items ready for listing, it's time to set up shop . . . virtually. Of course, just as any brick-and-mortar shopkeeper has to figure out their aisles, product arrangement, and stock their shelves, so does an Amazon zShop owner have to decide on categories, store layout, and how to add inventory to their store. So, let's start with the first task and figure out how to organize your inventory items into one cohesive category structure for your store.

How to Set Up a zShop

Before talking about the computer side of the equation, let's first discuss what will be going into your store—your inventory. One of the powerful features of Amazon zShops is that you, the store owner, can build your own category structure to organize your inventory and allow your customers to browse via the categories you've created. While Amazon has organized their catalog into overall categories, and subcategories, your goods may not fall into these pre-established configurations. Therefore, Amazon built the power for you to create your own structure. The best way to do this is to map out your category structure before you start entering in goods.

Once you create your categories, Amazon will present your users with a Browse box, similar to the one Amazon displays on their own home page (see Figure 6-2). Amazon will interpret the categories based on the items you've uploaded into your store, so they're always flexible, but you want to be careful and set up a good plan in advance. Every time you change the category path of an item and it doesn't match up to an existing category, you've now created extra subcategories and a potentially confusing category structure for your customers. For example, if your customers are expecting to find all your X-box video games in the X-box subcategory of your Video Games category, and you've changed category paths that don't correspond to this path, your customers may not see all your X-box video games for sale!

The key to curing these potential problems is to draw out a flexible but concise category structure and always look at that structure when creating or modifying

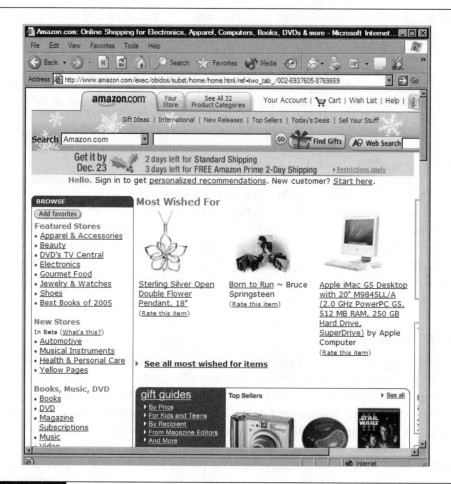

FIGURE 6-2   Amazon's Browse box allows people to browse by category.

your product listings. This structure should be part of your overall business plan, which can be as formal or flexible as you'd like. It should contain the overall vision and direction you see yourself taking with this Amazon business, however—for instance, what you plan on selling, how you plan on selling and marketing these products, and how you plan to evaluate your progress and make decisions towards the future of your sales efforts. While this may sound daunting, drawing up a business plan is an excellent way to gauge your potential, and it could save you lots of money once you begin implementing these plans. In other words, a solid business plan is well worth your effort!

To get started in your category structure, think of all the "top-level" or highest-level categories you plan to have in your store. For example, let's say you plan to sell video games and video game magazines. Video Games and Video Game Magazines would be your two top-level categories. Now, let's say you plan to specialize in first-person-shooter (FPS) games based on different game platforms. For simplicity's sake, you plan to start with four games—Halo, Doom, Final Fantasy, and Soul Caliber II—but want to add more games based on those already available for Microsoft's X-Box platform (like Halo and Doom) and Sony's Playstation 2 (PS2) platform (like Final Fantasy and Soul Caliber II). Your category structure for Video Games would look like the following:

Video Games:XBOX:Halo
Video Games:XBOX:Doom
Video Games:PS2:Final Fantasy
Video Games:PS2:Soul Caliber II

These strings of text are called your Browse Path, and they tell Amazon to do the following: Create a top-level category called Video Games. Create two subcategories underneath Video Games called XBOX and PS2. Under the XBOX subcategory, create two new sub-subcategories called Halo and Doom, and so on. This way, when people click Video Games in your store's Browse box, they can choose from PS2 or XBOX. Depending on which one they pick, they'll then see either Final Fantasy or Soul Caliber II, or Halo and Doom as the next set of subcategories.

NOTE   *You are allowed a maximum of 35 characters for each category or subcategory name, so be descriptive but not overly descriptive.*

As you build your Browse Path, put a colon (:) between each category, with no space before or after the colon. Be sure to capitalize your words correctly and consistently, as the slightest variation will tell Amazon it's another category and not the one you intended to identify. Don't create too many levels of subcategories since you want your customers to get to your items quickly, but use at least two levels so your customers can get a more precise listing of what they need, instead of having to dig through all your items to find the one they want.

NOTE   *You must enter the Browse Path exactly as it's written previously—with colons separating category names and no spaces before or after the colon—when entering your product information into Amazon.*

TIP   *If you're going to have several (more than three or four) different unique items that may be hard to classify, you may consider adding a category called Other to contain all the hard-to-classify entries.*

Create your list of categories and have it handy as you work through the zShop creation process. You'll be inputting your Browse Path for each individual item you add to the store. You won't be able to add or update the Browse Path during the customization process.

Seeing Your zShop Online

As soon as you've completed your Pro Merchant Subscription, you can view your zShop immediately online! Just go to your Auctions and zShops Seller Account, scroll to your last header—Your Storefront And Profile—and click the View Your Live Zshops Storefront link. You should see something like Figure 6-3, a basic frame to your store, with a Search box and a place where your feedback will appear. Amazon automatically creates this skeleton, which you're allowed to customize to make your own store. So, let's now tailor your store to your needs.

> **TIP** *Your constant Internet web address for your zShop, which you should give out to customers and advertise as much as possible, is simply www .amazon.com/shops/nickname (where nickname is the nickname you chose in Chapter 1 when setting up your Seller Account).*

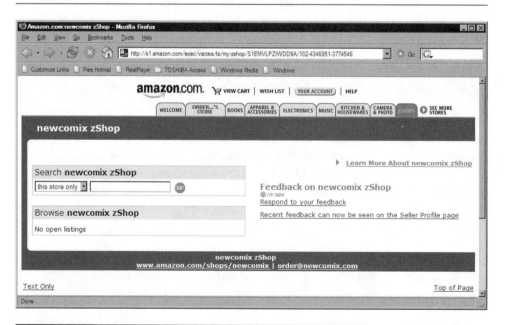

FIGURE 6-3   Your empty zShop is ready to be customized.

zShop Storefront Layout Customization

From your Auctions and zShops Seller Account screen, scroll down to the subheader Your Storefront And Profile, click the first link, which is called Edit Your zShops Storefront, to get to your customization screen, as shown in Figure 6-4. It should look similar to your skeleton storefront you just saw, except now there are Edit buttons. Clicking these Edit buttons will allow you to go in, add information, or select designs to customize your storefront so it represents you and your products in the manner you feel most appropriate.

Editing Your Brand Bar

Your first step should be to edit what Amazon calls your Brand bar. This is the bar that goes across the top of your zShop, identifying who you are and establishing your store's design—essentially what could be called the "look and feel" of the place.

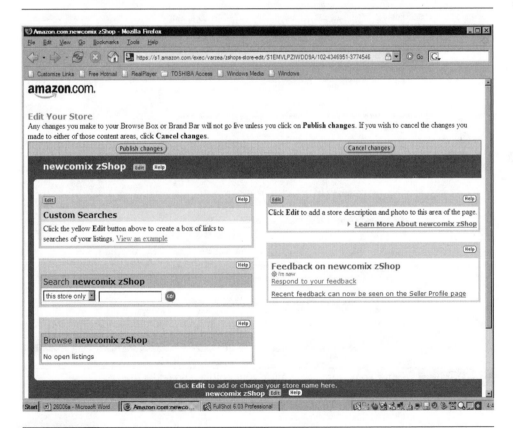

FIGURE 6-4 Customize your store layout and content here.

Click the Edit button next to the default of your store's title (in this example, NewComix zShop). Your default title will simply be the nickname you've chosen for your account followed by the word zShop. You'll be taken to a customization screen, like the one shown in Figure 6-5. From here, you can create your store name (which will be seen in your Brand bar), the text color of that name, and the background color for your Brand bar.

If you have a company logo, you can insert that logo into your zShop, which will replace your store name in the Brand bar. Fill out all the fields you'd like to change, and then click Preview in the middle of the page to review your changes.

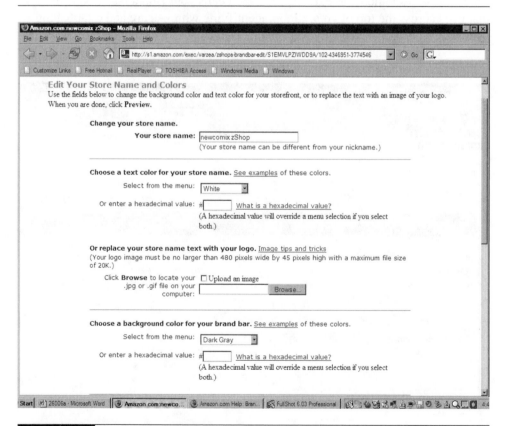

FIGURE 6-5   Enter your store name, pick your colors, and add a logo.

What's in a Name?

Your store name is the name that appears in the Title bar of a web browser when a buyer visits your store. It's also the name that appears in your Brand box at the top and bottom of your screen. You can use up to 40 characters for your store name, so make them count! Remember, picking this name does not impact your web address (or URL) at all; this is a visual aide to help you brand yourself to your customers and imply the purpose or inventory set of your store. You can use the same exact store name you have for your brick-and-mortar or e-commerce business. You can also create a new brand name that sets your Amazon store apart from your other endeavors.

You can either pick something generic, like "Joel's Stuff," to keep it clever, simple, and easy to remember, or you can pick something that incorporates your business name and product set, like "Joel's Cybernetic World of Games and Figures." Make sure you use your store name when pointing people to your Amazon zShop so they're not confused when they arrive. If you operate your own e-commerce site, you're allowed to use that name as your Amazon zShop store name. In fact, doing so is an excellent way to extend your brand name further.

TIP   *If you're having trouble thinking of the right color to use, just scroll to the bottom of this page, and Amazon shows you each color it has predefined in their system.*

Once you're at the preview screen, take a look at how your store name (or logo) appears on the screen, along with your color sections. If you're satisfied with your changes, click Continue to submit these changes. Otherwise, click the Edit button to go back and change your options. Once you're done, you'll go back to your zShops storefront, but with your Brand bar changes intact.

Editing Your Custom Searches

Next, let's take a look at your Custom Searches box. Every zShop will have a Search box so customers can enter their keywords and get to your items. However, you can help out your customers by creating a set of predefined searches, located underneath that Search box, where customers can quickly click to start their search. Click the Edit button in the Custom Searches box of your storefront to go to your Create Your Custom Search Box page, as shown in Figure 6-6.

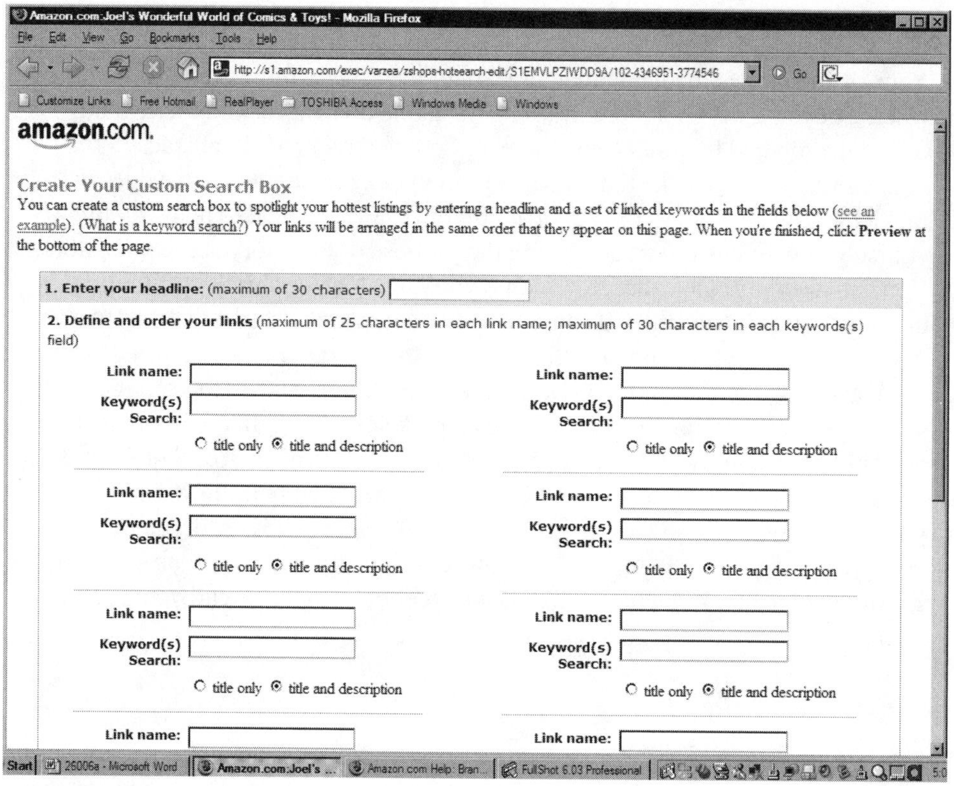

FIGURE 6-6   Create special searches based on your keyword combinations.

First, you can create a headline for all your searches. Some good examples here are "Featured Searches," "New Releases," or "Favorite Items." Next, you can create your individual searches. Each search gets a link name, which is what your customers will see, and a list of keywords, which is what Amazon will use to search your zShop when your customer clicks that Link Name.

As an example, let's say that Joel's Cybernetic World of Games and Figures store gets a lot of people looking for anything related to the Sony Playstation Portable (PSP) gaming system, since it's the newest handheld gaming platform available. You could create the link name "PSP stuff" and use the keywords "Sony PSP." Your last decision for each search you create is whether you want the search to look only at the titles of your inventory, or the title and description. In our example, we'll just look at the titles.

Once you've created all your searches, click the Preview button to see how your Favorite Searches box will appear on your store. Once you've gotten it the way you'd like, click the Continue button to commit those changes and move on. Once again, if you need to make changes, just click the handy Edit button to go back and make the necessary adjustments.

Editing Your Store Description/Photo

The next area of your zShop to manage is your Store Description section. After changing your Favorite Searches, you'll be taken back to your zShop storefront. In the top-right part of your zShop, you'll see a link called Edit Your Store Description. Click it to go to your Edit Your Storefront's Description And Photo page, as shown in Figure 6-7. From here, you can upload a picture of your store and add a lively description of it, using up to 1,500 characters. Give people an idea about what you sell, how you got started, and what people can expect when they shop with you. Don't add any HTML text to it though, since it won't be recognized when your description is displayed. Once you're done, click Preview to review

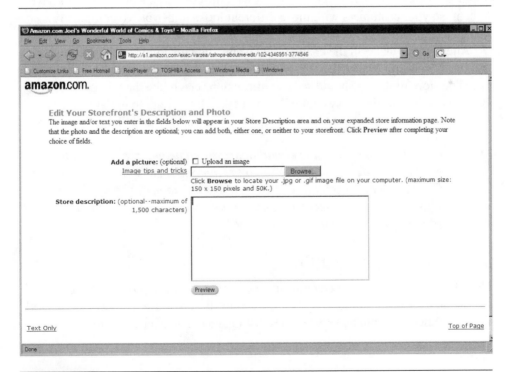

FIGURE 6-7   Describe your store in 1,500 characters or less!

your description and photo, and then click Continue to commit those changes and move to the next step.

If you don't have an actual store to feature, or don't want to use the picture of your storefront, consider using clipart images of your standard products, or an animation version of your products for sale, like a drawing of various computers or consumer electronics. Many people use their store logo in this area as a substitute.

NOTE *While you can (and should) include your own web site address in the store description, don't provide a specific link back to your web site's shopping cart or order form, as this is against Amazon zShop policy.*

One Final Review

Whenever you work on your zShop, there's one good rule to remember: Always publish your changes to make them live! Amazon allows you to make as many changes as you like, but won't promote those changes to their web site until you approve it. That way, you can experiment with different looks but you don't have to confuse your customers with those different looks until you've completely updated your site.

After you've made all the changes you want, click the Publish Changes button at the top of your Edit Your zShops Storefront screen to make those changes appear on your live storefront. You should see a confirmation screen like the one in Figure 6-8. Be advised that, while the system will say it takes four hours to update your store, some changes may take up to 24 hours to be reflected on your zShop.

TIP *If you want to change the e-mail address that people see at the bottom of your zShop page, you'll have to go to your Seller Account and click the Change Your Amazon Store-Wide Settings link to update that e-mail field. This way, you can specify an e-mail address that's dedicated to answering your Amazon customers' inquiries only.*

The Costs of Using zShops

Now that you've created your storefront, one big question you probably have is "What the heck is this going to cost me?" Luckily, the answer is "Not a heck of a lot!" Fees for zShops fall into three categories: listing, merchandising, and closing fees.

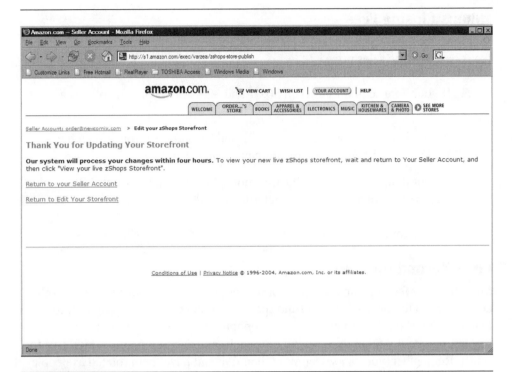

Your changes are now in the system and your store will be updated!

Listing Fees

There are no listing fees for selling at zShops. That cost is covered by your Pro Merchant Subscription.

Merchandising Fees

Merchandising fees, as of this writing, are also included. You can use the following features to draw additional attention to your most expensive or profitable listings. The time spent using these features is usually rewarded in the form of higher bids or turnover. (You'll find out more about these features in the next section.)

- **Featured Placement**   You can choose to highlight up to five items to feature in your zShop storefront. This service is free.

- **CrossLinks**   Insert a link to your listing on Amazon.com product detail pages. This service is free.

zShops Closing Fees

A closing fee is always assessed automatically when your zShops item sells. The fee is based on the sales price.

- If your item sells for between $0.01 and $25, Amazon.com collects a 5-percent closing fee.

- If your item sells for between $25.01 and $1,000, Amazon.com collects $1.25 plus 2.5 percent of any amount greater than $25.

- If your item sells for $1,000.01 or more, Amazon.com collects $25.63 plus 1.25 percent of any amount greater than $1,000.

Of course, your closing fee is refunded if your transaction is unsuccessful.

Costs Beyond the Fees

Since the only fee you currently pay for a zShops item is the closing fee, the other cost you need to consider is your time spent implementing the merchandising features. You should try to pick your most popular or highest margin items to feature in your store, but don't spend too much time agonizing over which five to select. Remember, you can select more than five and have them rotated as people visit your zShop.

Since CrossLinks are free to use, you should always try to find products to crosslink to your products, as long as the margin you're generating from these sales justifies the time spent finding such crosslink potential. Most of the time, it's worth your effort to crosslink these products.

How to Add Products to Your zShop

You've created your storefront and thought about your categories of merchandise, so now there's nothing to do but start stocking those shelves. Amazon gives you two ways of adding inventory to your zShop: an Inventory Loader that allows you to add multiple listings with one file, and a Single Item form that allows you to list each item, one at a time. We'll discuss the Inventory Loader later in the book. Right now, let's list your first inventory item.

From your Seller Account, click the List Single Items link under the Manage Your Inventory/Add New Inventory For Sale header. This takes you to the List Single Items For Sale page, as shown in Figure 6-9. You can choose to add something to the Marketplace, Auctions, or zShops. In this case, let's add a product you have in mind for your zShop. So, click the Amazon zShops link in the middle of the screen.

You've now arrived at the Sell An Item page. Amazon will prompt you either to list it in the Marketplace (using a UPC or ISBN number) or to add it to your zShop. Scroll down to #2 and start entering the item information, as shown in Figure 6-10. You'll probably notice that this form is very similar to the ones you've seen for an auction item and somewhat similar to your Marketplace item form.

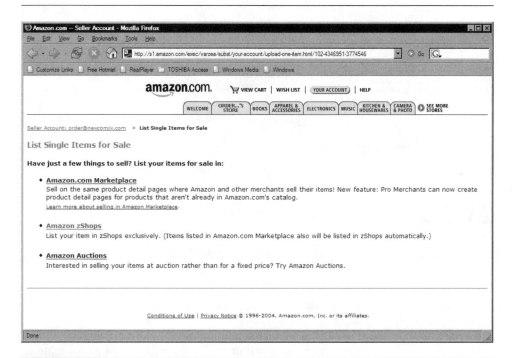

FIGURE 6-9   Pick where you want to list your items.

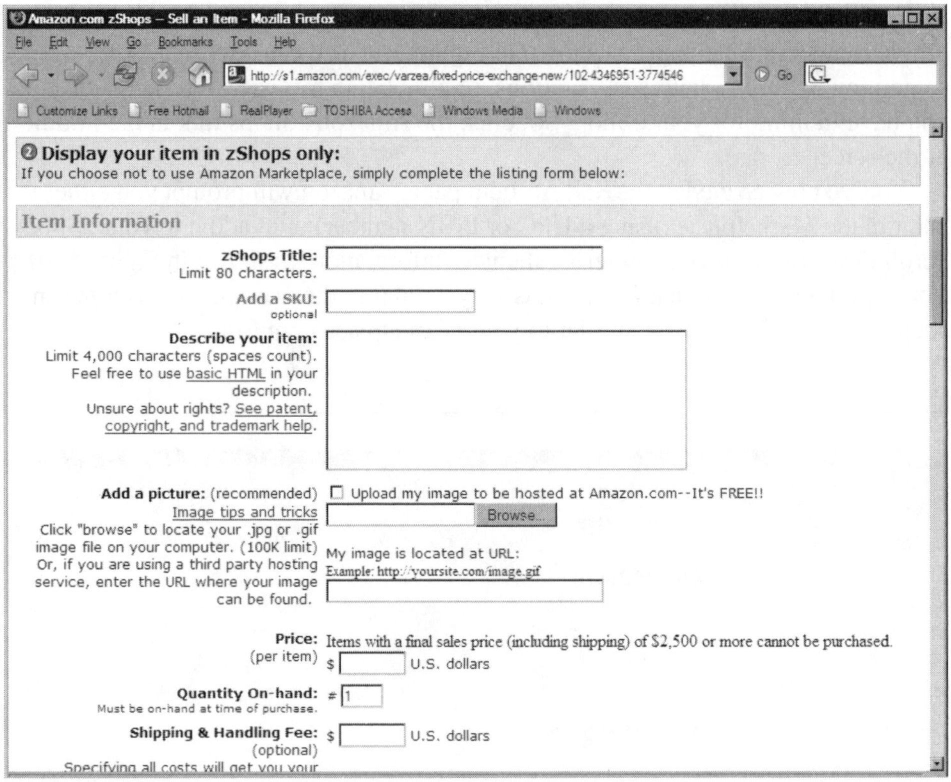

FIGURE 6-10   Start entering your information to list your inventory!

The key fields in the first section to fill in are the following:

■ **Title**   You can use up to 80 characters for the Title of your item. Remember to add important keywords to your title since this is how your customers will be searching for goods within Amazon.

■ **SKU (or Stock Keeping Unit number)**   Think of this as an identification number for your product. This number should only represent the particular item you're selling, so you can organize and retrieve records based on this number. In some cases, you can use the UPC code or ISBN number. Some people create their own SKU numbers for tracking purposes. This field is optional, so don't feel compelled to put something here if you're not going to use it. It's simply for your convenience.

For example, if you're selling Tools, you could create an SKU based on the manufacturer, model number, and size. Your 1/2" torque wrench from

Snap-On could have the SKU: SNAPWR05. This way, you could sort your inventory by your SKU and judge the results by the product line instead of the entire data set.

■ **Picture**   You can either upload one picture for your item, to be stored on Amazon's site, or you can specify the URL web address where your picture is stored online. If you upload a picture, be sure to mark the check box *and* use the Browse button to find the picture on your computer. While you're not required to add a picture, we strongly recommend adding one whenever possible. While there's no official study from Amazon about how a picture increases sales, other sites proudly boast statistics saying that including a picture raises sales by as much as 20 to 50 percent.

■ **Price**   If you're selling something that Amazon carries, you cannot charge more than they do, unless your item is collectible in some way. If Amazon doesn't carry the item or is out of stock on the item, you are free to price it according to its market worth, with one exception: Amazon does not allow any individual zShop item to go for more than $2,500 so every item is covered by their A to Z Guarantee program.

In the next section, you're prompted to assign a Location to your item, which is a category within Amazon's structure that will help classify your item. The main benefit of this is that when someone searches Amazon's overall categories, they can find your zShop item in that search if you've assigned it to a category. The important thing in this section occurs at the end of the category list, where you assign your own Browse Path, as shown in Figure 6-11. As we discussed earlier in this chapter, you should have a Browse Path consisting of your top-level category plus any subcategories, where this item is located in your overall structure. Enter that Browse Path in the box provided, and remember to use colons to separate each category.

In the last two sections, you're asked to specify your Selling Preferences and the Optional Features you want to use when listing this item. This looks almost identical to the Auctions listing form, with some minor changes. The main things to note here are

■ **Payments**   All Amazon zShop payments are now processed through Amazon Payments, so you don't have to worry about using your merchant account here.

■ **Shipping Information**   Here you can decide who pays for shipping, the buyer or you. Most of the time, the buyer pays for the shipping cost (and this is typically expected by the buyer), but you can specify this on an item-by-item basis if you want to cover the shipping cost. Be sure to enter the ZIP code where the item is being sent from so shipping costs are calculated correctly. Enter the appropriate fields, as shown in Figure 6-11.

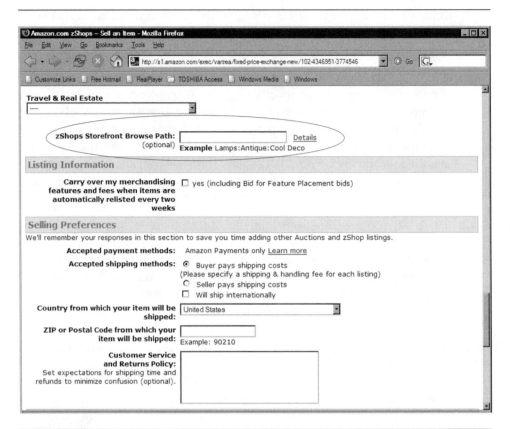

■ **Customer Service and Return policy**   Use this field to describe what your
overall policies are for returns and customer questions. Most people use this
field to state whether they take returns or not, what is expected of the buyer
when that happens, how long the buyer has to file for a refund or return, and
the average time it will take you to respond to customers' inquiries. (For
example, you could state "All questions answered within 48 hours.")

■ **Feature on Your zShops Storefront**   This is a unique feature to
Amazon's zShops. As a zShop owner, you are allowed to feature up to five
of your items directly on your zShop home page. The way to do this is to
mark the check box, as shown in Figure 6-12, next to the items you want
to feature. If you list more than five items with this check box on, Amazon
will rotate through these selections every time a buyer loads your zShop
home page.

Don't overlook this feature since it provides a fresh way to display different merchandise, especially once you've built up a loyal following to your zShop. This is a great way to promote new products or promote items whose sales are decreasing.

■ **CrossLinks**   Just like with Auction items, Amazon allows you to crosslink your inventory item with almost anything in their Books, Music, DVD, or Video store, as long as it's not one of the Top 500 items in those stores. This allows you to present your listing to a buyer who is looking for something similar in one of those four mentioned stores. For example, let's say you're selling a unique Fantastic Four toy, and you wanted to link that item to the *Fantastic Four* movie soundtrack. All you'd have to do is enter the UPC code of that soundtrack in the box provided (see Figure 6-12) and when people look for that soundtrack, they'll see the link to your item on the Detail page for that soundtrack.

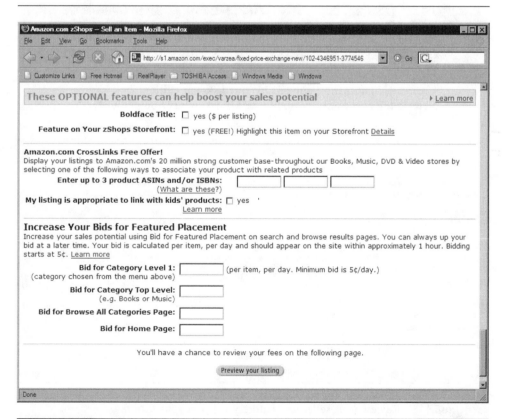

FIGURE 6-12   Select optional features like featuring your item on your storefront.

Once you've gone through the entire form, click Preview to review all the information you've entered. The key with this page is that you'll also see, at the bottom of the page, a summary of the fees you'll incur for listing this item, as shown in Figure 6-13. If you're satisfied with everything you've entered, just click Submit and your inventory item will be added to your store.

When you're finished, Amazon will display a confirmation screen for your new listing, like the one in Figure 6-14. You're presented with the key information about your new listing, along with specific URL web addresses to your item and your seller profile. Having the item URL is important to help direct people to your specific item listing. Below this information are three important buttons: Sell Another Item, Sell Another Item In This Category, and Sell Another Item Like This. These buttons make it easier to list similar merchandise without entering a lot of the same information over and over. We recommend using the Sell Another

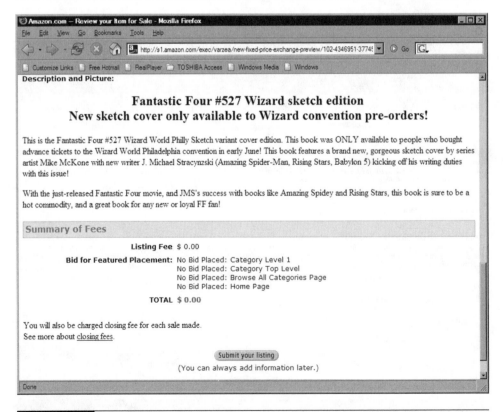

FIGURE 6-13   Review your seller fees before you list in your zShop.

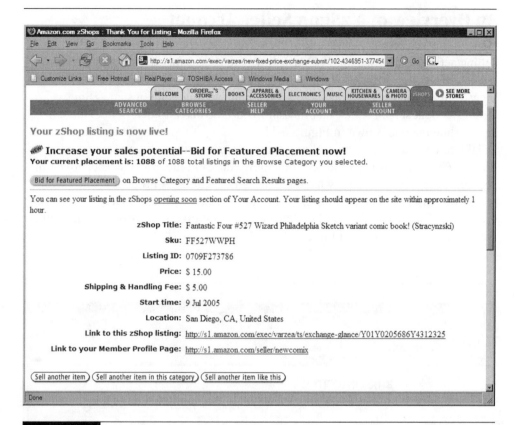

FIGURE 6-14   Your item has been listed! Use the buttons to list more inventory.

Item Like This button since it will copy all of the previous item's information into a new listing form, saving you a lot of typing but allowing you to make any specific changes and resubmit it quickly.

You're Selling... Now What?

Now that you've got your initial set of products up on your zShop, you should start to shift gears and think about the overall business you're receiving from the zShop and how to improve it. Some of this will come from monitoring the buying patterns and questions that come in from your customers. You may want to focus on certain sets of merchandise that are in higher demand than others, add merchandise, feature new items on your storefront, and so on. In order to do that, however, you need to know how to monitor your listings and make updates when necessary.

An Overview of a zShop Seller Account

As with the Marketplace or Auctions, your Seller Account is the hub of all your selling activities of Amazon. The easiest way to access this screen is to click the Your Account link at the top of any Amazon.com web page. Once you log in and view Your Account page, you should see a link for your Auctions and zShops Seller Account screen. Click that link and you'll be taken to that Seller Account screen, like the one shown in Figure 6-15.

If you compare your new Seller Account screen to the one you saw while reading Chapter 5, you should see some new entries in the Manage Your Inventory section. Specifically, you now have the link to the Create A Product Detail page, which was discussed in Chapter 2. You can also edit any Product Detail pages you created, and you can check on the status of your multiple inventory uploads, which we'll discuss in greater detail in Chapter 10.

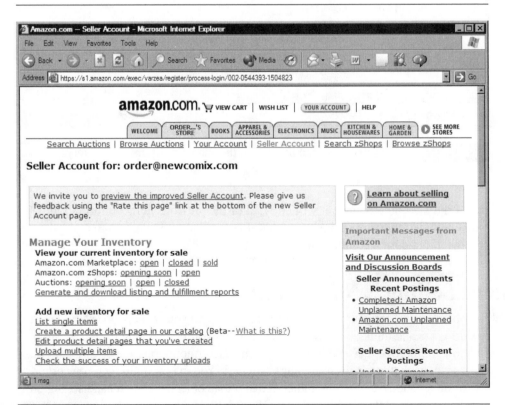

FIGURE 6-15   Your zShops Seller Account screen

How to Change a Store Inventory Item

From your Auctions and zShops Seller Account screen, you can look at any open items in your store by clicking the Open link next to the Amazon.com zShops title in the Manage Your Inventory section. You'll then be taken to a list of all your open (or active) zShop listings, like the example in Figure 6-16. This summary screen gives you a snapshot of everything you have for sale.

The last column, Edit, contains a link where you can reopen any listing and make any changes. Click the Edit link for the line item you want to change and you'll be taken back to the List Your Item form, which contains all the previous information.

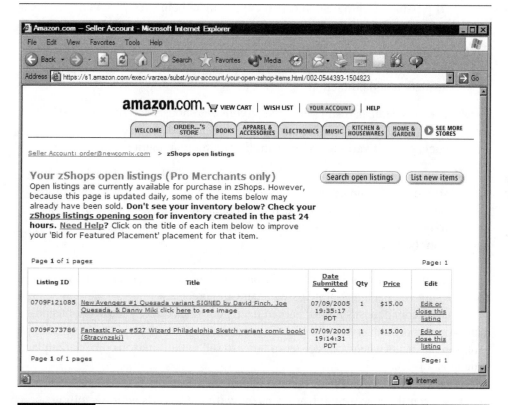

FIGURE 6-16 See all your active zShop inventory listings and make changes from here.

Now that You've Sold an Item

Essentially, you'll want to collect payment and ship your item out. Just as with Amazon.com Auctions, one of Amazon.com's latest policies dictates that all sellers must register to accept payment via Amazon Payments. As discussed in detail in Chapter 5, the use of Amazon Payments streamlines the buying process for both parties and ensures consumer confidence since all purchases are backed by Amazon's A to Z Guarantee plan.

When it comes to shipping out your items, the best way for you as a seller to get ahead is to create a systematic approach to warehousing, packing, and shipping your items. There are a few key elements to any successful Amazon business:

- Make sure your products are stored in a secure, protected environment. (If possible, a climate-controlled environment helps preserve your products and reduces the risk of damage due to extreme heat or cold.)

- Whenever possible, you should be able to pack your items for shipment at your warehouse, so you're not transporting raw products without proper insulation and protection.

- Create a dedicated shipping area at your warehouse, so you can easily organize all your shipping supplies and create a dedicated process to package your various products in the minimum amount of time possible.

- Always monitor the level of shipping supplies on hand and reorder your supplies with enough lead time so you don't run out of any items. Running out of key supplies can force your products to sit in your warehouse unable to be shipped, which can ruin your customer satisfaction and, ultimately, your bottom line.

We'll spend more time in Chapter 11 on setting up efficient back-room processes to make sure you handle your items with care and precision.

Amazon.com deposits money earned from your sales directly into your business bank account once every two weeks. There is no fee for this service. You enable Amazon payments when you register in order to sell in the Amazon.com Marketplace, Auctions, or zShops.

Since your buyers will use Amazon Payments to pay for your item upon purchase, you'll get an e-mail from Amazon with the buyer's address, telling you that it's time to ship out the item. While Amazon doesn't have a set policy governing your shipping methods, they strongly recommend you e-mail your buyer when you ship their item. Additionally, preparing your packages so that they look professional and will adequately protect the item is simply common sense.

One minor item you can do in order to impress upon the buyer their positive experience in buying from an Amazon.com zShops merchant is to prominently label your package: Your Amazon.com zShops Order.

To Sum Up

In Chapter 6, we walked through all the major aspects of opening up your own virtual storefront on Amazon, known as the zShop. We covered what it takes to sign up for the Pro Merchant Subscription and how to add it to your account. We then talked about how you should organize your inventory into your own categories, as well as discussed how to transform your bare-bones zShop storefront page into your own customized shop, full of information, logos, and colors. After advising you of the costs, we talked about adding your inventory into the store, using the categories you just thought of earlier.

We wrapped up by going over the Seller Account functions that help you manage your zShop activities, how to edit your existing inventory that's for sale, and what to do once you sell an item from your zShop. The functionalities involved in these processes are very similar to conducting Auctions on Amazon.

This marks the end of Part II, given that we've now demonstrated the three key areas to doing business on Amazon. As we venture into Part III, we'll discuss how you can position your activities on Amazon and draw in more people, both the loyal Amazon customer following and new customers who are looking for you and your products. Since you've now built the store and set up shop, it's time to get some people through that front door so you can make your fortune!

Part III

Use Marketing Techniques for Greater Profit

Chapter 7

Market Yourself Using Amazon

About three months ago, we stopped doing TV advertising . . . it worked, but not as much as the kind of price elasticity we knew we could get from taking those ad dollars and giving them back to consumers.

—Jeff Bezos, founder of Amazon.com

In Part III, we're going to look at various marketing techniques that other Amazon sellers are using. We'll do this by first discussing specific techniques in this chapter, and then by focusing on other Amazon programs like Paid Promotions (Chapter 8) and how Amazon can enhance a valuable marketing tool—e-mail campaigns—in Chapter 9.

It's an interesting fact that Jeff Bezos' attitude towards marketing is very much the same as the vast majority of people who sell on Amazon. Rather than spend money on advertising, prospective Amazon merchants decided to forego the chore of hunting for new customers and instead go where the action is—the Amazon Marketplace. Since the customers are already "on the river"—as those who work with Amazon like to put it—the remaining challenge is to steer these interested buyers to your particular store.

Become an Amazon Expert

To some it might seem ironic that in the new Information Age the most reliable way to attract customers who are strongly motivated to visit your store and purchase items is the time-tested tenet of word of mouth. In fact, this makes a great deal of sense—when there has been an explosion of goods and services along with a general cynicism of mass advertisements, personal recommendations do matter. Where a personal recommendation from a friend is unavailable, people more often than not will turn to the opinion of an "expert." Expertise in this context means a great deal more than a degree. In fact, it can refer to a great amount of real-world experience with a particular field or product.

An Amazon expert is like having a knowledgeable store owner who's able to answer all your questions, which results in you doing your business with him or her. For example, say you're a consumer who has an interest in growing exotic orchids. Which retailer would you do business with—the standard strip-mall garden warehouse supply store, or the store with an owner who not only can name the different types of plants you're interested in off the top of her head, but who has also been cited numerous times in the local paper as *the name* in orchids? When you become an Amazon expert, you help differentiate yourself based on your expertise and thereby give customers the confidence that shopping with you will be a good experience.

In addition, being an expert does more for you than simply allow you to retain customers who are looking for extremely specialized information or goods. There is also a halo effect created by the expert—in other words, if you're perceived as an expert in one area, then it's likely you're knowledgeable about closely related fields as well. In our example, if you know that the shop owner is an expert in orchids, you'll likely have a higher opinion of their knowledge about growing all sorts of plants— and you'll also be more likely to purchase tulip bulbs or grass seed from them.

Finally, Amazon experts benefit from a higher level of general visibility on the site. Much as local experts tend to get more business when they're noted in the newspaper, becoming an expert raises your profile when selling "on the river." It's this extra visibility that can steer people to your listings since they see you as an expert on a given product or subject area. Best of all for the business that is watching the bottom line, there is no required investment in cash—what you're leveraging is your own hard-won expertise.

In the brick-and-mortar world, the businessperson who offers opinions and advice gains a following. In Amazon, you can do that by becoming an expert. Amazon has three ways you can become a visible expert: by reviewing products, using Listmania, or creating a special Amazon "So You'd Like To" list. In each case, you'll be afforded an opportunity to gain more visibility—and offer a link to your store—on many more Amazon.com web pages than any other method.

Review Other People's Products and Gain Exposure

The simplest way to gain exposure on Amazon is by writing reviews. Every single page on Amazon contains a link next to the product description with a link to the customer reviews, where the latest reviews are posted at the bottom of the page. Reviews do not have to be long if they are informative, such as the example in Figure 7-1.

Each review will in turn have at least two links (the reviewer's name and See All My Reviews) that can take an interested reader to a profile of the reviewer, as shown in Figure 7-2. Notice that details about the reviewer are listed under the Browse column on the left. If this reviewer had an auction listing or a zShop, a link to the person's items would be listed here.

Amazon also rewards reviewers who give their real name or review multiple items with special links, called "badges." These items, discussed a little later in this chapter, give additional opportunities to read the profile of the reviewer.

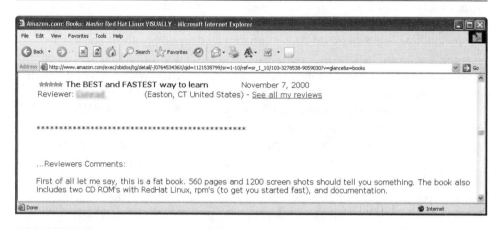

FIGURE 7-1   A sample product review

This in turn begs the question: why would someone want to learn more about a particular product's reviewer? At times, it is because you may have written such an interesting or controversial take on a product that a browser may want to read more of what you have to say. More often, it will be because Amazon buyers are,

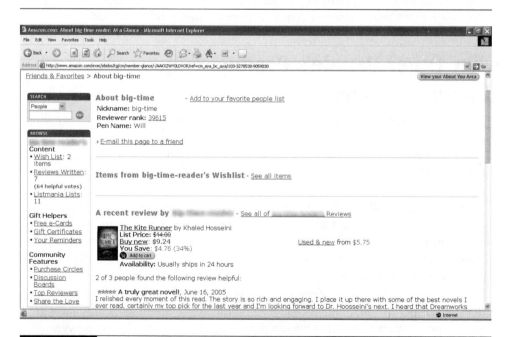

FIGURE 7-2   A sample reviewer profile

by and large, information-gathering people. Certain types of reviews will boost interest in your profile, which of course will link to your own listings or zShop.

Similar Product Reviews

How you write your reviews is important, particularly if you want to catch the attention of Amazon users. Writing a review that says "This item is great, and I have 50 of these on sale at my zShop!" isn't against the rules, but it will change your recommendation from an "expert opinion" into just another ad.

First off, the review must be a sincere appraisal of a product's strengths and weaknesses. Second, you can discuss your expertise in a positive, nonconfrontational way. You want to come across as a seller who likes the product line so much that you actually deal in it. Finally, you'll want to write reviews for products similar to the ones you carry, allowing you to catch the attention of people who may be drawn to buying widgets, but are not familiar with the brand you carry.

Here are two quick examples of reviews you could consider posting:

```
Excellent product so long as you can find it!
Reviewer: Widgetguy (USA)

I personally think the Black Edition widget is the hottest product
out there. It just looks so cool—and you'll differentiate yourself
from The Crowd. It's very capable and packed with features. I've been
carrying this widget for a while and it's always been a perennial
seller, so much so that I have to work to keep it in stock.


* * * * * * * * * *


An A for Effort
Reviewer: Widget_Expert (USA)

The Silver Edition widget works well and has a decent interface.
Having worked with widgets as a hobbyist and developer for a decade
though, it still lacks a couple of the colors that I've only seen
on Brand X models. I've had a lot more luck (and fewer returns)
from Brand X since it has a special feature that the others don't.
```

Become a Top Reviewer

You continue to gain more credibility if you decide to become one of Amazon's Top Reviewers. A Top Reviewer is someone who's contributed their knowledge and expertise to Amazon to achieve this status. You can't simply attain this rank by writing dozens and dozens of reviews. In the first place, as discussed earlier in this chapter, the content of your review matters a great deal. Simply posting a review that says "Thumbs up!" or "I sell these so I like them" is either dismissed out of hand or viewed negatively.

Second, Amazon allows its readers to weigh in on the judgment of the reviewers, allowing them to decide whether the reviewer does indeed know what they're talking about. Amazon provides small buttons by each review, encouraging people to vote Yes or No on whether a review was helpful to them. While the exact formula Amazon uses to tabulate how many Yes or No votes add or detract from a reviewer's reputation, it's obviously in your interest to convey accuracy and knowledge in your review when you post it on the site.

Top Reviewers are graced with a special badge, or symbol, that tells other Amazon.com customers that you've earned a Top Reviewer badge, or that you're willing to publicly be part of the Amazon.com community with the Real Name badge. Badges are a link placed by your name in your review, letting people know that you're a Top Reviewer or that you've put your Real Name out in the open. Some of the Top Reviewer badges are shown here:

#1 REVIEWER   TOP 10 REVIEWER   TOP 50 REVIEWER   TOP 500 REVIEWER   TOP 1000 REVIEWER

Listmania

A second way to raise your profile is to use the popular Listmania function to build lists of products you have an interest in promoting. Listmania is the option to create a list of items that have particularly influenced you as an Amazon.com reviewer—items you find personally or professionally important. Many pages on Amazon post these lists at the bottom of the product page, as in Figure 7-3.

If you've impressed upon a viewer that you're a reviewer who knows what they're talking about, they'll pay special attention to your list and consider purchasing what's on it. When they click your list, they'll see your entire line of recommended product(s) and your comments on each one, as in Figure 7-4.

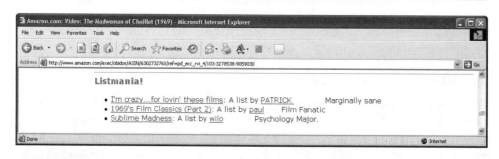

FIGURE 7-3   A sample Listmania listing at the bottom of a product page

FIGURE 7-4   A sample Listmania product list with comments

You can include items in any of the following categories in your Listmania list:

- Books
- Music
- DVD & Video
- Electronics
- Toys & Games

- Software
- Computer & Video Games
- Kitchen, Tools & Hardware
- Lawn & Patio

To add a list to your Amazon.com profile, simply click the Add A Listmania List link on the left side of the Friends & Favorites home page.

Create an Amazon Guide: So You'd Like To

A final option is to write a So You'd Like to . . . list. These lists differ from the straightforward Listmania list in that they're supposed to be written like guides to show people how a given product or products can enrich them or solve a problem. Because of this, they require a little more care in writing but come across as more

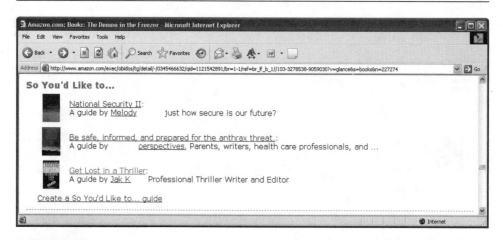

FIGURE 7-5   A sample So You'd Like To listing at the bottom of a product page

sincere and convincing to potential customers. Many pages on Amazon post these lists at the bottom of the product page, as in Figure 7-5.

When viewers click your list, they'll see your entire line of recommended product(s), and your comments on each one, as shown in Figure 7-6.

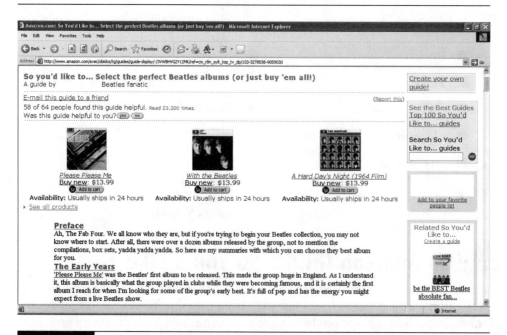

FIGURE 7-6   A sample So You'd Like To product list with comments

One thing to keep in mind is that creating a So You'd Like To list gains you immediate visibility without a corresponding level of trust. This is because anyone can create such a list. The way to impress upon a viewer that you're actually an expert is to add your comments to the items in your list in a way that highlights your experience and expertise.

This is similar to what we advise you to pay attention to when you're adding content in a product review. Once you've impressed upon a viewer that you're a reviewer who knows what they're talking about, they'll pay special attention to your list. For example, let's say you're writing a list called So You'd Like To . . . Build Your Own Music Studio.

One type of comment you could make, which wouldn't do much for your reputation as an expert, would be to say

```
I love Yamaha GX-1s. They're the hottest product on the market!
I think everyone reading this list should get one immediately.
I have LOTS of them. Check my link out *N*O*W!
```

On the other hand, you could make the comment extremely helpful by mentioning

```
The Yamaha GX-1 is a must for every aspiring artist. I've outfitted
every studio I've installed equipment in for the last six years
with a pair, and they reduce flutter and increase bass by over
30 percent. There's really nothing better for the price, which is
why I started carrying them in my store.
```

You can include any item from the Amazon.com store that has a ten-digit ASIN or an International Standard Book Number (ISBN). To create a list of this sort, click the Write A So You'd Like To . . . Guide link on the left side of the Friends & Favorites home page to start.

Advertise Your Amazon Listings Elsewhere

Now that we've talked about utilizing Amazon's site to gain you customers, let's shift gears and talk about the rest of the Internet—and the world. While Amazon attracts a healthy audience, you should also consider using many other avenues to promote your goods on Amazon.

Listing Your Amazon Items on Your Own Web Site

If you're already attracting people using your own e-commerce or content web site, it makes sense to utilize that traffic and guide them to your Amazon product listings to enhance your sales. Every Amazon seller has their own profile on Amazon, which you can think of as an online business card. By thinking of your profile as your own Amazon home page, you now have the perfect place to send your buyers, especially if you plan on focusing your efforts in the Amazon Marketplace. Your inventory will change greatly as you buy and sell more products, so building a solution only around specific products isn't the best way to go. Using your Amazon Seller Profile is a much better idea.

The URL web address for your Seller Profile is pretty simple: http://www .amazon.com/seller/*nickname*, where *nickname* is the Amazon nickname you gave yourself when you established your Amazon Seller Account.

At the very minimum, you can promote your Amazon listings by including a hyperlink on your web site that allows the user to go directly to your Amazon Seller Profile, like the one in Figure 7-7. A better solution would be to add a graphical

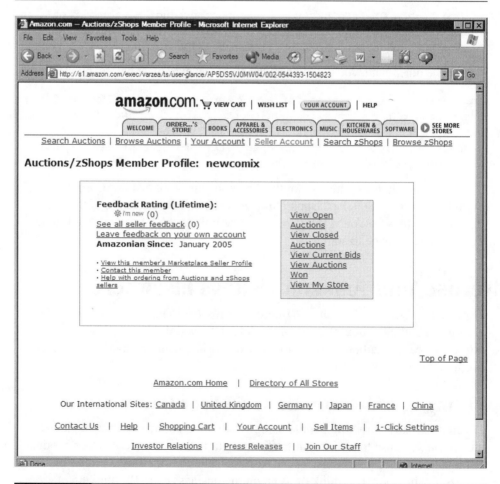

FIGURE 7-7   Your Amazon Seller Profile is your launch pad for sales.

element, like a button or picture, that, when clicked, sends the buyer to your Seller Profile so they can browse through your different items.

You can direct people to your listings beyond your own web site. As with your online presence, any printed materials you use to advertise yourself can promote your Amazon presence. You will want to work with any marketing people or printers that you may use in order to integrate your Amazon business sales into any marketing materials you use.

As a start, make sure you mention your Amazon presence as one of your sales channels in one or more of the following areas:

- Business cards

- Company letterhead

- E-mail signature files (taglines of text that automatically get appended to the bottom of e-mails sent out by you or anyone else from your company)

- Flyers

- Invoices

- Shipping labels

- Stationery

If you're just starting out on Amazon as a brand-new business as opposed to an established one who simply wants to add an outlet "on the river," then you need to determine for yourself whether or not these are necessary investments needed to sell on Amazon. You may find these extra items superfluous. On the other hand, should you find these items necessary, do your homework and find a good local printer to create them. Given the fluid nature of the Internet, we recommend you start by letting your fingers do the walking through the phone book as opposed to browsing online.

Directing People to Your Auctions

Since Amazon Auctions are a more fast-paced, dynamic format than selling items from your store, you're going to have different listing ID numbers every week (maybe more frequent than that), which could make it hard for you to update your web site every week with these new listings. Therefore, you can simply direct people to your Auctions seller page, where buyers can see all your auctions and decide from there what to bid on and try to win.

Amazon also gives you a large variety of buttons and graphics for you to take for free and put on your own web site. From the Amazon home page, go to the Help page and type **Promoting your Auctions listings** in the Search help box. Look for a page with this title and click it. Scroll down until you see the section titled Use Seller Graphics. Be aware of the rules governing the use of Amazon trademarked buttons.

Directing People to Your zShop

Just like with Auctions, you can direct people to your zShop with one handy, fixed listing. This listing will take people to your customized zShop storefront, which we built last chapter. You can add either a hypertext link, or boldly announce your zShop using premade Seller Graphics made by Amazon. Instructions on how to do this step are located at www.amazon.com/exec/obidos/tg/browse/-/1161362/#GuidelinesforUse.

When you use graphics, you're invoking the Amazon trademark, and in doing so, you'll need to follow specific guidelines to keep up the good name of Amazon and protect the investment they have put into their trademark. The web link just cited will also detail these guidelines for you.

In this case, the URL web address for your zShop is www.amazon.com/shops/ *nickname*, where *nickname* is the nickname you chose when creating your Amazon seller account.

In order to get to Amazon's seller graphics in this area, use the Help page, and enter the words **Promoting your zShops listings**. Follow the links and scroll down the page to find the Seller Graphics available for use, like those shown in Figure 7-8. Pick the graphic you'd like to use, and download it to your computer. You can normally do this by right-clicking the graphic and selecting Save Picture As, and then selecting the location you wish to save the file to. Finally, you'll need to visit your Internet service provider's online documentation to learn how to upload the graphic you've saved to your hard drive, since it varies depending on the service used.

Internet Message Boards and Forums

One way to get the word out regarding your Amazon product listings is to use appropriate Internet message boards and forums to inform people of your Amazon presence. By going to specific for-sale or auction forums, you can create a new posting which describes your products or sales and give a direct link to your zShop

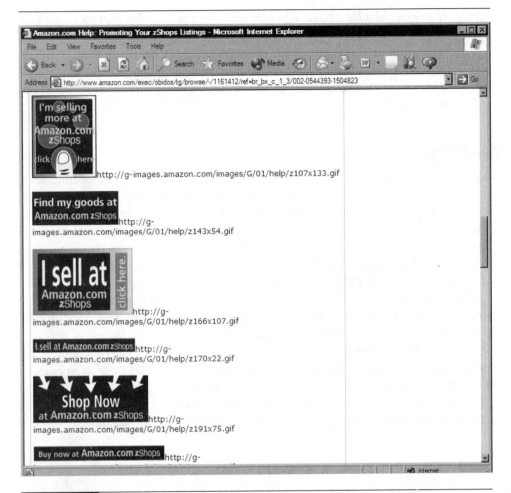

storefront, an auction item, or a specific product in the Marketplace. There are
several different pages listed for the Forums, which are subdivided by topic and
crosslinked to each other. Your best bet is to start at the New Sellers Discussion
Board, which is located at http://forums.prosperotechnologies.com/am-UShelpnew.

When you use any Internet message board, consider putting a link to your
zShop or auctions page in the signature you use on the forum. That way, every
time you answer someone's question or you're inserting your own ideas with
other similar-minded people, everyone browsing that forum will see a link to your
products for sale.

CAUTION

If you just blindly advertise products directly in most Internet message boards and forum, you're most likely violating the forum and damaging your reputation to Amazon and other sellers. Also, be aware that putting product endorsements in irrelevant message board or forum areas is considered spamming, which can negatively affect your sales performance.

To Sum Up

In Chapter 7, we talked about two main ways to bring attention to your listings and promote your Amazon presence. First and foremost is by becoming an "Amazon expert" and tapping into the rich, highly targeted, loyal Amazon customer audience of tens of millions of users. You can accomplish this by contributing to the site through product reviews, by answering questions on the boards, and creating functions like Listmania or So You'd Like To guides to direct people to a helpful set of products—that hopefully you're trying to sell.

The second method is to advertise your Amazon listings to people outside Amazon, both on the Internet and in your "offline" world. This can be accomplished by directing people to your Seller Profile and zShop storefront in a variety of ways. Amazon provides helpful graphics to enhance such messages and to encourage people to check out your listings. You can use those URL web addresses in any piece of literature you send out to promote your selling activities.

In the next chapter, we're going to talk about promoting specific items and actually getting paid when you refer buying customers using those links!

Chapter 8

Paid Placements: Create Targeted Advertisements to Generate Traffic

Long term, you can use the world's best retail rule of thumb: customers get what they want . . .

—Jeff Bezos, founder of Amazon.com

Ever since the early days, Amazon has understood the value of a well-placed advertisement. As the company was growing, Amazon would spend the money to advertise in the very small slots offered on the front page of the *New York Times*. Their ads would typically revolve around the birthday of a famous author, as Amazon would wish them a happy birthday and remind people to check out their site, dubbed Earth's Largest Bookstore.

Today, some of Amazon's best "advertisement pages" are their best-selling product pages. Amazon has therefore come up with a program where you can market your product by pairing it with a better-selling title and Amazon will sell it as a package deal. This way, your product can get prime "real estate" on a product page to help spur sales, you can pick the product that's relevant to your product, and here's the best part: Once your product placement has been reviewed by Amazon and no one else has already requested a placement on the same item, you've got a lock on it for at least one month. Since in this scenario you're essentially paying for a better placement on Amazon's site, this service is called a Paid Placement.

What Is a Paid Placement?

While reviewing a detail page for a product in Amazon's catalog, you may notice a "Best Value" offered to you a little further down the screen where you can buy that product, plus something else, for a savings off the regular price. This is one of Amazon's ways of encouraging more purchases (based on your past purchase history and shopping habits): recommending something you may like based on what other customers bought after purchasing the indicated item. They typically call this initiative "Better Together."

Other times, however, it's the result of a Paid Placement called the "Buy X, Get Y" program. This is simply a paid merchandising placement where you can gain attention for your product Y by offering it as a package deal with popular product X in the "Best Value" section of X's product detail page. The savings offered are covered by Amazon, in exchange for the membership fee you pay to use this program. In addition, it gives you excellent visibility. As part of your membership fee in this program, Amazon will offer an extra 5-percent discount to the customer if they purchase both products. In the meantime, your product (and the thumbnail photo of that product) will now appear on Product X's detail page, where people can click over and find out more about your product before deciding to buy.

What Does It Look Like?

Figure 8-1 shows an example of this concept at play. *The Mermaid Chair* is the newest novel from writer Sue Kidd. The author or publisher has created a "Best Value" where anybody who buys her second novel can get 5 percent off by also buying her first novel, *The Secret Lives of Bees*. This is a popular technique where you can use the publicity of a new project to bring attention to a previous project by the same author.

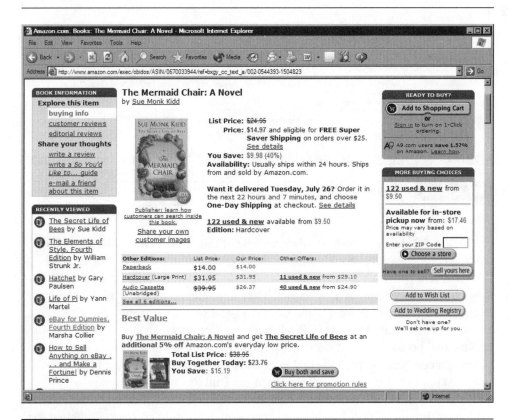

| FIGURE 8-1 | A Paid Placement to encourage sales of two of Sue Kidd's books |

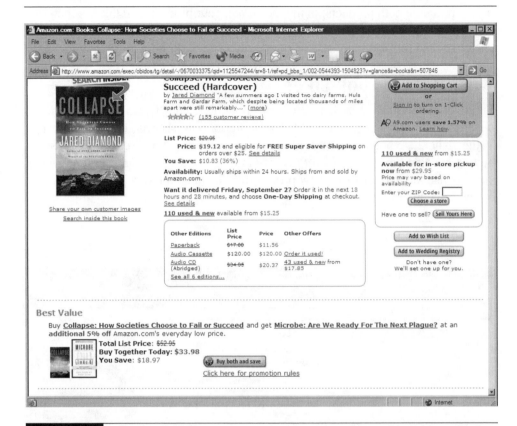

FIGURE 8-2　Another Paid Placement to encourage sales of a new bio-sciences book

Figure 8-2 shows a more popular example of this concept in action. Dr. Allen Zellicoff and one of this book's authors, Michael Bellomo, wrote a book entitled *Microbe: Are We Ready for the New Plague?*, dealing with modern plagues and how our health systems are responding. They have chosen to do a Paid Placement with Jared Diamond's newest book, *Collapse*, dealing with societies' reaction to catastrophes, because Diamond's book is a top seller on Amazon with high visibility, and the two books deal with similar macroeconomic crisis issues. These authors are offering a combination package that would appeal to most, if not all, of Diamond's potential readers, and is an excellent use of the Paid Placements program.

In any case, when you create a Paid Placement, you get excellent placement within the Product Detail Page. As you can see, the feature comes right below the main information part of the page. For many computer users, this feature is fully visible when they pull up the Product Detail page and will appear in the same screen, without the need to scroll down. In newspaper terms, this concept is called "Above the Fold," meaning this appears above the fold in a newspaper and is therefore more visible when the newspaper is open.

It's important to note that this feature comes above the Customer Recommendations, Editorial Reviews, and even the Product Details section. Remember, though, just because you've paid for such great placement doesn't mean you'll get lots of purchases. Your Paid Placement has to make sense and appeal to the customer in order to be effective.

In order to make the most of your Paid Placement, consider the following tips:

- Pick a complementary title based on subject matter, not because it's the best-selling book on Amazon. Ask yourself the question: "Would readers of product X even want to buy my product Y?" If the answer is yes, you're on the right track. If the answer is no, move on quickly to something else for evaluation.

- Timing can be very crucial. Ask months in advance for a prime holiday season month like November or December for your Paid Placement, or ask in advance to get the first month your product will be launched. Early buzz created from a prominent Paid Placement can help sustain your sales numbers for months to come.

- Do some research based on the Customers Who Bought This Also Bought list as well as the Customers Who Viewed This Also Viewed list when evaluating a potential partner for the Paid Placement. Are the customers who bought or viewed this book looking at other titles similar to the one you want to promote? Are they looking at your main competition? If so, you probably found your complementary product!

- Have backup products in mind before you submit your application. This way, if another promotion has your first choice, you can immediately give Amazon your second or third choice and lock out any other competition.

How Does It Work?

In fact, as mentioned earlier, you can't just partner any product with something else. If that were the case, every small vendor would be dying to partner with the newest Harry Potter book just to get the exposure. The first rule of Paid Placements is that the two products have to make sense as a bundle; they have to be somewhat related and relevant so that the customer would automatically think of buying them together. So you must decide what popular product would best complement your item. After registering for the small vendor co-op merchandising program, you would indicate what BXGY program (or Buy X, Get Y program; another name for Paid Placements) you'd like to institute. Amazon will review this request, and as long as the product pair makes sense, and no one else has previously requested this pairing for your time period, they will typically grant this request and implement the program.

In addition, once you partner your Y product up with another product X, you cannot initiate any more BXGY promotions with other titles until your current promotion period ends with product X. Amazon will also have to check with the corresponding label or studio from product X to make sure they don't object to the pairing. On your end, you have to make sure that the subject matter and/or audience is relevant to recommend your product as an add-on to the customer. You'll need to do some research into product X's content and description to ensure this fit exists. If, for some reason, Amazon cannot approve your request, they will notify you with potential alternatives. Otherwise, you'll be informed when your promotion period begins and ends.

NOTE   *This type of promotion is typically restricted to items in the following categories: Books, Music, Video, Software, Computer & Video Games, Tools & Hardware, and Outdoor Living. Check with Amazon to see if this list has changed.*

Typically, the review and approval process from Amazon will take a few days, but in rare circumstances, it could take a week or two. To be safe, you should request this promotion at least two or three months in advance if you're going after a hot product pair. If the product is more of a niche item, three to four weeks should be sufficient. Once it's approved, your promotion will be put into Amazon's system for the corresponding month and then launched on the first day of that month. The promotion will then appear on both your product Y's detail page, as well as product X's detail page, and whenever both products are added to the same order, the customer will receive that 5-percent discount off your product Y.

Best Uses for the Paid Placement

Now that you know how it works, the question is "When should I use this?" In some cases, you may want to take advantage of a specific event that will bring a lot of extra attention to a specific product or group of products. For example, the beginning of football season will spark interest in all the new football video games available, like Madden Football. If you're selling a similar software title, or an accessory for this game, using a Paid Placement would pay off the most in the summer months of July and August.

In other cases, you'll want to include this promotion in your overall product promotion strategy. Let's say you're planning on launching a new product for sale on Amazon. A Paid Placement is an excellent way to raise the visibility of your new item on top of your other launch promotions. Just make sure you provide enough lead time so this promotion will work in sync with other promotions that'll bring attention to your product.

In other cases, you may consider doing this type of promotion if the other product will get some temporary "heat" or attention. Let's say that a new trend takes off in music, and your product is a perfect complementary CD to one that's breaking the charts. If people are being introduced to a new kind of music, use that opportunity to feature your CD alongside something similar with more "heat" on it.

Finally, you may consider promotions of this kind for reasons that apply to you, your product area, or the market in general. If you feel a given product needs a "shot in the arm," or there's a new version you want to introduce to the world, a Paid Placement could give your product needed visibility that it didn't have before. For whatever reason you choose, your best laid plans will hopefully be put into motion when you try out this function.

Ideas for Initial Trial Runs

If you've only got one product to focus on, your trial run will simply be the first time you try out this Paid Placement. On the other hand, if you have multiple products, or multiple versions of the same product, you may want to consider doing what those in the technology world call a beta test, or a trial run, of this function. The key here is to pick a product, a good complementary (and popular) product to partner with, and do at least one test run to see what the results are.

If you have the time, we recommend picking one of your products that isn't the most visible, something that could really benefit from this promotion and that isn't getting its own big push. Thus, you should submit something in advance so you can lock in the desired date, and then be sure to monitor the results yourself as the month progresses. Keep track of the rank of your product, study the sales numbers that you'll have access to as a seller of this product, and see if there's any new mention of your product on the community boards on Amazon. The best promotions are those done with other efforts, but if you want to study the effect of this one promotion, try it by itself and see the net results. Compare the sales that month (and the rankings) with those from the previous month. Then, ask yourself, was the bump worth the cost? Try different combinations of products to see which ones work better or worse.

Now that you know you should monitor your Paid Placements, let's get down to the business at hand—building a Paid Placement.

How to Build a Paid Placement

Once you've decided that you're ready to try out this promotion plan, the first step is to register with the small vendor co-op merchandising program. This will allow you to create and manage your BXGY promotions, and fund your account so you can put on your various Paid Placements.

How to Sign Up for the Program

From the main Amazon.com page, click the See All 32 Product Categories tab. Near the bottom of its list, you should see a link that says Paid Placements. Click that link, and you'll be taken to the Paid Placements home page, as shown in Figure 8-3. This page will explain the current structure of the program and give you examples beyond what we've covered in this chapter. Click the orange Sign Up button in the top-left corner to fill out the application.

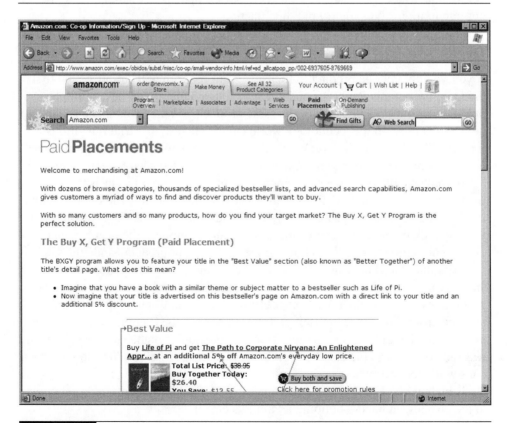

FIGURE 8-3   Home page for the Paid Placements program

Once you've clicked Sign Up, you'll be taken to the one-page form, as shown in Figure 8-4. You'll be asked to enter your contact name (or names), your business name, the category you plan to specialize in, and the ISBN or ASIN numbers of products you'd like to promote. In this case, enter the numbers of your Y products, the ones you want to increase visibility on through this promotion.

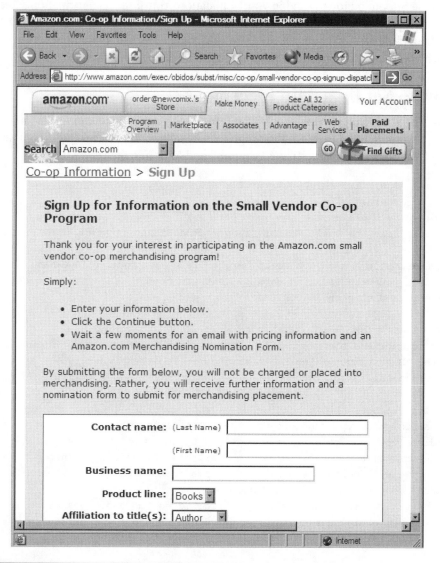

Enter your information to sign up for the co-op program.

Do NOT put in the ASIN or ISBN numbers of the Product X you wish to choose in order to promote your products.

Once you've entered all your information, click the Continue button to review your information. Make sure your contact e-mail and phone numbers are correct so Amazon can contact you directly whenever needed. If you need to make changes, it's recommended you use the Edit button on the page instead of the Back button on your browser. Once you're satisfied with all the information you've inputted, click the Submit button to send in your application. You'll see a confirmation screen with a copy of the information you submitted. Amazon will then contact you with additional information about the program, and a Merchandising Nomination form, which you'll use to submit your proposed merchandising initiatives.

How to Set Up a Paid Placement

Now that you've registered, check your e-mail for your welcome message and the blank application form for the program. The subject line should say "Join the Small Vendor Co-Op Advertising Program" and look like the following:

```
Date:    Sun, 01 Jan 2006 17:41:07 -0700
To:      yourname@isp.com
From:    sv-books@amazon.com
Subject: Join the Small Vendor Co-Op Merchandising Program

Welcome to the Amazon.com co-op merchandising program. This e-mail
provides you with specific details that you need to add your product(s)
for merchandising on Amazon.com.


Buy X, Get Y (BXGY)
Want to increase the visibility of your title on Amazon.com? Feature it
in the "Best Value" (also known as "Better Together") section of another
title's detail page.


Pairing Products
To participate, you must provide the ISBN/ASIN for both the X and Y
products you want to pair. Y titles can be added only to a single X title
at any one time. If a title is not available during the nominated time
frame, we will contact you.  A few things to consider when choosing a
product to pair with in a BXGY promotion:
     *      Consider whether your pairing makes the additional purchase a
            natural add-on for the customer. Consider whether the pairing
            makes sense in terms of subject matter and audience.
```

    *   In general, the higher the sales ranking of your potential pairing title, the more likely people are to see the promotion. Consequently, you will have more traffic redirected to your title's detail page.

Check out our Top 100 bestseller lists (see links below) for a current list of top-selling products to consider.

    * For books, use the Search Inside the Book feature for more information about a title's content. Enter keywords associated with your title and browse through the results. You can also use the "Sort by" box to view your results in different ways (e.g., by publication date, sales rank, etc.).

Top Seller Links:
Books:
http://www.amazon.com/exec/obidos/tg/new-for-you/top-sellers/-/books/
Music:
http://www.amazon.com/exec/obidos/tg/new-for-you/top-sellers/-/music/
DVD:
http://www.amazon.com/exec/obidos/tg/new-for-you/top-sellers/-/dvd/
Video:
http://www.amazon.com/exec/obidos/tg/new-for-you/top-sellers/-/video/

Timing
We ask that you carefully consider the timing of the promotion:
    * When is the best time to run your promotion? Will a Buy X, Get Y promotion be more effective at a different time of year or after a new title is released?
    * Are there other marketing campaigns that you are running separately? Time the programs so they are running simultaneously.

Cost
The cost for small vendors to run a BXGY promotion varies depending on the rankings of the paired titles:
    * If a product in the pairing is ranked in the top 250 titles on Amazon.com, the cost is $750 for one month.
    * If a product is ranked below the top 250, the cost is $500 for one month.

If you are not pairing your title with a higher-ranking one, we generally recommend that you use the BXGY program in conjunction with another

marketing effort. We have found that an additional effort to drive traffic
to Amazon.com detail pages is essential to the success of pairing two
low-ranking titles.

Additional options are available for those merchandising a DVD/VHS or
music product. Please contact sv-video@amazon.com for more information.

Important note: Although we will work with you to help make your
promotion a success, we cannot guarantee a response rate. Your submission
of this form acknowledges that you have read and understand this.

Nominations are reviewed on a weekly basis. Information about where to
send the Amazon.com Merchandising Nomination Form and payment is at the
end of this form.

If you have any questions, please be sure to review the FAQs at
www.amazon.com/coop by clicking the FAQs link.

Best regards,

Amazon.com Small Vendor Co-Op Merchandising Team
         http://www.amazon.com/coop

   Below the introductory nature of the e-mail, you will see the section on the
Amazon.com Merchandising Nomination Form, shown next. When you're ready
to start a Paid Placement, you have to fill out at least two sections of this form:
the Information section, detailing your information as the vendor, and the Co-Op
Nomination section, which you fill out for each promotion you want to implement.

NOMINATION FORM Amazon.com Co-Op Merchandising

Vendor:
Contact Name:
Contact E-mail:
Contact Phone Number:
Contact Fax Number:
Contact Address:
Total Merchandising Budget at Amazon:
Date Submitted:

Title 1: Co-Op Nomination

Co-Op Month:
Product Line:

```
Vendor:
ISBN/ASIN:
Title:
Author:
Product On-Sale Date:
Amazon Subject Category:
Merchandising Program: BXGY
BXGY: provide title and ISBN/ASIN for pairing:
Co-Op Cost:


Title 2: Co-Op Nomination
------------------------------------
Co-Op Month:
Product Line:
Vendor:
ISBN/ASIN:
Title:
Author:
Product On-Sale Date:
Amazon Subject Category:
Merchandising Program: BXGY
BXGY: provide title and ISBN/ASIN for pairing:
Co-Op Cost:


To nominate additional titles, please copy and paste Co-Op Nomination
details.


Example:
------------------------
Co-Op Month: June 2004
Product Line: Books
Vendor: Wet Feet, Inc.
ISBN/ASIN:
Title: The Mars & Venus Diet and Exercise Solution
Author: John Gray
Product On-Sale Date: 6/1/03
Amazon Subject Category: Books: Health, Mind & Body
Program Placement: BXGY
Coop Cost: $500
BXGY: provide title and ISBN/ASIN for pairing: The WetFeet Insider
Guide to Careers in Management Consulting: 1582072582
```

The Nomination Form—The Information Section

You can fill out the fields in the first section of the Nomination Form as follows:

■ **Vendor**   Enter the name of the business you've registered with Amazon, not necessarily the manufacturer or publisher of the item you want to promote.

■ **Contact Name**   You should put the name of whoever is the Primary Account Coordinator for your Amazon account (either yourself or anyone you've hired to handle the day-to-day activities on Amazon), or the Promotions/Marketing Manager for your initiative if you're working with other people on a big promotion for this product.

■ **Contact E-mail**   Put the e-mail address of the contact name you've just listed. Understand that this e-mail can be different from the e-mail you have on file with Amazon since this entry will be used to communicate directly with the small vendor co-op merchandising program.

■ **Contact Phone Number**   Pick the main contact number for the name you've listed. Like before, this number does not have to correspond with the main phone number on file with your Amazon account. They understand that you may have different people manage different parts of your Amazon sales strategy.

■ **Contact Fax Number**   Same as the others; pick a fax number for the main contact.

■ **Contact Address**   Pick the address where your main contact can receive mail regarding this promotion. If you want to review all the documents before anything is agreed on, you may want to put the contact address of your main headquarters here.

■ **Total Merchandising Budget at Amazon**   This field is to help Amazon gauge what kind of program you can implement on their site. Since the cost of the program depends on the popularity of the item you pick, they need to know which titles they can recommend if your first choice is taken or unable to be used.

■ **Date Submitted**   Put the date you plan to submit this form. Understand that this does not affect what date you want to begin your co-op promotion.

The Nomination Form—The Co-Op Section

For each promotion you want to implement, you'll need to fill out a Co-Op section of the Nomination Form. You can fill out the fields in this section like this:

- **Co-Op Month**   Insert the month and year that you wish to implement this program. For example, if you want to run a promotion during the holiday season of 2005, you would put "December 2005" or "November 2005" if you're gearing up for holiday sales.

- **Product Line**   In this field, they're looking for the main overall category in which to implement this promotion. Your options here include Books, Music, Video, DVD, and others.

- **Vendor**   In this field, you need to insert the publisher, manufacturer, or vendor of the item you wish to piggyback—the Product X, if you will. For example, if you hope to partner with the book *eBay Your Business*, you would put McGraw-Hill/Osborne in this field.

- **ISBN/ASIN**   In this box, you should either put the ten-character ISBN number (for books) or the Amazon Standard Identification Number of the item you wish to partner with. You can find this information on the Product Detail page of your Product X.

- **Title**   Using the same Product Detail page, enter the Title of the Product you're interested in promoting, as it appears on the Amazon Product Detail page for that item.

- **Author**   In this field, enter the Author (or Authors, if any) of the item you'd like to promote. In some cases, this field will be the musicians from the CD, or the actor or director of the movie you'd like to promote.

- **Product On-Sale Date**   In this field, put the date this product went on sale, according to the release date published on the Amazon product detail page.

- **Amazon Subject Category**   In this field, enter the precise chain of subcategories where this item can be found in the Amazon catalog. For example, if you were listing *eBay Your Business*, you would enter: Books: Computers & Internet: Digital Business & Culture: E-Commerce.

TIP

If you're trying to figure out which subcategory your item is in, try scrolling down the Product Detail page until you find the header Look For Similar Items By Category. In some cases, your item will be cross-referenced in similar categories.

- **Merchandising Program**   In this field, put BXGY, since that's the standard identifier for this kind of Paid Placement. Then, create a second line with the following information.

- **BXGY**   In this field, provide the title and either the ISBN or ASIN for the item you'd like to pair with the item just mentioned. For example, let's say we wanted to promote this book with our previous book, *eBay Your Business*, we would put in this field: *eBay Your Business, 0072257113*.

- **Co-op Cost**   If the item you want to piggyback on is in the Top 250 items for their category, Amazon will charge you $750 for one month of this program. If your item is not among the Top 250 at the time you want to submit this form, the cost is only $500. You would put either $750 or $500 in this field.

NOTE   *While this is a big chunk of change to commit, remember that you're getting a high visibility for your product, especially if you pick a Top 250 product.*

Submitting Your Nomination Form

Once you're done entering all the information, your section should look like the following:

```
Co-Op Month: December 2005
Product Line: Books
Vendor: McGraw-Hill Osborne
ISBN/ASIN: 0072262605
Title: How to Sell Anything on Amazon... and Make a Fortune!
Author: Michael Bellomo, Joel Elad
Product On-Sale Date: 11/15/05
Amazon Subject Category: Books: Computers & Internet: Digital
Business & Culture: E-Commerce
Merchandising Program: BXGY
BXGY: provide title and ISBN/ASIN for pairing:,. eBay Your
Business, 0072257113.
Coop Cost: $500
```

If you want to submit multiple initiatives in one Nomination Form, just complete one Co-Op section for each initiative. You would still put only one section for your Information. Once you're ready, you simply e-mail your Nomination Form to the following e-mail address:

If your initiative involves books: sv-books@amazon.com
If your initiative involves music, DVDs, or video: sv-video@amazon.com

TIP

If you want to suggest several initiatives across different categories, we recommend sending a separate Nomination Form for each category, as each category request is reviewed by different people.

You should hear back from Amazon with either an approval or a suggestion of viable alternatives. Once you've come up with an agreement, Amazon will send you an invoice, which you need to pay before your program date begins. Your invoice will also need to include a copy of your Nomination Form, and a review copy of the product you're trying to promote. Once that is sent in, you just need to sit back and see how your promotion fares on Amazon.

To Sum Up

In this chapter, we walked you through the function Amazon likes to call Paid Placements. This system allows you to place "co-op advertising" if you will, where Amazon will partner your product with a complementary product and offer buyers a discount if they buy both products together. This program gives your product visibility (and hopefully, traffic) on another Product Detail page and encourages more sales through this bundling program.

We've talked about how the program works, how to get involved, and how to construct your own Paid Placement campaigns. We presented this function to give you one more tool in your arsenal to increase the marketing efforts and awareness of your products on Amazon. In the next chapter, we'll talk about another effective set of marketing programs that you can control more: e-mail and direct mail campaigns, using products sold on Amazon.

Chapter 9

Generate E-mail and Direct-Mail Marketing Campaigns

If you do build a great experience, customers tell each other about that. Word of mouth is very powerful.

—Jeff Bezos, founder of Amazon.com

If you've ever been in a new town or city, you know the value of recommendations from people you know or trust. Since you're in a brand-new environment with no experience as to where to go, what to do, or where to get a good dinner, you're more likely to rely upon the experience of someone you trust. This is the same underlying principle behind much of the e-mail and direct-mail advertising you can use in conjunction with your Amazon.com sales efforts.

Customer Base Building Advantages of Amazon.com

By providing a positive buying experience to a customer, you've earned a certain level of trust you can build on. And if you've gained a repeat customer, then you have a very valuable commodity from both a financial and marketing perspective. Luckily, the nature of ordering items off of Amazon.com allows you to utilize three advantages you wouldn't find if, for example, your customer simply made a cash purchase from your brick-and-mortar store. The first advantage is that you gain access to customer information, which allows you to follow up with the customer. This is something you can't do with an anonymous customer who pays cash and walks away. Let's look at the other two advantages, trust and community, in some depth.

Zone of Trust

Another advantage to making a sale on Amazon is that you can measure, in a sense, the level of trust you've gained from an individual. You'll have records on how many times a specific person has purchased from you, and over what period of time. This willingness to purchase items from you marks them as someone who is more likely than not to be interested in related or complementary items. For example, if you sell vintage movie posters to a repeat customer, it is highly likely that person will also be interested in deals involving discounts on classic movie videos or DVDs.

Sense of Community

Just as Amazon merchants have a sense of community by terming their presence at Amazon as "on the river," buyers also become Amazon regulars to varying degrees. Some consumers may feel a vested interest in the site due to their many reviews of products they've ordered. For example, a buyer who is building their home DVD collection is more likely to return to Amazon.com and let everyone know what he or she thinks of a particular Special Collection Box Set of DVDs—and, if they liked it, to also see what other movies people are purchasing that may relate to the original title.

Other consumers have an even higher level of participation. Some decide to post on the Amazon discussion forums about their experience or to ask questions about topics of products they're interested in. For example, a consumer who purchases Season 1 of the *X-Files* might visit the forums to ask "Is Season 2 worth purchasing?" or "If I like this series, what other series might I enjoy?"

Finally, Amazon encourages this sense of contribution and creativity by allowing different forms of participation beyond the review—specifically, creating personalized lists of recommended products via the Listmania or So You'd Like To features (discussed at length in Chapter 7). Given these opportunities for extra participation, your chance to connect with an Amazon buyer is much higher than at many other places on the Web.

A Word about Direct-Mail Marketing Campaigns

There are two types of direct-mail campaigns available to you: the mass, or blanket, campaign, and the more selective targeted approach. Mass direct mailing involves purchasing either an e-mail list or related services in order to send out as many e-mails as possible to people, whether they're aware of your products or not. Targeted mailing involves simply sending out a letter, brochure, or discount offer to customers who have purchased from you before.

Many resources exist for both types of mailing. The Direct Marketing Association, found at www.the-dma.org, can provide you with a great deal of information on how to use this marketing tool. Marketing your products through direct-mail pieces offers advantages and disadvantages. One advantage to unsolicited direct mail as opposed to unsolicited e-mail is that it seems to generate less buyer distaste; while "junk mail" isn't exactly welcome, it doesn't taint a company the way a spam e-mail can.

However, it's likely that the disadvantages to direct mail outweigh the advantages for the average Amazon.com seller. The reason is that you've disregarded the twin benefits of e-mail's lower per-message cost and the fact that your customer base is already computer savvy and willing to purchase online. For these reasons, it makes more sense on the whole to pursue an e-mail campaign versus a "snail-mail" or direct-mail campaign.

E-mail Marketing Campaigns

While all types of direct marketing (e-mail and direct mail) are notorious for their low response rate, the advantage to using e-mail is that your costs are kept to an absolute minimum. Just as in direct mail, there are two types of e-mail campaigns: the mass, or blanket, campaign, and the more selective targeted approach.

Mass E-mail

The first type of campaign, which has fallen out of favor in recent years, involves purchasing either an e-mail list or related services to send out as many e-mails as possible to people whether they know of your products or not. Simply put, we don't recommend you follow this course, for two main reasons: the low success rate of these services, and the general image you're seeking to cultivate for your business.

Not to mention privacy issues, the costs and impact of spam today include the following statistics (found on anti-spam-software.com):

- In 1999, the average consumer received 40 pieces of spam. By 2005, Jupiter estimates, the total is likely to soar to 2000. *The Standard*

- America Online estimates that spam already accounts for more than 30 percent of its members' e-mail—constituting as many as 24 million messages a day. *The Standard*

- 74 percent of customers believe that their ISPs should be responsible for fixing spam problems. *Gartner Group*

- 7 percent of ISP churn (switching Internet Service Providers) was directly attributed to spam. *Gartner Group*

- 36 percent of e-mail users would switch ISPs in order to reduce the flow of spam they receive. *Gartner Group*

- 24 percent of users would be willing to pay an incremental fee to block spam. *Gartner Group*

- 250,000 spam-related complaints are reported every day at AOL alone. *PC Magazine*

- Nearly $2 of each customer's monthly bill can be attributed to electronic junk mail and other forms of spam. *Information Week*

Let's look at the first of these reasons. While direct response has a low success rate, this rate is normally made up by the sheer numbers of people contacted. The counterargument is that unsolicited e-mail marketing does appear to justify its costs for products which are pure commodities, such as certain kinds of pharmaceutical products. However, even if you sell this sort of product, consider that the low success rate promises to be even lower in the future as e-mail services, heeding the calls of their consumers, develop better barriers against unsolicited e-mail.

Second, and more importantly, there is both a philosophical problem and an image problem with mass e-mail. Among the many benefits of using Amazon as your marketplace is the ability to build trust among more customers than you would if you remained online in your own dot-com site. Trying to drive people to your site when they have not asked for your product is counterproductive at best, and destructive at worst. Plus, the image consumers have of companies who use unsolicited e-mail is about as low as one can get on the Internet—obviously not something you want associated with your company.

Remember, the marketing approach you want to take should be positive, not negative in nature. As we discussed in earlier chapters, your best bet is to identify your market and tailor your offerings to what the audience is actively seeking. Perhaps the kindest thing we can say about mass e-mail is that it is a technological quick-fix that looks interesting at first glance but is disastrous in the long run for you and your company.

Okay, we've made our point, but one last word: unsolicited e-mail is also known as spam—and even the government is taking legislative steps to deal with spammers. While we can't predict what the future holds for mass e-mail, we think it best to avoid the entire can of worms.

Targeted E-mail

Targeted e-mails "mine" your customer base (as it's termed in marketing circles). If you're really small or just starting out online, you can certainly send out e-mails yourself, but as you get bigger you should consider one of the many online services such as www.benchmarkemail.com that offer to handle these campaigns for you. These are particularly helpful in allowing you to manage your e-mail list—such as in removing duplicate or invalid e-mail addresses.

Your main concern should be to avoid sending unsolicited e-mail. You can accomplish this by only sending e-mail to your customer base—and giving them what is called the opt-in option. By opting in, the customer must actually click a link or check a box stating that he or she wants to continue to receive e-mails from you. And, of course, you want to make this option available to the customer when they purchase from you.

The opposite option is called opting out—which means that, by default, the customer will receive additional content unless they take action to *un*subscribe. While a legitimate option—it's used by many web and e-mail services when signing up new customers—we don't recommend it. No matter if it is straightforward spam, or opt-out e-mails, when the message arrives in the customer's inbox, it's seen as simply one thing: unwanted. Not only will this give you a low success rate but it may also annoy the customer and make them hesitant to deal with you a second time.

The Basics of an E-mail Marketing Campaign

Your e-mail marketing campaign consists of a few simple components. First, the e-mail itself, which will offer information to drive customers back to your product listings, or special offers such as product discounts. Second, be sure to know the exact web location of the page you want to bring people back to—whether it's your Amazon.com zShop page or a special Product Detail page you've created specifically to show off a particular product or deal. An exact web address is needed when you add it to your e-mails since a clickable hyperlink together with a non-clickable web URL can be pasted into the web browser's address bar.

Finally, you'll want to keep track of your campaign's effectiveness, which will be evident via the number of sales you take in from a given discount or product set that you're offering. If your offer is simple, then you can track it yourself in a spreadsheet program like Microsoft Excel. You can track results after the e-mail has been sent by simply comparing results to previous months to see if there's a bump. For example, if you made 300 widget sales this month versus 240 on an average month, it's a jump of +60, or a 20-percent increase. Monitoring your efforts over several months will also allow you to determine which e-mails generated the most response, and how the results are trending over time.

Responses to offers which are more complex (say, with multiple packages or price levels) can become more difficult to track. In these cases, the easiest solution is to purchase services from a company that handles targeted e-mail campaigns—specifically, those that know how to develop and track opt-in e-mail campaigns.

Some of the better known e-mail campaign services include the following:

- www.opt-in-email-marketing.org

- www.mailworkz.com

- www.benchmarkemail.com

- www.optinsystems.com

- www.wowbrand.com

No matter which service you choose, there are a couple basic items that should be kept in mind. First, be sure to ask for business references and whether you can contact them. A reputable company will provide this readily. Second, find out what kinds of fees are associated with the project from start to finish. As of this writing, fees vary widely among companies, and many offer different specialized services, such as crafting graphics for an e-mail that uses HTML (which can show fancy graphics or a company logo). Costs can also vary dramatically depending on your target demographics or market segment. However, as a rule, be cautious about signing up with a company that charges more than $200 per 1,000 image-rich HTML e-mails. A good rule of thumb is to expect rates of 5 to 20 cents per message.

HTML or Plain Text?

There's an ongoing debate as to whether one should send e-mails during an e-mail campaign that are plain text, or are HTML-enabled. HTML (Hypertext Markup Language) allows you to show pictures in the e-mail.

Whichever you decide is up to you, though there is a trade-off: HTML may make a more compellingly visual e-mail, but some people dislike the extra time the mail takes to load (especially with a big, complex picture), or they set their e-mail program to only accept text messages. The best policy is to make your decision based primarily on your target audience.

Pictures have the greatest impact on the mass consumer audience, who sometimes like more impressive graphics. On the flip side, corporate or technical clients prefer to leave out the graphics-based marketing hype. Stick to a concise, factually based text message and you'll be on better ground here.

And since marketing companies charge extra for designing HTML messages, it's not money well spent unless your product will greatly benefit from a picture showing what you're selling. Items with a strong visual component (clothing, art, semiprecious gems) are good candidates. Electronic circuits and reams of office paper are not.

See Figures 9-1 and 9-2 for an example of each.

TIP *If you've got a store or company logo, be sure to embed that graphic into all your e-mail marketing messages, since that will help build up your brand image. You can find lots of information on how to build your HTML e-mail messages from companies like ConstantContact (www.constantcontact.com) or HTML E-mail Marketing (www.html-email-marketing.com).*

Hit the jackpot with over 140 new beads and components, all up to 50% off. These specials are only available to you, our e-mail subscriber, for a limited time. After July 28, they will be made available to the general public.

FIGURE 9-1   An example of an e-mail using HTML

Shop Now and save on Great New Products! Exclusively yours for a limited time.

Hit the jackpot with over 140 new beads and components, all up to 50% off. These specials are only available to you, our e-mail subscriber, for a limited time. After July 28, they will be made available to the general public.

FIGURE 9-2   An example of a plain-text e-mail

Writing a Targeted E-mail

Many style guides and opinions exist about how to write targeted e-mails. That said, unless you plan to use an online service to handle your e-mail campaign, stick to a few simple guidelines. First, the subject line itself needs to be succinct and informative. Given the speed at which we all read through the subject lines of e-mail (especially if it isn't from someone we immediately recognize), it has to be something the reader won't have to guess at.

Second, make sure that the message itself isn't too long or rambling—again, consider how quickly we scan our e-mail today. It helps if the message is written with paragraphs containing no more than two or three short sentences. Larger blocks of text don't invite quick visual scans and are more likely to be deleted rather than read.

Third, it's best to have no more than two hyperlinks embedded in the content. Any more than this and the e-mail starts looking like just another piece of electronic junk mail—which can be confusing to boot. Fourth, it's always a nice touch to utilize a close and a signature thanking people for their time spent in reading your message.

Finally, consider personalizing the message by leaving a phone number and e-mail address that makes it obvious that the message will go to a "real" person. That is, the phone number should go to "Mike of A+ Items" and an e-mail to "JoAnn@Exclusivemotors.com" instead of "Marketing Department" or "customerservice@nameless.com."

Special Offers

One of the two main types of targeted e-mails is one that notifies the reader of a special offer. Special offers can be discounts on bulk purchases, discounts on a single item, or a notification of a limited quantity of a very special item. Whichever you use depends on the nature of your business—a discount on a bulk purchase of lawn furniture or the latest Harry Potter book probably won't get you many replies, unless you sell to resellers.

Note that there are three components to this e-mail (aside from the offer itself) that should always be on the message:

- A statement of limited product availability. Alternatively, if the product is available in unlimited quantity, highlight what makes the offer special, such as a bulk order, regional oversupply, or a seasonal discount.

- An option to opt-in to receive a company newsletter, articles, or special deals

- Hyperlinks to your store, or easy-to-read URLs that the recipient can cut and paste into the address bar of their browser

 *Make sure you don't use any white-on-white embedded characters or the user may run into difficulty cutting and pasting the URL into their browser.*

Newsletters

Another type of targeted e-mail is a newsletter, which can be a very powerful tool for building a strong, loyal customer base once you have allowed the customer to opt-in initially. If you have a very specialized product that has a devoted customer base (for example, civil war memorabilia, time-sensitive financial information, or collectible baseball cards), then you might be better off sending a quarterly or monthly bulletin, newsletter, or even a daily "tip sheet" to your customer base.

Your newsletter could provide a short feature article on a new development in the subject area. If there's a recognized expert in the field, it might be worth doing a special guest interview. For example, let's say your company manufactures products that prevent heart attacks. These could range from an herbal supplement to books and DVDs that show what kinds of fatty foods to avoid and what supplements to take to stay healthy. If customer John Smith has opted in to your messages, a sample newsletter might look as follows:

```
Hello John,

Top nutritionists at Harvard have stated as follows:

"By our most conservative estimate, replacement of partially
hydrogenated fat in the U.S. diet with natural unhydrogenated oils
would prevent approximately 30,000 premature coronary deaths per
year, and epidemiologic evidence suggests this number is closer to
100,000 premature deaths annually."

Tommy Thompson, the Secretary of HHS, said at a news conference on
January 12, 2005, that the FDA may recommend that the daily intake
of trans fat should be kept under 2 grams, perhaps less than 1 gram.
In effect, that would mean totally avoiding any foods containing
partially hydrogenated oils.

Trans fat can be found in many foods that you should avoid, including:

Margarine
Shortening
Cake mixes
Mixes in general
Many soups
Fast food
```

```
Frozen food
Baked goods
Chips
Crackers
Breakfast cereals
Candy
Non-dairy creamers
Salad dressings
```

```
Trans fats and high fructose corn syrup did not exist 30 years ago.
Today they are everywhere, and we are paying a heavy price. Let's
start getting rid of them, one at a time.
```

```
Bob Hartford, ABC Chief Nutritionist
```

```
P.S. Whatever your need, remember: http://www.abc123nutrition.com/
products.html is open 24/7 for your convenience. And don't forget
to check out my new book on sale at Amazon, The Top 100 Fatty Foods
in America.
```

```
Copyright, ABC Nutrition, Inc. If you no longer wish to receive
communication from us, click http://autocontactor.com and select
"unsubscribe."
```

Again note the components that should be in this type of e-mail.

- An initial option to opt-in and subscribe.

- In each subsequent e-mail, include an option to opt-out.

- One or two hyperlinks to your store or products on Amazon where the interested buyer can immediately purchase the items you're describing or view your information.

- Content! Remember, the key to a newsletter versus a discount offer is that you're not trying to close a sale in the e-mail but generate traffic back to your zShop, Auctions, or even your own company's web site. Instead of offering product, offer content—in this case, a new art design and an announcement that your site has over 200 web pages of information that the buyer could potentially use.

TIP

If you've created any kind of Listmania, or a So You'd Like to guide for Amazon, those can translate very well into newsletter items. Plus, you can embed the hyperlinks to your Amazon products in the newsletter to help drive sales!

To Sum Up

In this chapter, we talked about how the nature of ordering items off Amazon.com allows you to utilize three advantages that you wouldn't find if, for example, your customer simply made a cash purchase from your brick-and-mortar store. These advantages are a sense of community, gaining customer contact information, and establishing a zone of trust.

We also discussed the pros and cons of direct-mail campaigns (questionable), unsolicited mass e-mail (don't do it!), and targeted e-mails (a must). We also worked through the basics of your campaign, which is the e-mail itself, the web location of the offer, and a way to track its success.

The e-mail can be designed using plain text (boring but fast, and it gets to all web users) versus HTML (graphics-intensive, and more visually appealing). Of the two kinds of e-mails to use, either the offer e-mail or the newsletter approach can work for you, so long as you include hyperlinks to the offer or information you are touting, as well as an option to opt-out if the user so chooses.

Part IV

Grow Your Business on Amazon

Chapter 10

Become a Pro Merchant on Amazon

We look at other online companies to learn from, see what they're doing, and maybe adapt it.

—Jeff Bezos, founder of Amazon.com

As we start the fourth part of this book, we want to take you beyond the introductory steps we've already presented. At this point, we want you to start looking at the big picture—in other words, to start thinking about your overall business development on Amazon, not just about making individual sales. In the next few chapters, we'll talk about advancing your sales the same way Amazon did to grow beyond just selling books: by looking at entirely new areas to tackle.

This chapter is geared to helping you become a "pro" in every sense of the word. We've already discussed how to be a Pro Merchant on Amazon, but now let's talk about some methods that will make you a Professional Seller—someone who can grow their sales, gain new customer bases, and expand their product selection. We feel the topics here represent some of the best practices and habits of selling online. Try one, try them all, but definitely consider them, since most big sellers can't survive without some combination of them. And now, let's begin!

Finding Hot Products

Most merchants on Amazon are responsive to market prices—particularly when it comes to items whose prices have soared due to scarcity, or that have plummeted when an item has lost its often fleeting appeal. But the truly "pro" sellers are those who can identify and deal in trendy, hot products—in other words, tailoring what they offer to what the consumer most wants, as opposed to adjusting prices up and down according to random market demand. And, of course, your easiest resource at hand in identifying this level of market demand is Amazon's site itself.

Please note that this doesn't mean you should avoid common sense—if you see a particular item flying off your store's shelves (or a competitor's shelves across town), don't ignore what the market is telling you. Additionally, utilize your expertise in the real world as well as the online one if it's applicable. For example, let's say your company deals in preframed animation cels. If you've gotten a shipment of cels from an upcoming movie, and all the indications are that it will be well received when it comes out, then by all means, be ready to list these items on Amazon, and at a good price. In this particular example, you would probably want to capitalize on the pre-release hype by selling these items long before the film's release date. This way, you capitalize on other people hoping to stock up in case the movie does well, and protect yourself by unloading merchandise if the movie performs poorly compared to expectations (for example, the '90s remake of *Godzilla* got lots of hype but earned bad reviews and low audience turnout).

Amazon lets you see what's selling well in your market niche at any given time. Let's say you deal in exotic Columbian coffee beans, selling both ground and whole beans. Given your expertise, you know that some of the newly released coffees taste better than others, and that they'll probably sell well. When you do a search for the newly listed coffees on Amazon, you may see listings like that shown in Figure 10-1.

However, what you personally like and what's selling well on Amazon.com might be two different things. (Yes, like all experts, we know what the "right" brand is for any situation, but good luck imposing your wants on the market. The market always speaks louder!) Notice that there's always a Sort By pull-down menu that normally defaults to Newest Entries, Newest Releases, or Most Relevant, depending on what items you're researching.

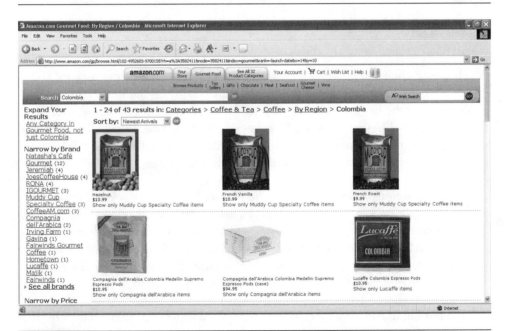

FIGURE 10-1   The newly released Columbian coffee items on Amazon

FIGURE 10-2   The listing of the best-selling Columbian coffee items on Amazon

However, click that pull-down menu and select Bestselling in the category you're interested in. You may see the results change significantly, as in Figure 10-2.

Notice that the brands which are selling—no matter what your opinion of them—are very different from what has been newly released. Repeat this type of search on the different areas where you plan to carry merchandise and you'll start to get a pretty good idea of what's selling, and at what price.

TIP   *Although items can remain on the Bestselling list for a while, they can also drop off and/or be replaced by new items. This is particularly true of items that don't get a strong (four- to five-star) customer rating. In other words, a best-selling item might be on the list because it's new, or because its price has been slashed. But if the product is essentially mediocre, then its prominence on the list will only last a short time.*

The bottom line to remember is this: successful sellers on Amazon deal in what their customers want, not with what they want. Sure, your knowledge in a specific area may allow you to get merchandise, pick out early hits, and describe your items better, but having the right policies, customer service, and knowledge of the system will allow you to excel in areas where you're just learning, and help you service new and growing groups of customers.

Good Customer Service Policies

It may sound a little too much like "marketing-speak," but it really is true that Amazon.com was founded—and continued to prosper—by providing an excellent online purchasing experience for buyers. Today, Amazon gets most of its press from its financial maneuvers, or from what new kinds of merchandise it will offer, or perhaps from what new services it will offer sellers who work "on the river." However, keep in mind that Amazon carved out its market niche in the early part of the dot-com revolution, when many consumers were hesitant to purchase items online, or to give out credit card information to people they had never seen (and never would see).

Dot-com firms were seen as fly-by-night, untested operators, and until their stock prices began to skyrocket, often viewed as objects of curiosity at best. It's only been fairly recently that that perception has changed. For example, the article "Internet—it's good for your social life" by Ahmed El Amin (*The Royal Gazette*, September 2, 2005) stated, "In 2001, Internet users bought online about 11 times each year. Now they buy online about 30 times per year." Today, buying online has reached the same level of acceptability as sending e-mail or reading news, since as general Internet use increases, buying online similarly increases.

Amazon.com overcame this initial hesitancy and built what is arguably the most solid customer base for retail sales online to this day. And it did this in no small part with its outstanding site, ease of transactions, and customer service. And since customers have come to expect this type of service from Amazon.com directly, it's in your best interest to provide the same level of treatment, especially if you'd like repeat business. The "best practices" of a good customer service policy can be summed up in the following subsections.

Being Responsive to Your Customers

Yes, we've already said this more than once throughout the book, but it's so important that we'll say it one more time: Answer all buyer inquiries within 24 hours of receipt. Remember, yet another of Amazon's credos (born from a time when people didn't have much faith in buying online) was that they should respond to customer inquiries as quickly as possible. Is it a little time-consuming to do this *all* the time? Yes, it can be. But maintaining good communication with your buyers promotes good feedback, which is a potent boost for your Amazon sales.

Managing and Shipping Your Orders Promptly

Of course, providing great customer service goes beyond simple e-mails—it extends to the management and fulfillment (a.k.a., shipping) of your orders. It's best if you don't take a completely passive stance on this issue and simply wait for e-mail notifications to arrive. Remember that you can access your Amazon Payments via your Seller Account to see what needs to be managed and shipped.

When it comes to fulfillment, the rule is simple: Ship your items *within two business days of order notification*. This should be an absolute rule for your organization—it's not a successful shipping policy to get about 80 percent of the packages shipped in two or three days. With the advent of instant everything, from online ordering to coffee to stock reports, the one thing people still notice is the wait for their merchandise. And, as we recommended in the previous section, don't forget to communicate with your buyer—send them a confirmation e-mail after the order has been shipped, and include tracking or delivery confirmation numbers if applicable.

TIP

Include a note in your package with your contact information and encourage your buyer to leave you feedback at www.amazon.com/feedback. It doesn't have to be complex. It can be as simple as "We at ABC Company have enjoyed doing business with you and encourage you to leave us feedback as to the promptness of our service and quality of our merchandise. Sincerely, President of ABC Co."

One final note about maintaining high-quality customer service. Remember that good customer service includes the prompt handling of refunds and returns as well as simple order fulfillment. We cover the topic of how to properly refund a customer's money and how to handle customer disputes in Chapter 4. Again, the same rule that applies to order fulfillment also applies to refunds: perform the action within two business days, and then notify the buyer that the action has been taken.

The Importance of a High Rating: Amazon's Feedback System

Without face-to-face interaction, or the name recognition of a major brand (and not just any major brand, but one that people consider trustworthy), buyers will often decide whether to make a purchase depending on the seller's feedback score. A high feedback score is vital to remaining competitive, especially when other sellers are competing for the same business, perhaps at similar or lower prices.

Once customers offer feedback on your service, it's a matter of public record. When your listing is displayed as one of the sellers offering a particular product, users can click the hyperlink connected with your company's name to see both your overall rating and every bit of feedback you've received from previous customers. Examples of these snapshots are shown in Figures 10-3 and 10-4. Imagine you're considering buying an item from one of these two sellers. After comparing the same item at the same price, whom would you buy from?

Your first reaction might be "But both have excellent ratings!" That's true, but we've picked these merchants out for that very reason. It's helpful to have a high rating, but it's equally important to maintain that rating for a substantial period of time to set yourself apart. Buyers not only look at the number of stars out of five, they also look at the total number of ratings to see how long the firm has been around, and whether they regularly fulfill customer requests. Thus, the first merchant's efforts are admirable, but 129 pieces of feedback pale in comparison to the over 43,000 comments given to the second.

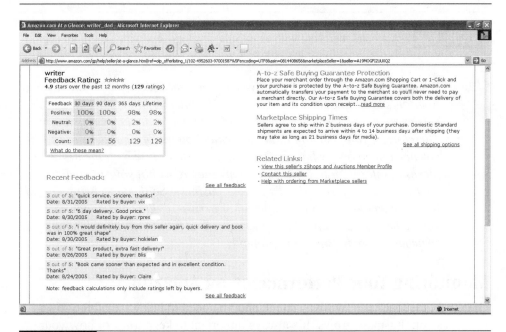

FIGURE 10-3   An Amazon merchant with an excellent customer rating

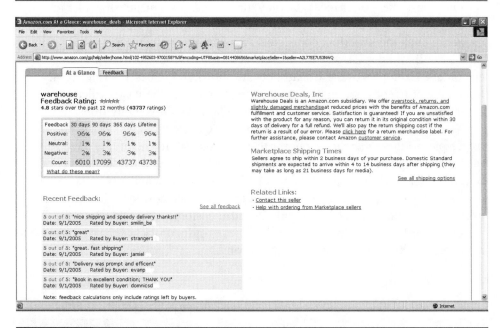

At a Glance | Feedback

warehouse
Feedback Rating: ★★★★★
4.8 stars over the past 12 months (43737 ratings)

Feedback	30 days	90 days	365 days	Lifetime
Positive:	96%	96%	96%	96%
Neutral:	1%	1%	1%	1%
Negative:	2%	3%	3%	3%
Count:	6010	17099	43737	43738

What do these mean?

Warehouse Deals, Inc
Warehouse Deals is an Amazon.com subsidiary. We offer overstock, returns, and slightly damaged merchandise at reduced prices with the benefits of Amazon.com fulfillment and customer service. Satisfaction is guaranteed! If you are unsatisfied with the product for any reason, you can return it in its original condition within 30 days of delivery for a full refund. We'll also pay the return shipping cost if the return is a result of our error. Please click here for a return merchandise label. For further assistance, please contact Amazon customer service.

Marketplace Shipping Times
Sellers agree to ship within 2 business days of your purchase. Domestic Standard shipments are expected to arrive within 4 to 14 business days after shipping (they may take as long as 21 business days for media).

See all shipping options

Recent Feedback:

See all feedback

5 out of 5: "nice shipping and speedy delivery thanks!!"
Date: 9/1/2005   Rated by Buyer: smilin_be

5 out of 5: "great"
Date: 9/1/2005   Rated by Buyer: stranger1

5 out of 5: "great. fast shipping"
Date: 9/1/2005   Rated by Buyer: jamiel

5 out of 5: "Delivery was prompt and efficent"
Date: 9/1/2005   Rated by Buyer: evanp

5 out of 5: "Book in excellent condition; THANK YOU"
Date: 9/1/2005   Rated by Buyer: domicsd

Note: feedback calculations only include ratings left by buyers.

Related Links:
· Contact this seller
· Help with ordering from Marketplace sellers

FIGURE 10-4 A second merchant with an excellent rating—but with a lot more depth

> **TIP**
>
> *What is a superior level of positive customer feedback? According to Amazon's Performance Target policy, "The number of negative feedback entries should be less than 5 percent of the total feedback entries received." Therefore, if you get more than five critical pieces of feedback out of 100, you need to go over what can be improved. Don't brush off the negative pieces of information if you don't think they're within your immediate control—they're just as deadly to your business! So if you're being dinged by customers for, say, slow shipment or arrival of damaged goods, and you've been scrupulous about packaging and fulfillment, then it's time you switched shipping firms, and promptly.*

Monitoring Your Performance on Amazon

Of course, feedback is a two-way street, and you need to be aware of your own results as your business grows. It's always important to keep track of how your customers are rating you, and that means more than just direct feedback ratings. Amazon keeps track of three basic areas when it comes to your sales: Refunds, Customer Feedback, and A to Z Guarantee or insurance claims.

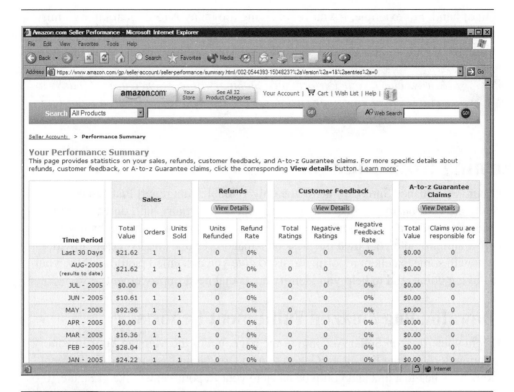

FIGURE 10-5   Take a look at your Amazon Performance Summary.

From your Amazon Seller Account home page, under the My Account header, click the link titled View My Performance Summary and you'll be taken to that summary, as shown in Figure 10-5. Amazon will show you your aggregate sales per month, and for each month, show you the breakdown of refunds given, the customer feedback received, and the A to Z Guarantee claims filed against you. Each of those figures will come with an associated percentage of total sales affected by each category. So, for example, if you had one refund in a given month of 100 sales, you'd have a 1-percent refund rate.

Your customer feedback score offers a little more detail since it displays your positive and negative feedback separately, and shows you the percentage of feedback that's negative. In this and the other two cases, Amazon is looking to compare your performance with other sellers so they can get a handle on which sellers are performing poorly against the rest and may present a problem. This is also done for your benefit so you can keep track of whether something is getting out of hand. For example, if you're receiving too many A to Z Guarantee claims, this may be a sign you're not describing your merchandise accurately, or you're using the wrong shipping company to deliver your products to the customer.

 *Always check your Performance Summary at least once every 60 days to get a sense of how your customers are responding to Amazon regarding your sales efforts.*

Learning from Your Data

Your Performance Summary is not the only valuable data report that can help you cultivate your business. Since Amazon's success is partially built on excellent data-gathering and analysis, it makes sense for you to employ the same technique to grow and promote your own business on Amazon. To that end, Amazon provides you with some excellent reporting tools to give you a detailed picture of how your sales are going, and to help you identify areas that need improvement.

Downloading Amazon Fulfillment Reports

From your Amazon Seller Account home page, under the Manage Your Inventory section, look for the link titled Generate And Download Listing And Fulfillment Reports. Click that link and you'll be taken to your Reports center, like in Figure 10-6. The basic system works as follows: You will request an activity report from Amazon. They'll go through their computer system and pull a report of all your order fulfillment records for the time period you specify. They'll then deliver that report electronically to your Amazon Seller Account, and you'll return to this page to log in and look at your generated report.

Click the Generate Reports Now link to get started. You'll be taken to a second screen, like the one in Figure 10-7, which asks you to select which report you'd like to generate. Typically, you can request reports detailing the last 15, 30, or 60 days worth of sales, orders, or cancelled listings. You simply pick the Yes radio button for any report you want generated. For example, if you want the Order Fulfillment report, detailing all sales you made where they paid through Amazon Payments (which, for you, is actually all sales, since you must use Amazon Payments), you simply click the Yes radio button under the Order Fulfillment Report heading and select either a 15-, 30-, or 60-day time period for the report.

Once you've picked all the reports you want to generate, click the Preview button to look over your selections. You'll be presented with a list of the reports

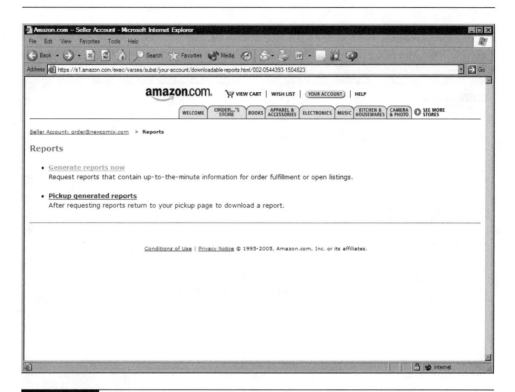

FIGURE 10-6   Your Amazon Reports page

you've requested, like that shown in Figure 10-8. Click the orange Generate Report Now button and Amazon will notify you when your reports are ready for viewing.

> **NOTE**   *In your Amazon Seller Account profile, make sure your e-mail notifications are going to the right e-mail address. Under My Account, click the link marked Turn On/Off My E-mail Notifications to make the correct adjustments, if needed.*

Once you've been notified via e-mail that your reports are ready to be viewed, go back to the Generate And Download Fulfillment Reports link from the Seller Account home page. Instead of clicking Generate Reports Now, click the other link, Pickup Generated reports. You'll be taken to a screen like the one in Figure 10-9, where you can review the results of each report. In order to view any particular report, click the link that contains the name of the report and the date it was generated.

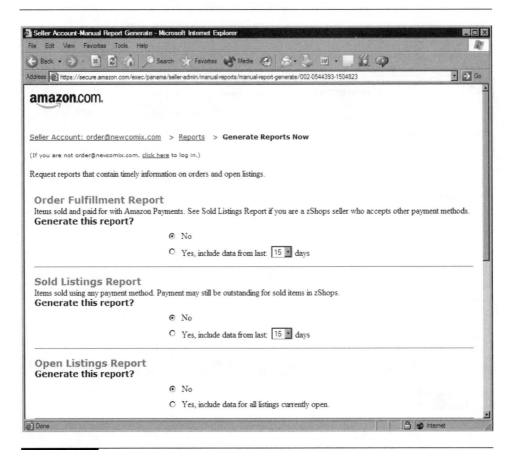

FIGURE 10-7   Here's your chance to order reports on your sales efforts.

Let's say that you want to see the order fulfillment report. You'd click the link titled Order—08/26/05 15:43:25 PDT from the example in Figure 10-9. This would open a File Download window where you could save the report to your computer. We don't recommend opening it into your Internet browser because it may not display correctly. Once this report is saved on your computer, use a spreadsheet program like Microsoft Excel to open the file, which should present the report in table format where each transaction is broken down into its critical fields. You'll get to see when each item was ordered, paid for, and the type of shipping the customer selected, along with all the key customer fields, and the different ID numbers Amazon uses to keep track of these transactions.

You can use Microsoft Excel to sort this field by any of the columns, and doing so can show some interesting results. Grouping your orders by date can show you

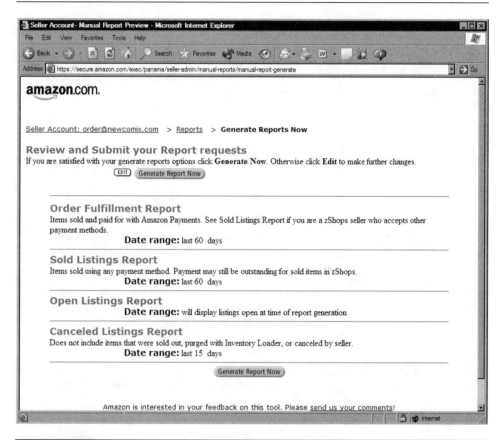

FIGURE 10-8   Review the list of reports you'd like generated.

peak times for when your products are being ordered (and by contrast, "dead" times when no products are being ordered), as well as a way to predict potential demand for shipping out products. This data can show you the average amount of orders you ship per day, as well as the minimum and maximum. Information like this is crucial if you're hiring people to help you manage your product shipments, because now you know what the busiest days can look like in terms of volume.

Other information can be pulled out of this report as well. You can sort your orders by Total Price, and get an idea of the Average Order amount your products are generating on Amazon. In addition, you can sort your reports by item name and get a glimpse into your most popular selling products (and if you don't see a certain product on the list, you know no one's ordered it in the last month or two) so you know what to stock and reorder.

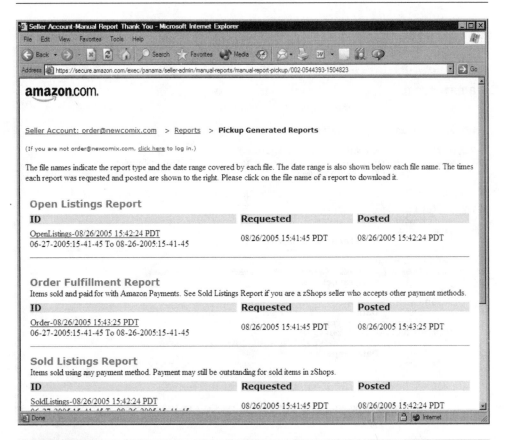

FIGURE 10-9 Pick the generated report you want to review.

Automating Your Selling Activities

One of the reasons we stress data analysis is because finding valuable, salable, and profitable merchandise is often what takes up the most time for an e-commerce business on Amazon. The best way for your business to grow is to automate the less profitable activities so you can focus your time on data analysis and finding the right products. That's why we're moving onto another important concept for people who want to build their business: automation. In other words, we want to help you find ways to handle some of the myriad tasks involved in selling online more efficiently, and (when possible) automatically, so you have more time to get inventory and handle more orders.

Thankfully, the rise of information technology has made automation a reality, and not just for big corporations with millions of dollars to invest. There are software programs in all shapes and sizes that can help you handle different tasks. We'll actually touch on the most sophisticated form of automation through information technology, called Amazon Web Services, in Chapter 11. Right now, let's start with that first step you need once you have your inventory… listing it on Amazon!

Amazon's Inventory Loader and Book Loader

In Part II of this book, we walked you through how to list an individual item in the Marketplace, Auctions, and zShops. We started you with that method to illustrate the important parts of a product listing and help you focus on optimizing each part. After a while, however, we're betting you're going to have lots of products you'll want to put up as fast as possible so you can work on the next batch. People sometimes debate the optimal number of listings you should do manually before changing over to use an automation tool. From our discussions, most people agree that once you hit 20 to 30 listings at a time, you should consider using an automation tool.

Amazon understands this need and has built a special function to help you load multiple items quickly and easily. It's called Inventory Loader. (Its first iteration, which is still around, is called Book Loader, since it was originally used just for books.) Inventory Loader lets you create a simple file and send it to Amazon. There, they dissect the file and simultaneously create all the different inventory listings specified in it so you don't have to walk through the form a multitude of times.

 *Because Amazon Auctions listings can be complex with lots of information, we're not recommending that you use this feature to upload auction items, though it is available to you. Use Amazon Help to search for Auctions Bulk Loader for more information on this feature.*

Creating an Upload File for Inventory Loader

Your first step in using Inventory Loader is creating your file to be uploaded. Your Inventory Loader upload file must be in the form of what's called a tab-delimited text file. That means the information has to be stored in a regular text file where each field of information is separated by a tab command. The easiest software program you can use to create this kind of file is Microsoft Excel, which allows you to create a spreadsheet of data containing your different products and will save your information in this special file format. Amazon even provides you with a handy blank template to get started. Just navigate to this URL with your browser to save it onto your computer:

http://s1.amazon.com/templates/MyAmazonInventory.xls

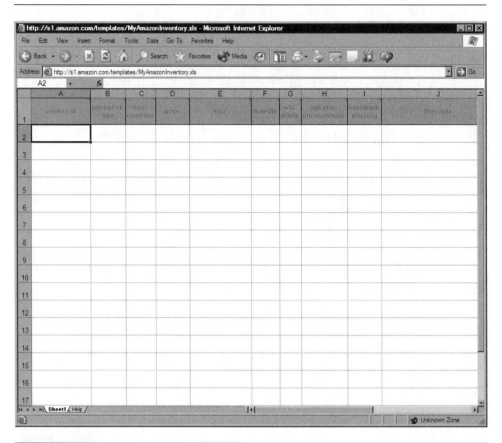

FIGURE 10-10 Amazon provides you with a blank template for your upload file.

> **TIP**
>
> *If you want to see what you're downloading before you save this file onto your computer, click this link but select Open. Use Microsoft Excel as the program to open this file with, and you'll see a file like the one in Figure 10-10. Think of this file as a blank report you need to fill in.*

Once you save this template on your computer, use Microsoft Excel to open and edit the file. Creating your upload file is like filling in an inventory report. Each line in the file represents a unique product. For each product you want to upload onto Amazon, you just have to fill in the following fields of information:

■ **product-id**   This is the special identifying number for your product, as we discussed in Part I. For books, you would put the ISBN number in this field. For most consumer products, you would use the UPC code. Most times, you will put the ASIN (Amazon Standard Identification Number) number in this field if the product you're selling already exists in the Amazon catalog.

■ **product-id-type**   Now that you've put in the identifying number for your product, use this field to tell Amazon which type of ID you used. For this field, enter one of the following values, depending on what you used:

   ■ 1 for ASIN

   ■ 2 for ISBN

   ■ 3 for UPC

   ■ 4 for EAN, a European Article Number similar to the UPC code in the U.S.

■ **item-condition**   As we've mentioned, condition is critical to your description. Amazon has devised a numeric code corresponding to their condition levels. Enter the appropriate number in this field based on your product's condition:

   ■ 1 for a Used Item that's Like New

   ■ 2 for a Used Item that's in Very Good condition

   ■ 3 for a Used Item that's in Good condition

   ■ 4 for a Used Item that's in Acceptable condition

   ■ 5 for a Collectible Item that's Like New

   ■ 6 for a Collectible Item that's in Very Good condition

   ■ 7 for a Collectible Item that's in Good condition

   ■ 8 for a Collectible Item that's in Acceptable condition

   ■ 9 for a Refurbished/Used product (only in Camera/Photo and Electronics)

   ■ 10 for Refurbished (Camera/Photo, Computers, Electronics, or Kitchen)

   ■ 11 for New condition

■ **price** Enter the numeric price of your product, dollars and cents only, no dollar signs ($) or other currency markers.

■ **sku** You need to assign a Stock Keeping Unit (or SKU) number to help you keep track of your inventory or help you match up your inventory with a current numbering system you may be using. This field cannot be left blank, so create a string of numbers and letters to help you keep track of your inventory. The system will not accept an SKU with spaces or other symbols in the string. For example, if you're selling different types of cell phones based on service providers, your SKUs can be CELVERZ01, CELSPRT01, and CELCING01 to represent Verizon, Sprint PCS, and Cingular phones, respectively.

■ **quantity** Enter the numerical quantity of the product you want to sell.

■ **will-ship-internationally** The contents of this field tell Amazon whether you're willing to ship this product internationally or not.

   ■ Enter y (or 2) if you're willing to ship internationally.

   ■ Enter n (or 1) if you're only willing to ship inside the United States.

■ **expedited-shipping** The contents of this field tell Amazon whether you're willing to offer expedited shipping in the U.S. for this product.

   ■ Enter y if you're willing to ship this product expedited (through programs like the U.S. Postal Service Priority Mail).

   ■ Enter n if you aren't willing to offer this shipping option for the product.

■ **item-is-marketplace** This field tells Amazon whether to insert this product into Amazon Marketplace. Enter y if you want it there; n if you don't. (By entering n, Amazon will insert it as a product in your zShop.)

Amazon also requires you to have three empty columns with the following headers:

■ item-name

■ item-description

■ category1

Amazon will fill in these fields as you upload your file to them and use that information to help create your product listings.

Optional Information for Your Upload File

If you're planning to upload listings specifically for the Amazon Marketplace, there are three optional columns of information you can add, as shown in the following:

- **add-delete**   If you want to delete a listing from your Marketplace inventory, create a line in your file with that product ID and put the letter d in this column. Doing so will delete this listing.

- **image-url**   If you need to use your own picture to depict your product, instead of Amazon's stock photo, you need to put the URL web address where your picture is being stored online. You should enter something like this:

  http://www.*yoursitename*.com/*imagename*.gif

- **item-note**   You should enter any comments about this product that describe the item or condition better. You have up to 200 characters to say things like "BRAND NEW SHRINKWRAPPED" or "UNREAD 1ST EDITION FOR SALE WITH MINT DUST JACKET" to help sell your product.

If you're planning to upload listings specifically for Amazon Auctions or zShops, there are some optional columns of information you should add, as shown next:

- **image-url**   Same as with the Marketplace (see earlier entry).

- **shipping-fee**   Enter the amount you're charging to ship out the item to U.S. buyers, in dollars and cents, no symbols.

- **browse-path**   This allows you to create your own categories separated by colons. You would enter a value like: Video Games:Xbox:Strategy.

- **storefront-feature**   Enter the letter y in this field if you want to feature this product on your zShop storefront page. Remember, you can have up to five featured items at one time. If you pick more than five, Amazon will rotate them on the page for you.

- **boldface**   Enter the letter y in this field if you want your Auctions item (or zShops item, for that matter) title to appear in **Boldface** to distinguish itself from the rest.

When you're done creating your file, use the File | Save As command in Microsoft Excel to save your file, and then pick the file type: Tab Delimited. Excel will display some messages saying it can't save the entire file in this format. Just click the OK button to save the worksheet you've created as a Tab Delimited file. You can save the entire file later as an Excel file for future usage.

Uploading Your File to Amazon with Inventory Loader

Once you've created your inventory file, it's time to send it to Amazon. Go to your Seller Account home page on Amazon and in the Manage Inventory section click the Upload Multiple Items link. You'll be taken to a screen that looks like Figure 10-11,

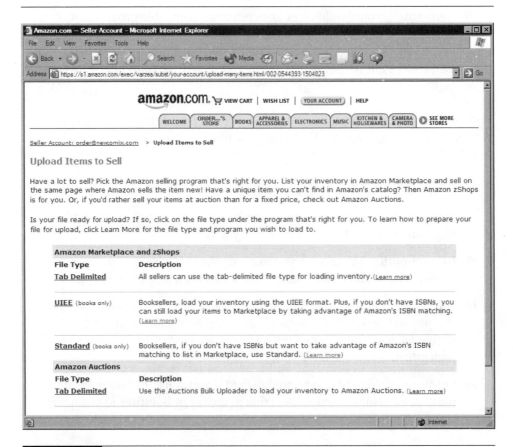

FIGURE 10-11 Pick the appropriate link to send Amazon your inventory file.

where you have to tell Amazon, through your selection, what type of file you're sending it and to which area(s) of the Amazon site your products should go.

If you're uploading products into Amazon Marketplace or zShops, click the first link marked Tab Delimited. If you're only uploading books into the system, you can click on the Standard link to use the same file you just built. If you're uploading items into Amazon Auctions, click the Tab Delimited link next to the Auctions header.

Once you click the appropriate link, you'll be taken to a page that will ask you a few final questions before uploading your file. Once there, you'll have to make a few selections, such as:

- **Select Your Program**   If you're only uploading items into your storefront, select zShops Only. Otherwise, select the second option, Amazon Marketplace And/Or zShops.

- **Upload Option**   Here, you'll select one of three actions for Amazon to take once it receives your file:

   - **Add/Modify/Delete**   Amazon will analyze this file and add, modify, and/or delete your listings based on the information in it.

   - **Purge and Replace**   Amazon will delete any current Marketplace and zShop listings and "replace" them with the products listed in your file.

   - **Modify/Delete**   Amazon will only modify or delete listings based on products in your upload file, it will not add any products, even if your file specifies products to be added.

- **File Path**   If you click the Browse button, your computer will prompt you to select the appropriate file. Use the window provided to find the file you want to upload, and then click OK.

Once you've specified all these fields of information, click the orange Upload Now button to send the information to Amazon. You'll get a confirmation screen regardless of how you created your upload file. If there was a missing field of information that was required, or incompatible or excessive data, you will see errors in your Error Log, which you can view once Amazon has finished processing your file.

Once you've uploaded your file, Amazon will process the listings, usually within minutes, though it could take up to 24 hours. In most cases, you can review the status of your uploading within 15 minutes or so by clicking the Review Inventory Upload Status button from the confirmation screen or by clicking the link Check The Success Of Your Inventory Uploads on your Seller Account home page.

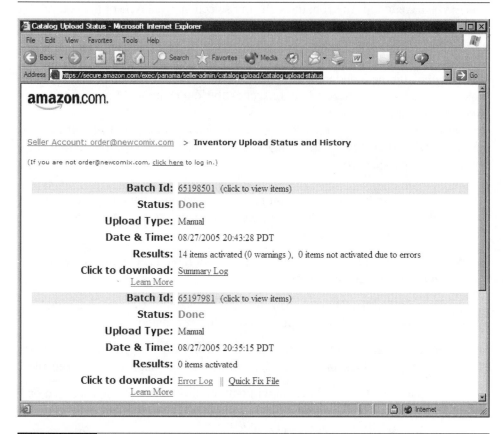

FIGURE 10-12   Check the results of your products' upload!

When you've done so, you should be taken to a confirmation screen like the one shown in Figure 10-12. This screen shows the result of two different uploads, the first one being successful, and the second one resulting in errors. If you click the Batch Log ID number, you'll see the results of your upload. Notice the link to the Error Log near the bottom of the screen. When there are any problems with the upload, like a missing value in one of the lines of the file, you'll see the description of that error in the Error Log. If you click the Quick Fix file, it'll create an upload file of the entries that got rejected, so you can save that file, fix it, and upload the Quick Fix file to complete the process.

Of course, once all your intended products have been uploaded to your account, the same rules apply to maintaining your listings. You should always check in and make sure you've priced your items appropriately, especially if you're not achieving the same sales numbers you had in the past. You have the ability to end any listing at any time as long as nobody's purchased the item yet. But this way, using some quick manipulation with Microsoft Excel (which can populate many fields quickly if the information is the same), allows you to add inventory quicker so you can worry about increasing your sales and making your fortune.

Other Automation Techniques

Inventory Loader can do more than just load your inventory: it can help you prune and maintain your listings. Remember, the add-delete field can be used to remove listings, not just add them. The Purge and Replace option for uploading your Inventory file can dump all your current listings and replace them with new ones, in case you need to swap out your previous inventory for a new batch because your previous inventory got damaged, stolen, or lost.

One great trick people use with their Inventory Loader files is to create instant sales. They'll open up their previously uploaded file, use Microsoft Excel to quickly discount all the prices by 10 or 20 percent, and then save the file and modify all their listings with one upload. Thus, you've just used Inventory Loader to change all your listings without manually going in and fixing the price on each one!

Now that we've talked about how to automate inventory loading and management, the next logical step is to talk about automating the "back end," or what happens after the sale has been made. The next chapter is going to focus on how to handle these different procedures, so your e-mails and communications get boiled down to a science, freeing you up, again, to focus on the important aspects of your business.

To Sum Up

In this chapter, we moved away from the basics of Amazon to focus on the habits and techniques that help Amazon sellers move beyond the casual sale and grow into a sustainable business. We started urging you to think more like a business at every step, where you present nothing but professionalism and courtesy to your customers while cultivating that relationship. We talked about keeping ahead the curve by finding and stocking the hottest products, and reviewing your data to make sure you're both hitting the goals you want to achieve and identifying any problem areas. Finally, we discussed automating some of your processes so you can focus on increasing your business further. We'll next talk about how to manage the process that starts when you get that wonderful e-mail saying your item's been sold!

Chapter 11

Systemize Your Back-End Processes

Work hard, have fun, make history.

—Jeff Bezos, founder of Amazon.com

In the last chapter, we introduced the concept of automating parts of your business so certain tasks happen "on their own" without your direct involvement, allowing you to spend your valuable time instead buying inventory or making strategic partnerships. In this chapter, we'll take that concept further by talking about what you can do on the "back-end"—in other words, those processes and tasks that happen after the sale has been made, which are invisible to the average consumer but that nevertheless keep your business running.

In that vein, we'll discuss three major areas every professional Amazon seller can benefit from through automation: communicating with your customers, shipping out your products, and communicating electronically with Amazon's computer systems. For each of these, you should read through the material, implement what you feel comfortable doing, and use the resulting time savings to cultivate your business in new and exciting ways! Remember, this isn't about getting rid of work. It's about creating processes that routinely take care of necessary tasks on their own so you don't have to do repetitive and time-consuming steps yourself!

Automating Your Customer Interactions

In the world of retail, the chime that goes off when a customer opens the front door is your indicator that it's time to interact with them. In the world of e-commerce, the "chime" is the e-mail you receive. Customers like interacting with their vendors, whether it's to find out more about the product they want to buy, or to find out about the seller they're about to do business with, sight unseen. Building a good customer rapport is just as important in e-commerce as it is with traditional retail, and more so because you don't have that direct contact. Therefore, as your business grows, it's important to look at automation to make sure your customers get their questions answered in a quick, efficient, and professional manner.

Handling Customer E-mails Both During and After the Sale

You should expect two main classifications of e-mail communication from your buyers: inquiries during their shopping process and follow-up communications after the sale is made. Each area is important since inquiries can lead to sales, and good customer service after the sale can lead to repeat customers, a high feedback rating, and great word-of-mouth—so both should be respected.

When it comes to inquiries about a product for sale, response time is the first important factor, especially for a time-sensitive sale like an auction. Therefore, whatever e-mail address you use in your Amazon account must be highly accessible. Preferably, it should be an account you can check on the road (if you travel a lot), or an account that isn't exclusively yours, so other people like employees or colleagues can monitor the account for you.

Once you check the e-mail regarding an inquiry, the first thing you need to assess (and this may sound silly) is whether you have enough information from the buyer to answer the question. Because a buyer has to contact you through their e-mail program and not through a pre-filled form, you may get questions where you're not sure what item the customer is referring to with their question. In situations like this, immediately respond with a nicely worded reply reassuring the customer you're responsive to their needs, but asking for clarification on which item they're referring to. You should have an e-mail like this already handy so all you have to do is cut and paste it into your reply.

If the customer inquiry is complete, meaning you know which item they are asking about, and their question isn't too vague, then you have two options: Figure out the answer and respond as soon as you can, or, if you're unable to find out the exact answer, e-mail an update to the customer explaining the situation (for example, "Thank you for your e-mail inquiry. Unfortunately, I am away for the next 36 hours. The moment I return, I will take those measurements you requested and e-mail them to you right away."), and then follow up with the information as soon as you can. Don't worry about hitting the customer with two rounds of e-mails, they'll appreciate the update and the fact that you took the time to initially respond.

> **NOTE** *While some people consider using automated e-mail replies, which send a generic e-mail every time someone e-mails their account to reassure people quickly, this strategy usually backfires. As a great example, eBay used to send out automated e-mail replies whenever someone e-mailed their customer service department. They eventually unplugged this service because of backlash from their customers.*

Regardless of the situation, you should have preformatted e-mail responses ready to go that handle 90 to 100 percent of what you need to say so you're not typing the same message over and over again, risking spelling and grammatical errors each time that could make you look bad. Also, if you're getting the same question more than once, after you reply to the potential customer, go immediately to your product listing and update it based on the question being asked. This should be an automatic process that you do at least once a day or two to keep your items as up-to-date as possible.

Finally, remember that your e-mails regarding product questions should deal primarily with that particular product, and not attempt to bring that customer into your overall store. The main exception to this rule is when a customer is asking about one product, and you have another product for sale that fits their need. In that situation, be sure your reply steers them towards the correct product. (For example, "Thanks for your inquiry regarding the Beethoven Masters boxed set. Unfortunately, this collection does not have Beethoven's Ninth Symphony. However, I am also selling a CD of the New York Philharmonic performing Beethoven's Ninth, which is currently on sale for $10. If you're interested, please follow this link: www.amazon .com...) Focus only on the one sale to be made. Your e-mails after the sale should work on converting them into a repeat customer.

Amazon E-mail Confirmations: How to Respond Properly

When it comes to e-mailing after the sale, that process begins when you get an e-mail confirmation from Amazon announcing that a sale has been made. Depending on where the sale occurred (Marketplace, Auctions, zShops), you'll get a differently formatted e-mail, but in all of them, you'll have the basic set of information you need to complete the sale. When you get one of these e-mails, look for the following information:

- Name of the product(s) that have been purchased
- Buyer's e-mail address
- Buyer's name and physical address
- Type of shipping for the item

Another way you can get this information is to routinely log into your Amazon Seller Account and view your Amazon Payments account page. In fact, you should check this page after you get an e-mail notification, just to make sure the transaction is completed and aren't waiting for funds to clear. Also, you can double-check the buyer's e-mail and physical address to make sure you have the correct information.

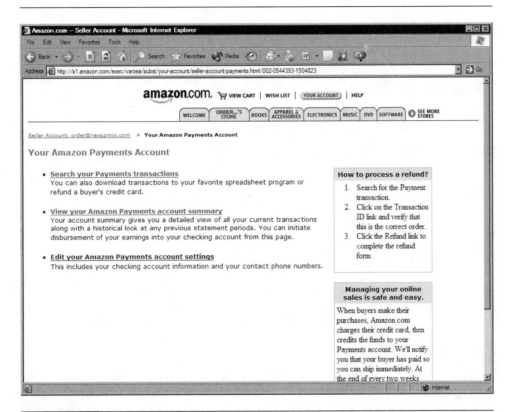

FIGURE 11-1 Use Amazon Payments history to get a view of all your recent sales.

As an example, let's say you're viewing your Amazon Payments account and billing history page, like in Figure 11-1. If you click Search Your Payments Transactions, you can log into your account and do a search for all your transactions from the last day, week, or month.

Once you pick the range of time you want to review, click Search to get a list of orders, like the one in Figure 11-2. While it's not visible in the figure, this table has all the critical information you need to get started. You can see the listing and order ID information, as well as the title of the item that sold. If you scroll to the right, you'll also see the buyer's e-mail address, quantity ordered, the total amount collected (and fees deducted), and whether the status is completed.

At this point, you can send out the first of a few automatic e-mails to complete the sale, such as the "Payment received/order is to be shipped" e-mail. We use the words "can send out" because this is an optional e-mail. Amazon has already sent

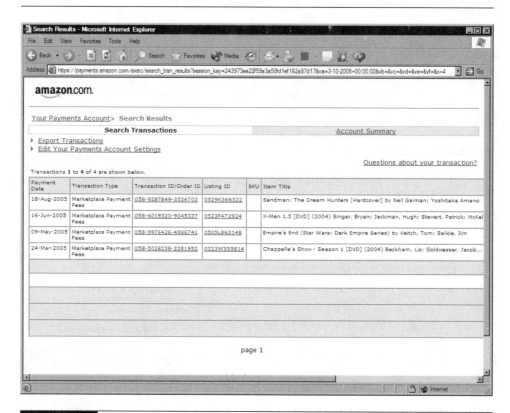

FIGURE 11-2   Get a list of all your recent Amazon sales.

the customer an e-mail invoice with their purchase, so the customer knows that their order was confirmed. The purpose of you sending out a Payment Received e-mail is to establish a connection with the customer and let them know that their order is going to be sent soon. Any e-mail of this nature should give a clear timeline as to when the order will be shipped (for instance, "Your order will be shipped out in the next 24 hours" or "Your order will go out as soon as we get our new stock in next Tuesday").

You should definitely include the shipping address you have on file for this order so the customer can verify that address and respond to you if there are any mistakes or necessary changes. One thing you should definitely not do is try to upsell them on other products in that first e-mail. Your job is to fulfill that initial sale, and only that initial sale. Once you've established a relationship with the customer after the sale is over, then you can contact them later with new and exciting deals.

After this step, you should focus on shipping out the product (which we'll talk about in the next section, "Automating Your Shipping Processes"). Once you've done so, it's time for a very important e-mail, the "Order Has Been Shipped" e-mail. Sometimes, this is the main e-mail you will want to send your customer, if you decide not to use the "Order is to be Shipped" e-mail first. Regardless, this e-mail needs to accomplish three very important points:

■ Thanking the customer for their order

■ Providing tracking information so the customer can monitor their order

■ Giving the customer an "actionable" item to keep them in your customer set.

The first task is self-explanatory, and is usually accomplished with the opening sentence of your e-mail. (For example, "Thanks again for your recent order with Joel's Stuff about the video games.") This can often be overlooked or ignored, but really it should never be omitted. In order to build up that customer relationship, you should always start with a Thank You.

Next, you need to provide the tracking information on the order you shipped out to the customer. This accomplishes several things: it signals the customer that you've already put the order in the mail, and it allows them to instantly monitor the progress of their package, 24 hours a day, seven days a week, without asking you and waiting for a response. In the world of e-commerce, where instant gratification is an important measure to live up to, the ability to monitor the package is crucial. It takes the burden off you, the seller, to complete the order in the eyes of the customer.

When doing this, give the actual numerical or alphanumerical string, the name of the shipper (whether it's the U.S. Postal Service, UPS, FedEx, and so on), and a web address URL (not necessarily a clickable URL) where they can go to enter their tracking number (such as www.usps.com, www.ups.com, or some other).

Last, but definitely not least, you need to give the customer something to do, or an "actionable" item, that will encourage them to stay a part of your customer base. Most of the time, it can be as simple as "Hey, send me your e-mail address and I'll add you to my monthly newsletter list where you can read articles and get exclusive discounts on hot new products in the marketplace." You can also offer a direct-sale product, perhaps one that is an excellent up-sell or cross-sell to the product they've ordered.

For example, if someone has just ordered the new Apple iPod 5GB digital music player, you can run a special in your e-mail that states the following:

As a thank you for buying the newest Apple iPod, we're offering a special 25-percent discount on iPod carrying cases. Use the code XYZ at my web site to achieve this instant savings! For new Amazon buyers only!

We use the word "actionable" because you want to present an offer or a request that requires the buyer to take an action to get involved. You don't want to include every buyer on your massive e-mail lists and announcement bulletins just because they ordered a product from you. As we discussed in Chapter 9, that form of e-mail marketing is considered spamming and is basically illegal. Instead, use the opportunity of this e-mail to encourage continued participation from this buyer, and come up with standard offers in your e-mail templates that you can use over and over again so you're not constantly thinking of new offers every time you make a sale.

Systemizing the Feedback Process

While we talked about the three important parts of the "Order has been shipped" message, there's a fourth part that should also be part of every e-mail: asking the buyer to leave you feedback once they receive the item. Once you've sent this e-mail, and there are no problems reported by the buyer, that's the end of your communication unless they've signed on with your "actionable" item to stay in touch with you or take you up on a new product offer. Therefore, you definitely want to make sure that you've asked the buyer to leave you favorable feedback at the end of your e-mail. (For example, "Please take the time to leave me feedback on Amazon once you've received the item, and I am leaving you positive feedback for your quick payment.")

While this technique usually helps remind your buyers to leave feedback, Amazon will also follow up with your buyers with an e-mail reminding them to rate the transaction, like that shown in Figure 11-3. Amazon will send this reminder out one month after you've ordered so that enough time has elapsed and the buyer typically has their order by that point (if the buyer hasn't already left feedback).

Regardless of this e-mail, you should have a preformatted e-mail template ready to go that's your own version of the Feedback Reminder e-mail. Use this opportunity as one more chance to follow up with your buyer and build that ongoing relationship. Start the e-mail with something like "Dear Bob, Thanks again for your order from our Amazon store of the new video games. We want to make sure that everything has arrived in excellent condition. Please let us know if there were any problems with the products when they arrived."

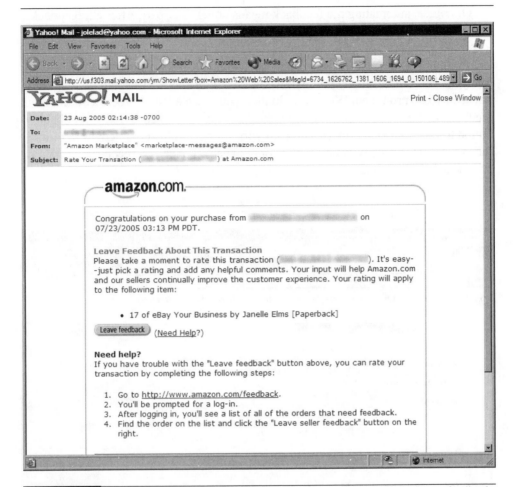

Then, use the rest of the e-mail to gently remind them that you could really use the feedback. Remember, don't tell them to leave you a five-star positive feedback, and definitely do NOT threaten to leave them poor feedback if they don't leave you super-positive feedback. Just point them to www.amazon.com/feedback and ask them to contribute their comments to help your reputation and business. Thank them again, perhaps cite another product offer or a reminder to join your e-mail newsletter, and then insert your electronic signature. This e-mail should then be ready to go, only needing the person's name and e-mail address to send it off.

Of course, automating the feedback means doing your part. After all, feedback on Amazon is a two-way street just like on other sites. Once you start dealing with a volume of transactions, you want to handle your feedback postings in a systematic and routine way. Once a week (or more depending on your volume), you should log into your Feedback page by going to www.amazon.com/feedback and logging into Amazon when prompted. When you do that, you'll see a list of orders awaiting your feedback as a buyer, like the one in Figure 11-4. Click the Leave Seller Feedback button to rate your seller on a scale from 1 to 5, along with a comment as to how the order went. As a buyer, feedback is only expected once you receive the order and the sale is complete.

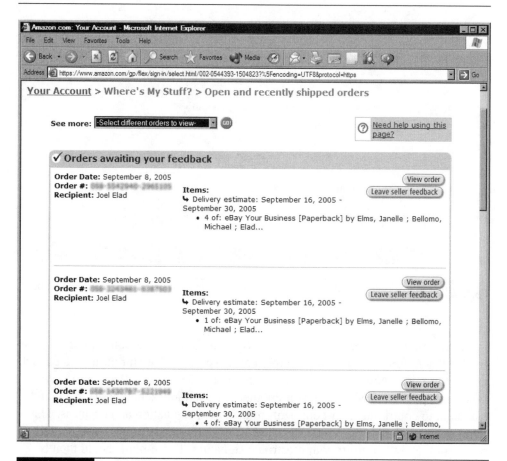

FIGURE 11-4   Amazon gives you a list of orders that are awaiting your feedback.

As a seller, you have to log into your Seller Account, and pull up each individual order, in order to leave the buyer feedback. Under the Manage Your Inventory heading, you can go to the Marketplace inventory that is sold, zShops items that are closed, or check on Auction items that have closed. Once you go to any of these lists, click an Order ID to see an individual order, like the one in Figure 11-5. You should see a Leave Buyer Feedback button in the upper-right corner of the order. Click that button to rate your buyer on a scale from one to five, and add a comment if you like.

As a seller, as long as you were paid immediately from your buyer with Amazon Payments, you should be satisfied with the buyer's performance. Most sellers leave feedback after the buyer's payment has cleared, but some sellers have waited until

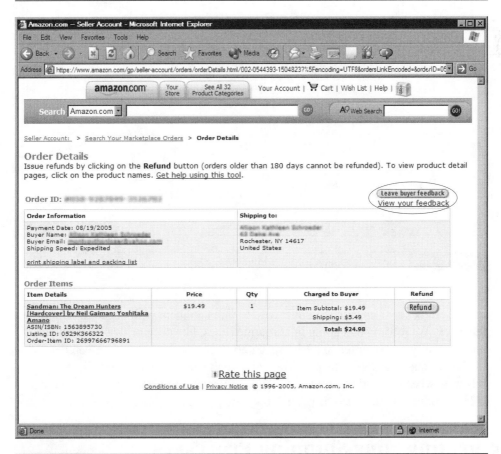

FIGURE 11-5   Amazon lets each seller leave their buyers feedback as well.

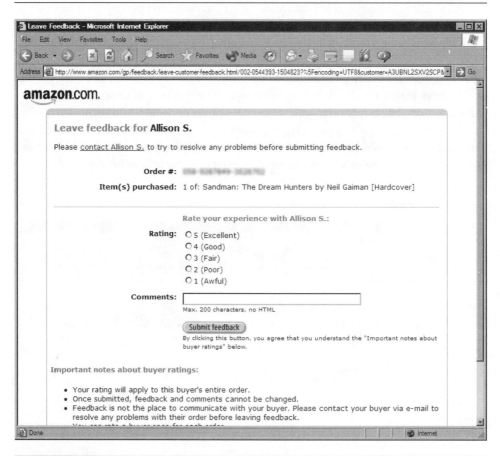

FIGURE 11-6   Leave feedback for your buyers.

the buyer goes first, in case the buyer tries to threaten them with negative or poor feedback. We recommend going in at routine times, like once or twice a week, and handling all your buyer feedback immediately, once the payment has cleared. Click the button and you'll get a feedback screen like the one in Figure 11-6. Rate your buyer between one and five and also add a comment, up to 200 characters (with no HTML coding instructions), if you're so inclined.

Automating Your Shipping Processes

Now that we've talked about e-mail communication and feedback, it's time to shift gears and talk about the other main part of a back-end Amazon sales operation: shipping. You've listed the item, achieved the sale, gotten paid, and established a relationship with your new customer. Now it's time to seal the deal and get their product to them quickly and in excellent condition. The best way to ensure this, sale after sale, is to organize your shipping process so it can run smoothly and be scaled with your business. You don't need a full-service shipping department to handle your sales, but you do need to organize your efforts.

Building Your Shipping Station

What better way to organize your shipping efforts than to start with a home base? One of the keys to a successful shipping operation is to establish, at the beginning or early on in the game, a fixed, centralized location where you plan to pack and prepare all your sold items. The last thing you want when scaling up your business is to always have to take over the kitchen table, dig up your supplies, and frantically prepare your orders while not spilling any food or drinks on the merchandise. You may laugh, but we've seen it happen. We acknowledge that not everyone will have the space to set up a dedicated shipping area, but we urge you to think of it as an investment. The time spent having to take over an area, lay out your supplies, then pack your items and totally clean up, is time better spent running your business, making new deals, and getting new merchandise.

If you're trying to decide where to set up this area, the following are a couple of helpful pointers:

- Pick an area that's close (or in the same room) to where you store your inventory, if possible. This way, you're not spending lots of time moving inventory to the packing area, and you can easily grab items that may suddenly need to be shipped out.

- Pick an area where you can have a big desk or table for preparing your orders and which has enough space to store shipping supplies near your packing area.

- Pick an area where you can have your computer, Internet connection, and printer handy, if possible. This should not be considered a deal breaker, though. For example, if you're maintaining goods in a storage locker and have enough space there to establish a shipping area, you can prepare your labels at home with your Internet connection and printer and bring them all to the storage locker.

- If you have employees (or plan to hire some soon), establish an area that can be easily accessible to them as well as yourself. Remember, your bedroom may not be the place for your new employees to spend the day.

Once you pick a shipping area, the next job is to stock it with supplies. For this, you will first need to consider what you'll be shipping out. If the main product area is books, focus on heavy-duty envelopes and labels. If it's bulkier merchandise, stock up on big rolls of bubble wrap and Styrofoam peanuts. If you're shipping expensive and/or fragile items, stock up on tissue paper, foam dividers, and lots of different-sized boxes.

> **TIP**
>
> *One of the easiest ways to stock your area is to order supplies from your favorite shipping company:*
>
> *Go to http://shop.usps.com to order free envelopes, boxes, tape, and more from the U.S. Postal Service.*
>
> *Go to https://www.ups.com/labels?loc=en_US to order free boxes and envelopes from UPS.*
>
> *Go to www.fedex.com/us/officeprint/packship/supplies.html to order free Federal Express boxes and packs.*

Once you've stocked your area, make sure everything is within reach of the main packing area, but outside of any walkway. This way, you can just bring your products to the same area and focus on packing instead of "Oh, yeah, the roll of tape is upstairs. Let me stop what I'm doing, go upstairs, get it and come back" only to be followed by "Oh, now I have to go to the basement to get my envelopes." This is the first way you can save time through an efficient shipping operation.

Printing Your Shipping Labels from Home

Another way you can save money through efficiency is to print out your shipping labels and postage from home so you're not always stuck in line waiting to send out your packages. Thanks to high technology and the Internet, the postman is not the only way to get postage anymore. All the major shipping companies have come up with ways for you to create your shipping labels online, print them out with any regular printer, and pay for postage as well so you can hand off the package and move onto the next task.

You'll need to invest in a couple of things for this: mainly, a computer, Internet access, a printer, and a weight scale. Most likely, your only purchase will be the scale and maybe a new printer. If you're wondering what type of scale to get, once again it goes back to the main types of products you'll be shipping. If you're only going to sell light products, focus on a scale that weighs accuracy from zero to five or zero to ten pounds. If you're going to be selling heavier items, get a scale that can handle 50 or 100 pounds. While some of you may be thinking that the bathroom scale is an okay substitute, we still recommend another scale that's more accurate.

Some of the services we'll soon talk about will offer a free scale as part of your package. Investigate these solutions first before buying a new scale.

You actually have many options nowadays for purchasing your postage online and creating your labels from home. Here are some of the more popular ones if you plan to use the U.S. Postal Service to handle your packages:

- ShipOK (www.shipok.com)

- Stamps.com (www.stamps.com)

- Endicia (www.endicia.com)

- USPS Click 'N Ship (www.usps.com)

In addition, you can create accounts directly with the larger shipping companies such as UPS (www.ups.com), FedEx (www.fedex.com), and DHL (www.dhl.com), where they bill you monthly and allow you to print labels directly with the postage charged to your account. The benefit of signing up for one of these accounts is that, depending on your volume, you can usually get a corporate or discount rate off the retail price of mailing out packages with these shippers, not to mention a consolidated statement to track your charges and the need to only pay once per month instead of every time you have to mail out an order.

Some of the USPS online postage solutions, like Endicia and Stamps.com, charge you monthly to use their services, either by the amount of stamps you purchase, or by using a flat rate for unlimited usage. Once you log into your account, they'll guide you through the process of preparing a label. The key pieces of information that you'll need to generate each label include the following:

- Name of recipient

- Street address, city, state, and ZIP code of recipient

- Weight of the package

- Type of shipping service to be used

- E-mail address (see sidebar for why)

- Value of the package (mainly for international shipments)

One of the great features of services like ShipOK is that they'll interface directly with your Amazon account, and allow you to print multiple labels on one piece of paper. You just specify the speed of delivery and the weight of the package, and ShipOK will pull the delivery address directly from Amazon's data banks. In addition, services like Endicia will also print out the necessary customs forms, filled out, that you can affix to your package so you don't have to write out one customs form after another. Based on the value, Endicia will print out the correct form you need as well.

Spend some time up-front shopping around for a service you like, and establish an account as soon as possible. This way, you can create clear, professional labels and even hide the amount of postage you paid, without scrawling their name on the box, risking an error that could delay your customers from getting their package, and waiting in line to pay for your postage.

Automating the Tracking Number E-mail

As you're creating your shipping labels, there's one last feature we want to call to your attention. When you're filling in your customer's shipping information and are about to create that shipping label, look for a field that asks for their e-mail address. The reason they're asking for this address is that the shipping company can automatically send that person an e-mail with the tracking or delivery confirmation number, and instructions on how to access their web site to see the real-time status of the customer's package.

In some cases, you'll want the ability to send your own "Order Has Been Shipped" e-mail so you can bring that customer into your own database and control the look and feel of your interactions with the customer. However, ordering this e-mail can be an extra check, an extra step of protection, to make sure your customers are fully informed. After all, when that customer sees an e-mail from UPS, FedEx, or the USPS, they'll know it's because they're about to receive something, and they can easily click the link to check the status of their package. Your own e-mail can be a follow-up to this e-mail, reiterating the information or just telling them that a separate e-mail is coming with the tracking number.

By using this function, you're not forced to record these numbers and enter them again into your own e-mail program when sending out e-mails. And when you start sending out hundreds of packages a week, this is one critical function you might enjoy outsourcing to your shipping company.

Arranging for Automatic Pickups

Now that you've printed out your shipping labels and paid the right amount of postage, you might be headed to the car, thinking, "Okay, time to drop off the packages." However, there is a final step you can take to save yourself that trip. UPS, FedEx, and yes, even the U.S. Postal Service, allow you to arrange for a carrier pickup, where they'll send a driver out, just to get your packages. Now, each carrier has their own rules and regulations about this, but here's the main idea.

If you're shipping out packages through the U.S. Postal Service, once you know you're ready to go, look for the Carrier Pickup option. This can be found on their web site at www.usps.com/pickup/ under Carrier Pickup. As long as you request a pickup by 12:00 a.m. Pacific Time (or 3 a.m. Eastern) on the day you want the packages picked up, a postal employee will come to your address, when they come to deliver your mail, and get all your Express Mail, Priority Mail, and international packages. Remember, all your packages have to have the postage-paid labels on them and be ready to go before the postal employee arrives. If you can't wait all day for the carrier to come out, you can request Pickup On Demand service for an additional $12.50 per pickup, regardless of the number of packages you have. With this service, they'll give you a two-hour timeframe where someone is guaranteed to come pick up those packages.

If you're shipping out packages through UPS, you can usually schedule a pickup in the process of creating your shipping labels, or you can go directly to https://wwwapps.ups.com/pickup/schedule?loc=en_US when you're ready to schedule a pickup. You'll basically specify the day you want the pickup, the earliest the driver can come, and the latest the driver can arrive. You can order a pickup up to five days in advance, but it can't be a same-day request. You'll have to fill in information telling the driver exactly how many packages to expect, and what each package weighs. Of course, if you've just created your labels, the UPS web site will have that information already.

Once your volume increases through UPS, we recommend asking them for an automatic daily pickup account, where a driver will always come by your business each workday, at roughly the same time, to see if you have any packages to send. This way, you don't have to think about ordering the pickup; you only have to get your packages ready by your designated time. You will need to negotiate with your UPS account manager if you want this service for free. They usually ask that you ship a minimum number of packages each month. We've talked to businesses that use this feature and only ship out 10 to 20 packages per month, while we've talked to others where the minimum is closer to 50. Even if it costs money for an automatic daily pickup, this could pay off because it frees you and your employees up from one less task and enforces the right behavior of getting your packages ready for the driver.

If you're shipping packages through FedEx, ordering a pickup will depend on the type of shipments you make. Express Service, meaning any next-day, second-day, or third-day select service through FedEx, is ordered through one service, while Ground packages are actually handled by another department. To get started, just use your web browser to go to www.fedex.com/PickupApp/ and choose the appropriate link. One thing to remember for Ground pickups is that FedEx will ask you to print a log sheet detailing your Ground packages for that pickup so it's available with your packages to give to the driver. When you set up a FedEx Ground account, you'll get a log book that you can manually fill in as well, but their web site also allows you to print a log sheet once you're done creating all the labels.

Automating Sales with Amazon Web Services

Now that we've covered how to establish processes, shipping stations, and templates, it's time to shift gears and talk about your other vital "back-end" system, which you, personally, may not use all that much—your Information Technology architecture. By this, we mean the computer systems that hum all night and keep your business on the Internet. For some people, it's simply the web server hosting their web site and an Excel spreadsheet on their laptop with their finances. For others, it's a dedicated computer that hosts their web site and inventory programs, does their credit card billing in batch orders every night, and runs QuickBooks and all the other software. Yet for others, it's multiple computers or an outsourced operation where someone, somewhere, with a room full of servers, is maintaining all your applications, from payroll to inventory to accounting and marketing, for a monthly fee or percentage.

In all of these cases, you've got computer software programs working for your business. And in some cases, having a dynamic, intelligent, "always-on" connection from your IT to Amazon's IT, can greatly expand your business potential. Imagine if your computer and Amazon's computers could talk without you being in the room, be able to share information instantly, provide you with updated prices, specials, reviews, and inventory levels, and allow you to take advantage of more of Amazon's operations. Now, Amazon is making that possible.

One fascinating development that is still being fully rolled out as of this writing is Amazon Web Services. These are web-browser based services designed for merchants who want to maximize their sales. For example, Amazon has patented a one-click purchasing system as one web service. Also, albeit in limited release, there's another service that will permit sellers to quickly tap into Amazon sales data for particular products, allowing the merchants to identify sales opportunities. A final program makes it even easier to list products for sale on Amazon.

By making the development of these tools public, Amazon is attracting independent programmers to contribute to the product. In this way, Amazon's services could end up growing "organically," much the same way the Linux operating system did in the 1990s. There are indications that Amazon is succeeding in its efforts in this area. According to *Business Week*, as many as 35,000 programmers had downloaded Amazon services software in the first 18 months of their offering, which is open to those developers writing new applications based on the code.

Why Amazon Developed Web Services

In a way, Amazon's entire web site is already a kind of web-based application. Given the level of functionality on the site, matched only by a couple others such as eBay, Amazon is practically what Larry Ellison of Oracle described back in the 1990s as a "network" computer, in which people access programs online, rather than from their personal hard drive. By building a stable suite of software on which Amazon.com merchants can develop businesses, Amazon CEO Jeff Bezos is seeking to create a platform that would become the standard in online business transactions.

The open-source model allows Amazon to harness development expertise from interested developers without cost. However, it may surprise you to learn that Amazon doesn't make money (at least directly) from Web Services. Essentially, the merchants who sell "on the river" make use of the developments to more easily list and sell their products…and since Amazon takes its commission from the sales, the revenues generated are substantial.

How to Subscribe to Amazon Web Services

Signing up for Amazon Web Services (AWS) is easy, since all it requires is that you acquire a subscription ID number. This ID is always needed to access any of the web services. Begin by navigating to the following web page: https://aws-portal.amazon.com/gp/aws/developer/registration/index.html.

You should already have an Amazon account to log in to here, as shown in Figure 11-7. If you don't have an account yet, you can create one by selecting the No, I Am A New Customer option.

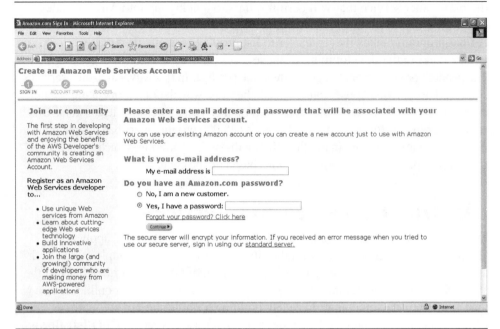

FIGURE 11-7   The AWS Sign-In screen

Once signed in, you'll have to fill out a form and then read through and sign the licensing agreement by clicking the check box and then the Continue button at the bottom of the page. You'll then be granted your subscription ID number, which you can use from now on to select whichever Web Services you may be interested in, without any additional charge.

Can You Benefit from Amazon Web Services?

Over 65,000 people have already registered to use Amazon Web Services. Whether it's right for you depends on your specific needs as a business. For example, if you do a volume business, selling hundreds or thousands of dollars of merchandise on Amazon on a regular basis, you're bound to reap much greater gain from web services than if you're just dipping a toe into the e-commerce world.

Because we don't want to focus on the actual details of implementing Web Services within your computer organization, we'll simply give you an overview here. Would your current computer operations and e-commerce setup benefit from having your computer automatically talk to Amazon's system, retrieve information, and pass customers directly to your Amazon listings any time of the day? If so, we recommend giving this service a try, and also talking with whoever helps you with your back-end computer operations and/or e-commerce web site setup when you sign up for Amazon Web Services.

Thankfully, there are easier ways to take advantage of this powerful new concept. Companies have created new business models by developing software programs and services that take advantage of Amazon Web Services to help other businesses do their job better. Take a look at some of the exciting new possibilities Amazon Web Services has enabled to help your business grow and prosper.

Bargain Hunting On-the-Fly

Other services may be more niche, but they're fascinating nonetheless. For instance, a company called ScoutPal (profiled in Figure 11-8) offers cell phones with barcode scanners to Amazon booksellers so they can remain in touch with the Amazon marketplace no matter where they are. If you're into the selling and buying of high-end or collectible books, this is the invention for you.

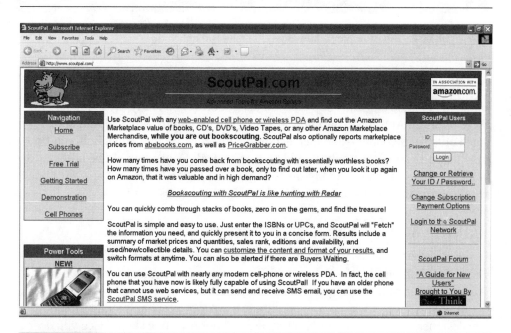

FIGURE 11-8   The ScoutPal homepage at ScoutPal.com

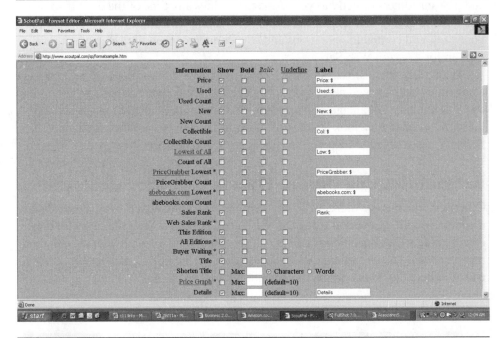

FIGURE 11-9   An example of how ScoutPal data is displayed

For example, let's say you're at a book fair and you come across a crate full of medieval-style atlases. They look valuable, but what's really the going rate for these items on Amazon? By simply pressing a few buttons, you can find out as you stand outside the booth—and then act on the information immediately if you find out that purchasing the books would be a great deal. Depending on the criteria you want to display, as shown in Figure 11-9, you can instantly see the price the book is selling for as new, used, or at multiple online book sites.

Making Money Through Referrals

Another interesting niche player is the site AssociateShop.com, shown in Figure 11-10. AssociateShop builds you special web pages where you can sell products from Amazon and earn up to 7.5 percent in referral fees.

In order for you to participate, you must use AssociateShop's straightforward site designer, shown in Figure 11-11, to create your own free shop. Once you do this, enroll in Amazon's "associate" program and any sales made from your site will earn the referral fees, which are paid via check from Amazon on a quarterly basis.

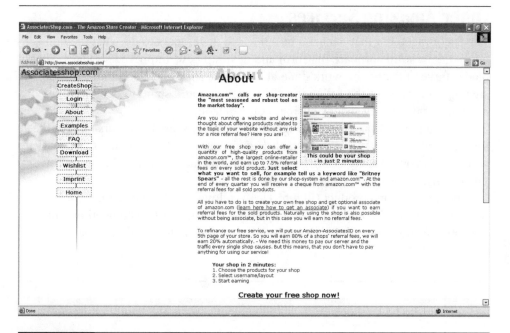

FIGURE 11-10   The AssociateShop.com site

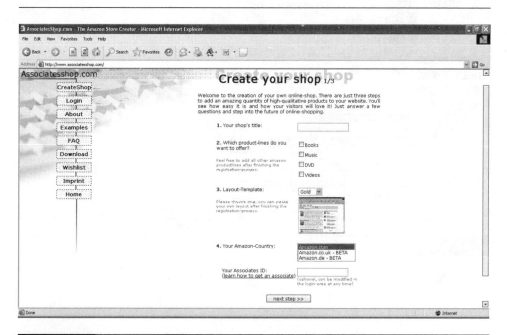

FIGURE 11-11   AssociateShop.com's web site builder page

Other Amazing Services

The encouragement that Amazon has given to developers to do what they do best—take a solid software platform and develop new, improved services—has paid off even beyond the work done at AssociateShop and ScoutPal. Consider signing up for any of the following services that could stand to benefit your company and the way it does business on Amazon.

For example, Monsoon.com (Figure 11-12) allows small retailers to have the same advantages as larger, more established businesses when it comes to a complete scanning barcode system. Using barcode labels and their software, Monsoon can provide inventory analysis and reporting.

The SellerEngine product (Figure 11-13) allows you to manage inventory in real time from your computer. Not only do you get access to a competitor's price, you have the option to adjust an item's price on-the-fly to remain competitive.

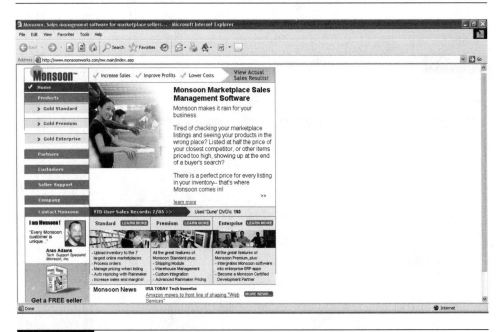

FIGURE 11-12   The Monsoon home page

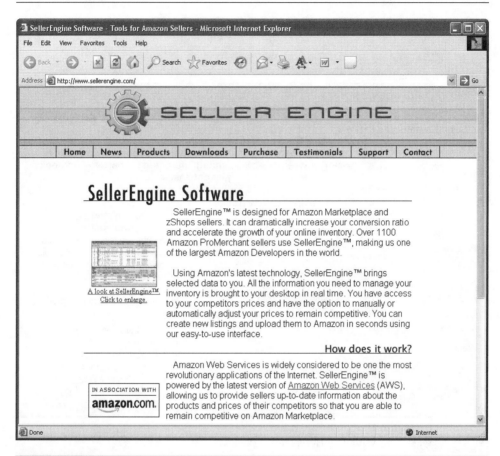

The SellerEngine home page

SellerEngine claims to be one of the more popular software developments from Amazon, with over 600 Amazon Pro Merchants signed up for its services.

One final product worth mentioning has been developed specifically for book sellers. WhiteOakBooks, featured in Figure 11-14, charges a small monthly fee to maintain your Amazon Marketplace book inventory, thus relieving you of time-consuming maintenance. The product also supports Marketplace and zShops listings, so you can provide transactions on your site.

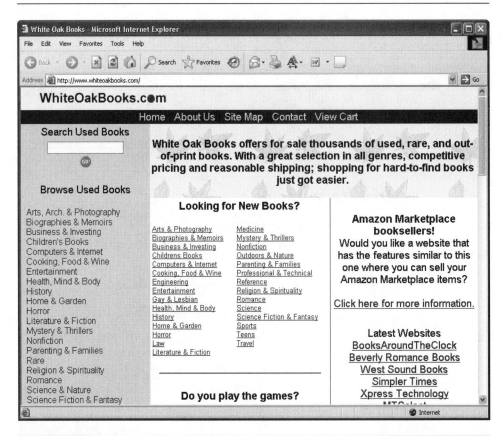

FIGURE 11-14   The WhiteOakBooks home page

To Sum Up

In this chapter, we've talked about three critical areas you can improve and systemize to allow you to cultivate your business and spend less time doing routine tasks.

First, we talked about creating a system for your customer interactions. We demonstrated several areas where you can create solid, dependable e-mail templates with the right text, which you can use over and over again to handle customer inquiries or keep your customers informed of the process after the sale has been made. We talked about the extra value you can create by using these customer interactions to build a closer tie between your customers and your business, whether it's getting your customers to sign up for more e-mails and newsletters, or up-selling another product once the primary sale is complete.

Second, we talked about the importance and value of automating or systemizing your shipping activities. Whether it's establishing a solid shipping area, getting an account to print out your own postage from home, or having your shipping company come to you instead of the other way around, these steps will allow you to reduce the amount of time you spend getting your orders ready to go, which can give you more time to get the rest of your business growing.

Finally, you learned about Amazon Web Services (AWS), which were designed for merchants who want to maximize their sales by allowing their IT systems to interface directly with Amazon's platform to gather information, prices, and more.

Whichever services you choose to use will depend on your specific needs as a business. For example, a company called ScoutPal offers cell phones with bar-code scanners to Amazon booksellers so they can remain in touch with the Amazon Marketplace no matter where they are. AssociateShop and other companies offer similar niche-oriented programs that could benefit your business, depending on your sales numbers and the type of merchandize you deal in. Finally, you can write your own customized application that hooks directly into your business and allows you to build onto the Amazon platform directly.

Chapter 12

Amazon Advantage: Sell Your Own Intellectual Property Direct to Consumers

A brand for a company is like a reputation for a person. You earn a reputation by trying to do hard things well.

—Jeff Bezos, founder of Amazon.com

If you're interested in adding yet another possible revenue stream to your business, Amazon has opened the door for you. Under the Amazon Advantage program, you can promote and sell your books, music, or videos direct to consumers under the auspices of Amazon.com. So long as you have the distribution rights in at least North America, you can take advantage of this amazing opportunity.

How You Can Use Amazon Advantage to Increase Revenue

Now, you may at first think this program isn't for you. Maybe you don't have a new DVD showing off the latest work of your garage band, or a great American novel that's ready to print by the thousands. But the products you can use to build up your business don't need to be so esoteric or artsy. They may simply be a new way to sell your expertise and gain more exposure on one of the most viewed web sites around.

Selling Expertise

Many Amazon sellers are so involved with selling their products on a day-to-day basis that they don't realize how potentially profitable it is to sell information. It's highly lucrative in part due to its incredibly high margin. After all, what you're really selling is your hard-won expertise in a given area. A $5 booklet on how to make French pastry, set up a wireless router, or how to value Shaker furniture can be published for literally pennies on the dollar—because your total material outlay sometimes amounts to just the paper it's printed on.

Selling your expertise on Amazon is also easier than one might first believe, because many people think in terms of full-length books, CDs, or videos. But you don't have to be the next Leo Tolstoy—far from it! When attempting to solve problems or get good advice, brevity is the norm. You'll do much better selling a 75-page booklet on how to buy snowboards than a 500-page, all-encompassing tome on the subject.

Examples of Selling Your "Knowledge Niche"

One final item to keep in mind is that your thoughts—at least in your certain area of expertise—are of value, if only because your knowledge lies in a particular niche. For example, let's say you sell digital cameras on Amazon.com. Now, there are literally dozens of books on how to take great digital pictures on the market. It'd be tough to compete with any of those books if you go "head-to-head" with one. But how many books might there be on tricks and tips for using the main product you sell—the Nikolta Shutterbug?

Another example could be one Amazon Advantage member who sells products related to managing stress, improving relationships, and quitting smoking. Rather than restrict herself to marketing the products of others, she's also put together a 50-page booklet, *Life Skills for Peace of Mind*, and sells it for a very reasonable $6.95 (shown in Figure 12-1). As the seller, D. Papin, notes, "The only real outlays I had for this product were registering the (ISBN) number, signing up for the Amazon program, and the initial publication cost, which came out to less than $1 per booklet. Total out of pocket was very, very small. Probably the only real challenge was the week spent culling my knowledge to create the booklet itself."

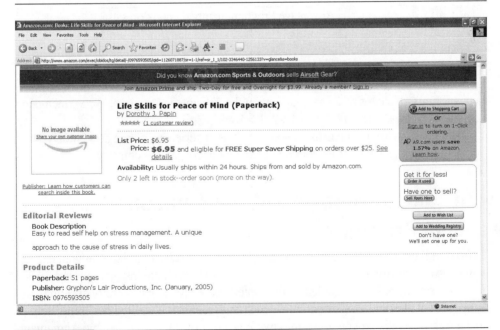

FIGURE 12-1   An example of a booklet published under the Amazon Advantage Program

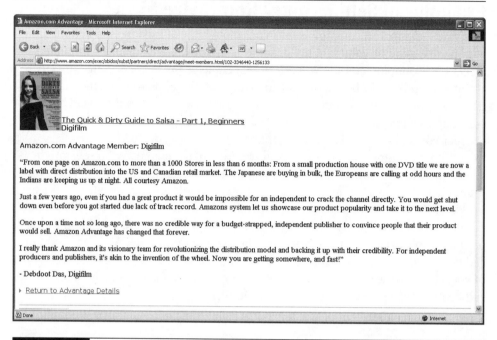

FIGURE 12-2   An Amazon Advantage Program member's book on salsa

Ms. Papin isn't alone in her use of Amazon for marketing complementary products for her company. Consider how others have put to use their knowledge of salsa dancing, fine cuisine, or financial planning in the Advantage Program. We've included a couple of their profiles in Figures 12-2, 12-3, and 12-4.

Alternatively, Amazon has listed some of their experiences online at www.amazon .com/exec/obidos/subst/partners/direct/advantage/meet-members.html.

How to Take Advantage...of the Amazon Advantage Program

To make full use of the Amazon Advantage Program, start by familiarizing yourself with the Amazon Advantage agreement, then look over both the instructions and rules of the agreement. They're detailed (selling intellectual property is a pretty exacting prospect), but they're fairly straightforward. The agreement is spelled out completely on the web page. It's broken down into two main sections: the Membership Agreement

FIGURE 12-3   Another Amazon Advantage Program member markets their knowledge of fine cuisine for a good cause.

itself, which goes over everything from Order Shipping to the Limitation of Liability, and the Advantage Instructions and Rules, which details how Amazon handles the Advantage accounts.

CAUTION   *Although it may look like a really boring document, force yourself to read it. If you have any doubt whether you can sell your intellectual property on Amazon, this should give you an answer.*

You apply online to the Advantage Program by submitting at least one of your titles in the application. The annual fee is $29.95 and Amazon's commission rates are 55 percent. As long as enough stock is on hand when Amazon customers make a purchase, an order is processed and shipped within 24 hours. In order to ensure prompt service, Amazon recommends you ship to them as many units as you believe will sell.

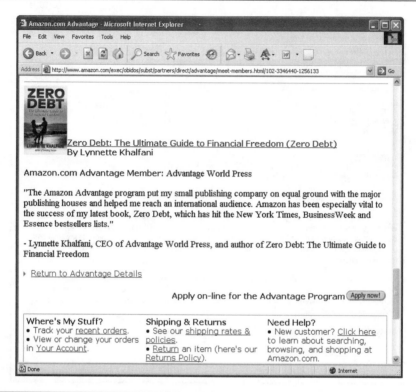

FIGURE 12-4   An Amazon Advantage Program member shares her experience in getting out of debt.

Amazon has a tendency to be a bit vague in their requirements here, which is surprising given the detail in their Advantage agreement. Essentially, having "enough stock on hand" means "one copy or however many is needed to fill a customer order," and there is no timeframe for the requirement of sending them "as many units as you believe will sell." Since there has been no reported case of Amazon running out of "shelf space," we recommend that when you ship to Amazon's warehousing department "as many units as you believe will sell," send as many as you believe will realistically sell within one calendar year.

Applying for Membership in the Program

Once you've read the agreement Instructions and Rules, you can then fill out your application. Completing the application is very simple, and consists of marking check boxes and filling in empty text boxes with your information, as shown in Figure 12-5.

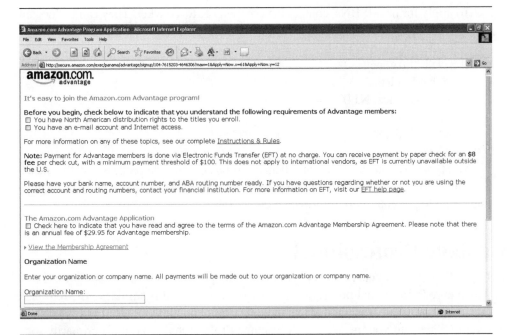

FIGURE 12-5 The Amazon Advantage application

After receiving the electronic application, Amazon indicates whether your titles have been accepted into the program by e-mailing you. The typical time it takes for a title to be accepted is two to three weeks, so factor this time into your schedule if you plan to make your product available on Amazon.com before making a big push to market of your information or work of art.

Getting an ISBN Number

In order to sell your written or audio work on Amazon, the final item you'll need is an ISBN number. ISBN stands for International Standard Book Number and is the accepted global standard by which books are cataloged. ISBNs are useful not only in identifying book titles, but also the publication format (the number of the edition, hardcover, softcover, mass paperback, or audio).

To apply for new ISBNs, contact the company R.R. Bowker. They can be located at www.bowker.com, or contact them directly at:

U.S. ISBN Agency
121 Chanlon Road
New Providence, NJ 07974
Tel: 908-665-6770
Fax: 908-665-2895

You typically can buy ISBN numbers in groups of ten. The process usually takes from three to five weeks, so be sure to do this as early as possible so you're not ready and raring to put your work on Amazon but still waiting for a response.

Advantage Professional

Depending on what kind of content your company provides, you may qualify for the Advantage Professional program. Advantage Professional is similar to the regular Advantage program, because it offers more flexibility on the discounted prices you can offer to better suit your needs. The Advantage Professional program is primarily for two types of potential sellers: those who want to sell products with visual content, and publishers who want to sell specialized professional or technical books with limited appeal but a high markup.

Advantage Professional Books

If you're a small, niche publisher who wants to gain extra visibility via listings on Amazon, this is the program for you. For example, let's say you publish books that teach people how to work in very specific areas, such as books on network routers, different aspects of the tax code, or the human nervous system. While the cost to publish these books can be extremely high due to the small size of the audience, the technical complexity of the work, or the heavy graphics requirements (especially in medical texts), you can offset the costs of production somewhat by selling more copies—hence the advantage to working with Amazon.

In order to become an Advantage professional, you simply fill out the application so you can be placed under consideration (for some reason, Amazon calls it a survey, but it's really an application form). The top of the form is shown in Figure 12-6.

CAUTION   *To be considered for this program, you must enroll at least five qualified titles and have the North American distribution rights for those titles.*

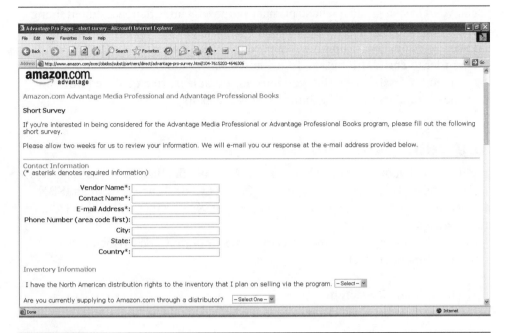

The top portion of the Amazon Advantage application

As with regular Advantage merchants, Advantage Professional users get to add their products to the stock at Amazon's fulfillment center, where they will have 24-hour access to it at Amazon.com. They also get quick payment terms, and complete reporting on sales and inventory.

 Amazon also points out that nonprofit groups may also qualify for joining this program. Be sure to note this status on your application form.

Advantage Media Professional

Let's say you've developed a brand-new video method of teaching people how to pass the Advanced Placement college tests in mathematics. This educational content is valuable, but only to a small, select group of people who are looking for information to pass a specific exam. When searching online for help, where do you think prospective students will go? Obviously, a well-known supplier of study aids: Amazon.com.

If you apply for status as an Advantage Media Professional, you can put your service on Amazon and get increased exposure to the market, as well as the bonus of complete sales and inventory reporting. Any provider who publishes content on DVD, video, or CD-ROMS can apply. The key to being accepted under this program is that you have to have a product whose primary purpose is informational. Entertaining educational media is okay under Amazon's criteria. But content that is designed to entertain by itself—or to simply sell a product—likely won't make the cut.

In order to enroll, fill out the form shown earlier in Figure 12-6. Just as with Advantage Professional Media, you must enroll at least five qualified titles and have the North American distribution rights for them.

Getting Your UPC Number

In order to sell your DVD or video work on Amazon, the final item you'll need is a UPC number. UPC stands for Universal Product Code. Much as with an ISBN number, it's an all-numeric product-identification system standard used to identify, track, and manage products.

To apply for new UPC numbers, contact the Uniform Code Council at www .uc-council.org or contact them directly at:

Uniform Code Council Inc.
8163 Old Yankee Road, Suite J
Dayton, OH 45458 USA
Telephone: (937) 435-3870

To Sum Up

In this chapter, we've taken a look at how you can use Amazon to create a whole new stream of income to supplement what you sell on the site. Under the Amazon Advantage program, you can promote and sell your books, music, or videos direct to consumers as long as you have the distribution rights in North America. Selling your expertise on Amazon is also easier than one might first think, because your knowledge may constitute a particular niche.

We then discuss the Membership Agreement, costs of the program, and how to join. We talk about the Advantage Professional program and how it benefits publishers of highly visual content or specialized and expensive textbooks. Finally, we cover how to get an ISBN number through R.K. Bowker (www.bowker.com) so you can sell written works on Amazon, as well as how to get a UPC number through the Uniform Code Council (www.uc-council.org) so you can sell audio or video works on Amazon.

Chapter 13

Take Advantage of Amazon's Global Market

International sales represent 36 percent of overall sales, and by 2005, they may be 50 percent. Our competitive position in Germany, Japan, and the UK is stronger than it is in the U.S.

—Jeff Bezos, founder of Amazon.com

In this final chapter, let's shift focus to a topic on most people's minds when selling online: international sales. After all, customers in Beijing can shop on Amazon just like someone in Boise, right? International sales are spurring revenue for most e-commerce sites such as Amazon, and is one the company has been addressing for years.

Amazon has established separate international sites for some of the biggest economies in the world. They've enabled people in over 24 countries around the world to open an Amazon account and buy from any of their sites, as long as those customers pay the shipping and any additional fees and duties. Globalization is very important for Amazon, and every U.S. e-commerce company for that matter, to continue to grow and expand their services, revenue, and profit. More importantly, selling internationally has allowed entrepreneurs and sellers such as yourself to tap into an immense customer audience with very low transaction costs, and to allow you to reach more interested buyers than you could ever reach here at home. In some cases, your international buyers will be even more valuable to you if their currency has a favorable exchange rate with the U.S. dollar. To them, your items will seem cheaper by comparison, and, therefore, more desirable.

In this chapter, we're going to take a little trip around the world and show you Amazon's different international sites, as well as explore matters of shipping, customs, and other things you need to know to reap a healthy fortune from customers the world over.

An Overview of Amazon's International Sites

The Internet has allowed everyone to live and compete in a global economy, and e-commerce is no different. Because the Internet is being adopted and used by billions of people around the world, it's only natural that those users would consider doing business and conducting commerce transactions over the Internet. Considering that most money is being moved electronically every day, global shipping companies are delivering packages continuously, and importing and exporting are big parts of most countries' economies, the infrastructure for global e-commerce is there to support these transactions.

To truly compete in this economy, however, Jeff Bezos saw that you can't just throw up a bookstore in one language and expect everyone to conform to your standards. Instead, he sought out local teams in the countries he chose to expand Amazon into, to make sure that the content and selection matched the country Amazon was entering, and that it was truly serving its customers with the appropriate and valuable merchandise they were shopping for online. Figure 13-1 offers a snapshot of Amazon's current international presence, and the categories each site serves. We're going to walk through six of Amazon's most promising and important international sites, and show how they serve the citizens of their country while serving Amazon's goal of being "Earth's Biggest Bookstore," and more.

One of the biggest benefits these international sites give their local customers is that all the prices will be reflected in their local currency. From pounds to yen, each item displayed on an Amazon international site will be displayed in the currency

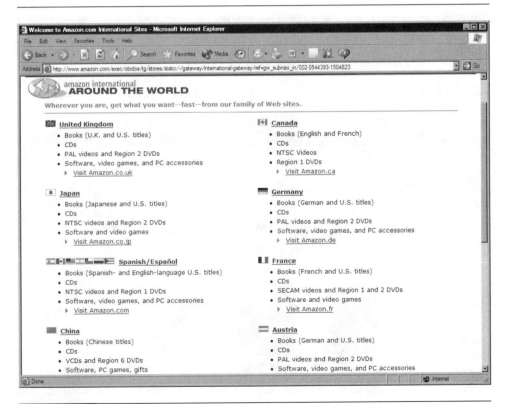

FIGURE 13-1   Amazon gives you an overview of their international sites.

for that country. The user has the option of having Amazon convert that price to any other currency, but this is one more way Amazon lets their international customers feel like they're still shopping at home.

Amazon Canada

One of the most identifiable traits of a Canadian web site is the need to service both English-speaking and French-speaking Canadians. As you can see from the Amazon Canada home page in Figure 13-2, they do just that. Amazon offers pages in both English and French and basic commands are shown in the two languages on the home page. Canada's range of categories is similar to the U.S. site, carrying the main categories of Books, Music, DVD, Video, Software, and Computer & Video Games.

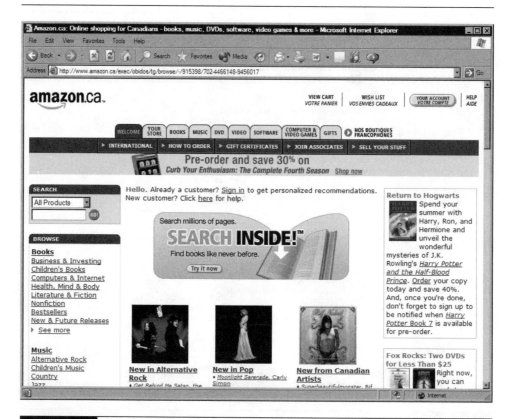

FIGURE 13-2   Bonjour! Welcome to Amazon Canada!

However, international sites like Amazon Canada allow the company to try out different positioning for new and established features. In this case, Amazon Canada features a Gift Suggestion tool right on their home page as its own tab. And keeping with the bilingual culture in Canada, their Gift Selector has recommendations "En Francais" as well as in English. The "En Francais" gift selection at the moment is focusing on arts and culture, but curious customers can find out more based on Amazon's rich customer history of similar interests.

Amazon UK

Hopping "across the pond" from North America, we find Amazon's United Kingdom site, as shown in Figure 13-3. While their language is similar to the main Amazon.com site, the vocabulary and words used reflect the British or Queen's English as opposed to the American vernacular used on Amazon.com. This way, UK customers don't have to translate in their heads what the "Yanks" are trying to sell to them.

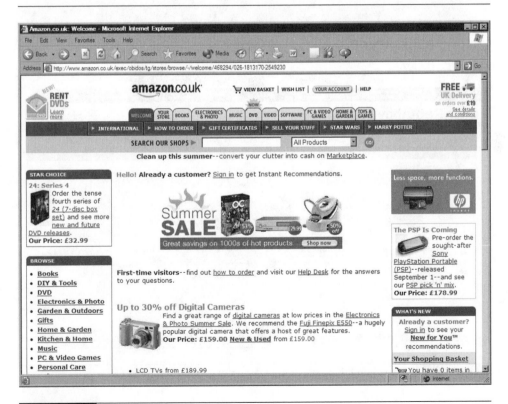

FIGURE 13-3   Amazon UK bids you a fair hello!

When shopping for items on Amazon UK, local customers don't have to worry about things like whether their DVD is encoded in the right region, or whether the consumer electronics will work with their wiring system. Products sold on Amazon UK are those geared for use in the UK.

Always looking to expand, Amazon UK is an excellent testing ground for Amazon to try out new services. One such example is how Amazon has gotten into the business of renting DVDs to Amazon UK customers. Featured prominently as an ad on their home page (as shown in Figure 13-3), this new service works like NetFlix here in the United States, where people can have DVDs mailed to their door, and they simply "drop them in the post" when they're done, to get new ones. The whole system is outlined in Figure 13-4. This way, Amazon can test this functionality in one country and possibly roll it out to other countries after a successful trial run.

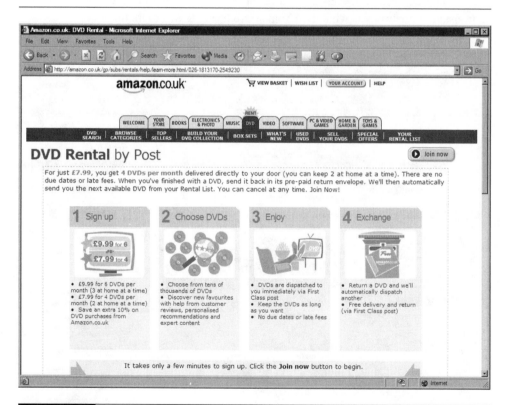

FIGURE 13-4   Amazon UK is starting a DVD rental business in the UK.

Of course, *your* business can test the waters just like Amazon. Amazon UK makes it easier for a U.S. seller than some other sites, given that both sites use English. You can research the best-selling items for Amazon UK's site, just like Amazon.com's site, and see if you can stock and sell some of these items, for example. We'll talk later in this chapter about the requirements for establishing an account for an international site.

Amazon France

As we move through the Chunnel, we arrive at Amazon France, where a multicolored adventure awaits us, starting at the Amazon France home page, as shown in Figure 13-5. The site, entirely in French with prices in Euros, allows any French citizen, from the Parisian to the rural vineyard operator, to keep up with the latest in literature,

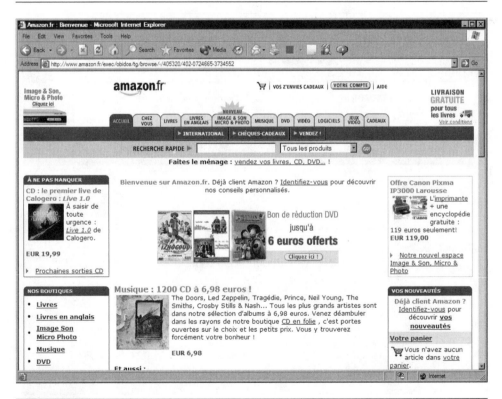

FIGURE 13-5   Bonjour a la Amazon France!

cinema, and now camera and photo equipment (the newest category to Amazon France). They highlight both American entertainment as well as French cinema in their DVD and Video sections, and offer *Jeux Video*, or Video Games, based on the release dates set for France, not the U.S.

One noticeable difference here is that Amazon France has set up two book categories: *Livres*, the default for books written in French, and *Livres en anglais*, for books written in English. If we take a look at the *Livres en anglais* category page (Figure 13-6), we start to recognize more of the titles available. This allows French customers to either shop for books in their native language, or experiment by trying out a book written in English.

But when it comes to French culture, Amazon is not lacking. If you look at their Browse box from their home page, their top three categories are

FIGURE 13-6   You can find books in English on Amazon France. Check it out here.

■ Art, Music, and Cinema

■ Humor

■ Food and Wine

Typically, these are not the highest-selling categories of books in the U.S., but these are the most popular categories in France, as these categories are filled with local French publishers and European publishers that cater to this audience. One look at the *Cuisine et Vins*, or Food and Wine, category in Figure 13-7 shows subcategories dedicated to Cheese, Pate, Sauces, and Wine. Amazon France stocks the categories of what their citizens are wanting.

FIGURE 13-7   From *poisson* (fish) to *fromage* (cheese), it's all here.

Amazon Germany

As we move through the European continent, we find one of Amazon's most successful international sites—Germany. You can see from their home page in Figure 13-8 that they feature CDs, books, and other products based on local artists, with some influence from American entertainment, evident by the *Star Wars: Revenge of the Sith* icon. Like Amazon France, they maintain two book categories, one for books in German (*Bucher*) and the other category listed simply as "English books." Unlike Amazon France or Canada, Germany has already started to expand into categories like Kitchen, Home and Garden, and the renting of DVDs, just as we saw with Amazon UK.

FIGURE 13-8   Wilkommen to Amazon Germany!

<table>
<tr><td>**FIGURE 13-9**</td><td>*Eisbar* the bear has his own home at Amazon Germany.</td></tr>
</table>

While Harry Potter is selling well in Germany (just like in the rest of the world), Amazon Germany does focus on more local characters that don't have worldwide recognition. *Der Kleine Eisbar* is a polar bear character popular with German kids, and as you can see from Figure 13-9, Amazon Germany has their own *Eisbar* page where kids and their parents can find the latest videos, DVDs, books, music, and even software related to *Eisbar*. In addition, Amazon Germany fills this page with content such as interviews, reviews, and other information.

Amazon Japan

Let's change course for a moment and head to the other side of the world. Amazon Japan services their nation's citizens from a familiar home page written in their kanji (letters/characters) and offering a service very appealing to people who live

FIGURE 13-10   Konnichiwa! Welcome to Amazon Japan!

in a very small area. Because there isn't a lot of real estate to build the "big box" retailers like Best Buy and Home Depot for Japanese consumers to shop in, a site like Amazon that allows shipping right to someone's door is very appealing. Amazon Japan offers a wide array of products without worrying about turnover on their shelves (like most retailers in Japan including "7-11 Japan"), and this allows Amazon to compete very effectively. (See Figure 13-10.)

Amazon Japan understands Japanese customers' desires to be able to order American products, which is why they set up their "In English" category on their home page. Click this link and you're taken to your own "American store," like that shown in Figure 13-11, where customers can buy imported books, CDs,

FIGURE 13-11   Shop "In English" to get American products in Japan.

dictionaries, DVDs, and more. You won't find these products in Amazon Japan's main categories since they focus on their own artists and entertainment sources. While a few worldwide icons pop up, like Harry Potter, you can find a cornucopia of Japanese singers, writers, filmmakers, and animators.

Amazon China

Unlike the other countries, Amazon's presence in China isn't called Amazon China, it's called Joyo.com. In early 2005, Amazon bought Joyo, which was the leading online bookseller in China at that point. While they've kept the Joyo name, when you go to the Joyo.com home page (see Figure 13-12), you can see the overall Amazon

FIGURE 13-12   Ni hao! Joyo.com is your Amazon China connection!

"style" with the tabs along the top of the page denoting categories, the Search box in the top-left corner ready to guide customers to the right product, and the Browse box underneath it, listing the different categories.

Unlike Amazon.com, Joyo will organize content based on the type of consumer. In the U.S., there's a special page for Baby items, but on Joyo there's a shopping portal page for men, women, and even the business professional. Note the Manager page in Figure 13-13, showcasing different products important to the working professional in China. Joyo also focuses on Community, which has its own Club page with pictures, discussion boards, and more. It's helping Chinese customers reach out through the Web to find both products and each other while they shop.

FIGURE 13-13   Chinese business professionals can start with the Joyo Manager page.

Adding International Capability to Your Marketplace, Auctions, zShops, and Inventory Listings

If you're ready to push your potential and sell to customers outside the United States, the key thing that Amazon is looking for is whether you're willing to ship internationally. Amazon is not going to display your product for sale to international customers if you won't ship to them, so the first thing you have to decide is whether you want to handle international shipments. If so, make sure you check off "International shipping" as a shipping option when you post your item for sale, especially when doing Marketplace sales.

Currently, Amazon offers an International Standard Shipping credit for books, music, DVDs, and videos only.

If you live outside the United States, you currently can't list items on the U.S. Amazon.com site unless you operate a business with a U.S. address and a U.S. checking account. In such cases, you're directed to Amazon's other international sites, as profiled earlier in this chapter. The reverse is true for U.S. sellers who want to sell directly on one of Amazon's international sites. If you want to sell directly to international customers using one of Amazon's international sites, you need to establish some form of operations in that country, including a valid address and bank account there. Something like this should not be taken lightly, and will cost some money and time to establish. It's not as cost-prohibitive as setting up full-fledged operations overseas, and is definitely possible for a small business. The profit potential grows when you have region-specific products that appeal directly to an international audience, but which have zero to little appeal in the United States.

As it stands, Amazon has extended several of their selling programs, such as Marketplace, Auctions, and even affiliate programs like Associates to most, if not all, of their international sites. If you've got items that appeal to a given international audience, or fit their needs, consider looking into a partnership with a distributor in that country that can help give you an international presence. Setting up international operations is a topic worthy of its own book, but to add international sales capability, where your products actually sit on one of Amazon's international sites, start by looking for trade associations through the United States Chamber of Commerce. They operate a directory of American Chambers of Commerce abroad, also known as AmChams, which you can find by going to this web address: www.uschamber.com/international/directory/default.htm.

Shipping Issues for International Customers

Overall, there are some significant pros and cons to pursuing an international presence, particularly regarding shipping. In general, when it comes to sending products to customers in foreign countries, there are a couple extra steps you need to be aware of to make your shipment a smooth and easy one. Most shipping companies will offer assistance with these extra forms and requirements, they'll usually advise you whenever necessary, and many of them are adding these capabilities to their online systems to make the process even easier. This is enabling the rapid adoption of e-commerce around the world and can expose you to millions of new, potential customers who are interested in your products, especially those with favorable exchange rates towards the U.S. dollar.

Confirming Shipping Information

Amazon allows you to confirm the shipping address and shipment choice by looking up the transaction online. Once on your Account page, simply click the Your Seller Account link. After reaching your Seller Account, click the link marked Manage Your Amazon Payments Account/View Billing History. Your Amazon Payments Account options will appear on the next page. You'll find your orders listed with the following information:

- Payment Date

- Transaction Type

- Order ID

- Listing ID (disregard this for Marketplace orders)

- SKU

- Buyer (e-mail address)

- Quantity

- Amount Due Seller

- Status

Once your buyer has submitted payment, transaction information will appear. Funds will show up in your Payments account as soon as the buyer's credit card is successfully charged.

According to Amazon, international shipments are expected to arrive in three to six weeks, giving you a lot of flexibility. However, be sure not to abuse this extra time allocated since extensive shipping delays can result in buyers leaving a negative rating on your account. This in turn could lead to the termination of your account on Amazon and the revocation of the shipping credit by Amazon offers.

The best way not to fall behind is to complete the paperwork and ship out the products as soon as possible. When you're planning to sell internationally, be sure to stock your shipping station with enough customs forms. You can even go one step further and fill out the Sender information section for these customs forms with your information. This way, when it's time to fulfill an order, your customs form is already half filled out. By using some online postage sites like Endicia.com, you can also generate and print out completed customs forms to stick on your packages.

Be sure to pack your items extra carefully and add some more packing material, since your packages can suffer more damage going across the ocean than just going across the country. If you're worried about going every day to mail one or two international packages, prepare your packages like always, but hold onto them and take them in batches two or three times a week.

Even if you don't have a delivery confirmation or tracking number to give, you should always send out an e-mail to your international customers stating that the order has been shipped. This way, they know the item is on its way and not still being packaged up. Let them know what service you used, and even the type of packaging, so they know what to look for in their mail. Acting quickly and efficiently when preparing your international shipments will help keep your service levels and customer feedback high from your international buyers.

Shipping Credits

Amazon.com gives you a shipping credit to help cover your shipping costs when you sell your item. This allows you to cover standard shipping costs. Amazon collects a shipping fee directly from the buyer at the time of purchase, passing on to you the shipping credit. The amount of the credit depends on the product you're selling, as shown in Table 13-1.

Shipping Options

It's very easy for any Amazon seller to get overwhelmed with shipping activities when there are lots of other aspects to be concerned with in your business. Even if you're a start-up company with some personnel, there will come a point, especially if you begin to generate mass sales on Amazon.com, where it makes less and less sense to have your $50/hour contracts manager or $75/hour code designer spend a couple of hours a day packing boxes for shipment.

In addition, the nature of the product will often dictate how you ship. For example, if you ship a product that needs little or no packaging and comes in one standard size, keeping things in-house may be ideal. However, if you run a company that produces goods that are fragile, perishable, and come in all sorts of bizarre shapes and sizes, you may be better off handing the operation over to one of the mass-market shippers we'll discuss next.

The U.S. Postal Service

Of course, the most universally recognized and capable shipping service around is the U.S. Postal Service. They will deliver to almost any country on Earth, and in

Merchandise Type	International Standard
Books	$8.95
Music	$4.95
Videos	$4.95
DVDs	$8.95
Video Games	Not available
Software & Computer Games	Not available
Electronics	Not available
Camera & Photo	Not available
Tools & Hardware	Not available
Kitchen & Housewares	Not available
Outdoor Living	Not available
Computer	Not available
Sports & Outdoors	Not available
Cell Phones & Service	Not available
Musical Instruments	Not available
Office Products	Not available
Toy & Baby	Not available
Everything Else	Not available

TABLE 13-1   Credit Awarded Depending on Merchandise

some cases, you can choose to send items by air or by boat (economy shipping).
Other services like UPS or FedEx only offer airmail shipping, which can be very
expensive. Of course, when using the U.S. Postal Service, once it arrives at the
destination country, they will hand it off to the local post office and you won't be
able to track the item to the final destination. Other services such as Insurance and
Certified or Registered mail differ from country to country.

The downside can be that the Post Office doesn't have a reputation for speed
and may not ship to all countries. You can determine whether the country you
wish to ship to is available, and the cost of shipping the item there using the USPS
online shipping calculator at the web page http://ircalc.usps.gov/, shown in
Figure 13-14.

FIGURE 13-14   The USPS international shipping calculator

UPS

A second option is to use UPS, especially if you need to ship to a location that the U.S. Post Office does not handle. Additionally, UPS offers tracking information for every package, as well as up to $100 of package insurance, which is automatically included in the price of each shipment. When you create your online shipping label, UPS will prompt you for the customs information and print out the customs forms to include with your label. The link to UPS' international shipping calculator, shown in Figure 13-15, is located at http://ups.com/using/services/rave/rate.html.

FedEx and DHL

FedEx and DHL have some of the strongest brand recognition and client integration. Many overseas companies already use these services, are familiar with the process, and have integrated their systems to be able to create labels online, print out the shipping

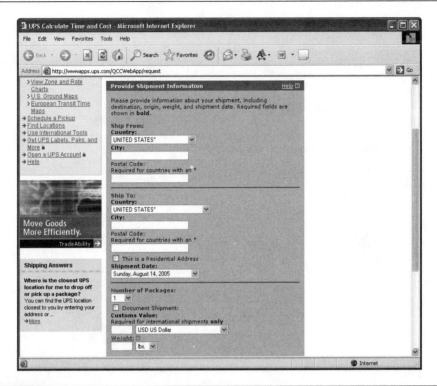

The UPS international shipping calculator

labels, and be able to get their product to one of innumerable drop boxes across the globe. And like UPS, FedEx and DHL give you $100 insurance automatically on each package, which is included in their cost. The FedEx international shipping calculator is located at www.fedex.com/us/international/ and is shown in Figure 13-16. DHL's international shipping calculator is located at www.dhl-usa.com/shipping/.

Choosing Among the Various Providers

Given all the options we've presented, you're probably wondering which service to use. We've found that the biggest determiner of service provider is the shipping cost. If it's not a valuable item (let's say under $100) and easily replaceable, the U.S. Postal Service is probably your best bet. They are definitely the choice for

FIGURE 13-16   The FedEx international shipping calculator

heavy items, such as books, that would be too expensive to send via air mail with any service. Besides, for inexpensive items, the customer isn't going to want to pay a high surcharge for shipping and they'll be more willing to wait for surface or economy mail.

The best time to use a service like UPS or FedEx is when you're shipping out more valuable or hard-to-replace items. When you need verification that the customer received the item, we recommend one of these shippers. Also, if you've consolidated all your shipments to go through one provider, using them for your international shipments makes your life easier. If that shipping company offers you a discount for having your account, compare your costs to the U.S. Postal Service and see if it's comparable in price to do all your shipments through one company.

Customs Forms and Duty Taxes

Next, we're going to take a look at the two main issues that most sellers will face when shipping goods outside the United States: customs forms and the duties/tax question. Basically, customs forms provide a way for you to declare what you are shipping to a foreign buyer, along with the value of the item, in case that country has any import tax and duties. Secondly, we'll look at the overall issue of duties and/or taxes that your buyers may face when they receive your products and what the general expectations are regarding how this should be handled.

> NOTE
>
> *Be aware that when shipping computer hardware and/or software outside the U.S., there are some restrictions regarding any encryption software that can be sent, including encryption used by basic programs like Microsoft Internet Explorer. Check with the U.S. Government's web site for exact details, and be sure to remove any software that's not allowed to be exported to another country.*

Forms to Expect

There are different kinds of customs forms that are required, depending on the shipping company as well as the content and weight of the items being shipped. Despite these differences, every customs form shares the basic requests for pieces of information:

- Description of the item
- Quantity of the item
- Value of the item
- Sender's address (that's you)
- Receiver's address (that's the buyer)
- Weight of the package (usually filled in by the shipping company)
- Signature of the sender

In some cases, you'll be asked for specific codes, the country of origin for your product, insurance numbers, the speed of delivery, and what to do if the package is undeliverable. The pieces of data above are basically mandatory, so you can expect to fill out these fields whenever you ship a package outside the U.S.

When it comes to the description, give a basic overall depiction of what the item or items are in the package. You shouldn't spend more than a sentence or six to ten words to describe your products. Descriptions such as "Kodak Digital Camera" or "1 ruby and diamond ring" are usually sufficient for this field. Your quantity may or may not be part of your description, so check your customs form for more details.

Note that some buyers have been known to ask sellers to claim that your shipment is something other than what it is, such as a gift or commercial sample. As a consequence, if the destination country inspects the package and finds the customs form to be fraudulent, you could face unexpected fees and penalties. This in turn can affect your feedback and customer relationship to say the least. In a worst case scenario, you could also be indicted in the U.S. (or other country of origin) for mail fraud. So, bottom line, you should always fill out your customs forms accurately and follow U.S. law, and explain that to your buyers.

Your quantity, when listed separately, should match up with the description you've given. If you're shipping two music CDs and one DVD, make sure your quantities are in the right place. Don't just write "3 items" on the form. The customs agents in both the U.S. and the buyer's country will want to know exactly what's in the package, so details are important.

When it comes to the value of the item, you have several options. You can either put the price you paid for the item, the price the buyer paid for the item, or the retail (or replacement) value of the item. For example, if you bought a laptop computer for $300, sold it for $600 to a buyer, but it costs $1,000 to replace if something happened to it, you could reasonably argue that the value of the item is either $300, $600, or $1,000. As a point of reference, most people list the price paid by the buyer as the value, and will also insure the package for that same value whenever necessary. In the example we just described, you would put the value at $600.

CAUTION *Some foreign buyers may ask you to write a lower customs value on their customs form, in order to avoid paying more duties or tax. This practice is frowned upon and should not be done, especially when you need to insure the package. Once you write a lower value, you cannot insure the package for more than the stated value.*

While the recipient's address should be obvious, the only note to make regarding the sender's address is this: You should write the address where you're doing business from, even if it isn't your home address. You want your shipping activities to correspond with where you organize your selling activities, whether that's from home, a P.O. Box, an independently rented mailbox at a place like the UPS Store, or a physical office location. The address used on your customs form should match the one you've listed as the return address on the form, so be sure to follow this same practice when putting return addresses on your packages.

U.S. Postal Service Customs Forms

Since many of you might use the U.S. Postal Service (USPS) to send your international packages, we thought we'd take a closer look at the two customs forms that they employ for international shipments.

NOTE

In some cases, the U.S. Postal Service is your only option for certain countries, as private shipping companies like UPS and FedEx don't service every country in the world. In addition, countries served by these companies may require the use of expensive air mail options, which could be price-prohibitive for your buyers.

The main difference between the two customs forms for the USPS has to do with the weight of the package. If your package is four pounds or less, and does not require insurance, you will use a small form known as the "green customs form" due to the green section of the form. Otherwise, you'll use the larger "white customs form" that makes three copies when you press down and write out the customs form.

The green customs form is easy to complete. On the left-hand side, in the green portion, you simply fill out the quantity, description, and value of each item in your package. (Don't worry. You don't have to declare things like packing material, Styrofoam peanuts, or packing paper.) You pick one of the four check boxes to declare what kind of shipment this is: Gift, Commercial Sample, Documents, or Other. At the bottom of the form, you add up the values of the objects in your package and state the total. Finally, you sign this section and put the date you're mailing out the package. The right side of the form is where you should complete the sender's and receiver's address. You then sign and date that section as well. The green section is then affixed to the package, while the right section is kept by the local post office where you mailed your package.

TIP

The Automated Postal Centers found at most post offices can accept most international packages weighing one pound or less. Just be sure to affix your green customs form to the package before you drop it in the slot. This way, you don't have to wait in line to mail light packages overseas.

The white customs form asks for a little more information. At the top of the form, you complete the sender's and receiver's addresses, line by line as prompted by the form. Near the middle of the form, you fill out a detailed quantity, description, and value for each item in your package. You then have to mark several check boxes on the form: whether the item is being sent by air mail or ground, whether to have your package returned to the sender or treated as abandoned if the receiver can't be reached, whether your item is a gift, documents, commercial sample, or other.

Duties and Taxes

Your goal is to make paying duty tax the buyer's concern, not yours. Even though as a business, you're probably used to making that process as smooth as possible for the customer, this is one case where the profit may not justify the added service.

You should always be clear what is your responsibility (as far as taxes go), as well as the buyer's. And of course, be leery if you find yourself dealing with a buyer that wants you to lie on their customs forms so they can avoid duty taxes. The last thing you need is your shipment seized by customs.

Because the taxes and rules for duties differ widely from country to country, the intricacies of this topic could also take up its own book. When it comes to sales that are generated from Amazon.com-posted products, the safest bet is to always have the buyer be responsible for any duties or taxes. If you expand your presence overseas, once again you should consult an international distributor who can walk you through each country's rules and regulations, or outsource your products to that distributor, have them cut you a check, and let them worry about the different collection processes and so forth.

To Sum Up

In this chapter, we've taken a look at the major sites that Amazon has created to target specific world economies. We've talked about how you can access those international customers, both through selling on the U.S. site Amazon.com, and by looking into partnerships to post products directly on an international site. We've discussed shipping options for reaching international customers, and shown you the biggest players in that market for U.S. sellers. We've even gone in depth about the customs forms you can expect to fill out when shipping a product overseas.

We hope that, armed with this information, you can make an educated guess and decision about whether to sell overseas. It's a great potential market, full of eager customers and higher revenue, and all it takes is some knowledge and time to service it correctly.

Conclusion

In fact, this brings us to the close of the entire book, and our overall goal: We wanted to present you with the critical facts, steps, and information to allow you to join this vibrant e-commerce community and earn some money by partnering with one of the best e-commerce sites around and thus serving that community. Amazon's strength now depends on eager sellers such as yourselves, who add products, information, reviews, and opinions to this global network. We hope that we've given you a well-rounded picture of what to expect, and how to dive in and make a successful run on Amazon.

Now it's your turn. The best knowledge can only be gained by venturing onto the site and trying it yourself. But don't worry, you can always flip back to a given chapter if you're stuck in a certain area, or use Amazon's help system to give you more information. That said, we wish you the best of luck as you and your products help make Amazon.com "Earth's Greatest Selection."

Part V

Appendixes

Appendix A

Amazon Associates: Amazon Will Pay You to Sell Products for Them

Before Amazon expanded their site to allow outsiders to sell merchandise, they got these savvy entrepreneurs and business owners involved in another way—Amazon signed them up as affiliates. These affiliates help recruit customers to come to Amazon's site and buy something, and in exchange, Amazon will pay these recruiters a small commission on the sale. Amazon affiliates got the chance to market merchandise without investing in capital, while Amazon dramatically increased their reach and exposure without an initial investment. After all, Amazon never had to pay an affiliate until a sale was achieved.

A few years ago, Amazon renamed this program Amazon Associates, but the core remains the same: Affiliates place targeted advertisements on their web sites, in e-mails, or newsletters, for specific products, categories, or stores within Amazon. Every time a customer reaches Amazon through an affiliate, that customer's sales are tracked with a special identifier. When the customer buys something, Amazon credits the affiliate with a specific commission, and then makes a payment to the affiliate either once a month or once a quarter.

NOTE   *You only earn a commission when a referred customer buys something from Amazon, not one of their Marketplace or Auction sellers.*

The Basics of the Program

Amazon Associates is a free program to join, but requires a separate registration process (which we'll discuss in the next section, "How to Join the Associates Program") from the regular setup process. The program is ideal for businesses and entrepreneurs in the following situations:

- If you own or operate a popular web site related to your industry, hobby, or interest, you can use Amazon Associates to refer your readers to targeted products that relate to your web site. These usually pay off better than a targeted advertisement and it relates to your web site better than a generic ad, which makes it less intrusive to your readers.

- If you currently use e-mail and/or direct marketing to move one or two specific products, you can use Amazon Associates to increase the quantity and quality of products offered, and earn commissions on related products your customers are already buying.

■ If you're using Amazon to distribute your own products (the Amazon Advantage program is discussed in Chapter 12), you can earn an extra commission by advertising your products and sending people directly to your product detail page on Amazon. Be aware that you do not earn commissions when they shop from your Marketplace items for sale.

There are other scenarios that have worked well for Amazon Associates. Nonprofit organizations often use this program for charity fund-raising drives to have their members shop through their affiliate web page, with the commissions going to their organization. Manufacturers put links on their site to books or products that feature their company to help promote their brand. Whatever the case, Amazon Associates allows you to make money by earning customers, even if they're not buying one of your products.

Types of Referrals Available

There may be 50 ways to leave your lover, but currently, there are only five distinct methods that Amazon Associates offers their affiliates to bring in these referrals:

■ **Product Links**   These links create special windows on a person's web site that display a product image and take people directly to a specific product from Amazon's catalog. The Associate gets to pick the exact product to be displayed via this link, and Amazon coordinates all the images, buttons, and necessary pricing information to dynamically present this information on the Associate's web site. Because Amazon sends all this information automatically from their servers, it's a very visual and dynamic way to refer people based on their interest in specific products. (For an example, see Figure A-1.)

■ **Recommended Product Links**   Like Product Links, these types of referrals are all dynamically generated from Amazon's servers. Unlike the specific Product Links, in this situation the Associate specifies the type of product they want displayed on their web site, Amazon picks the appropriate best-selling products for the specified type, and then it displays them in a graphical format, along with cover images, buying buttons, and dynamic pricing information. The Associate can decide whether to sponsor Recommended Product Links by category or by specific keyword, and Amazon coordinates the colors, design layout, and content of these ads, keeping it fresh for the consumers. (For an example, see Figure A-2.)

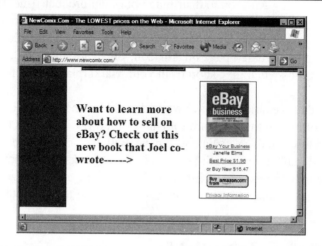

FIGURE A-1 See how co-author Joel Elad uses a Product Link to advertise his book *eBay Your Business* on another e-commerce web site.

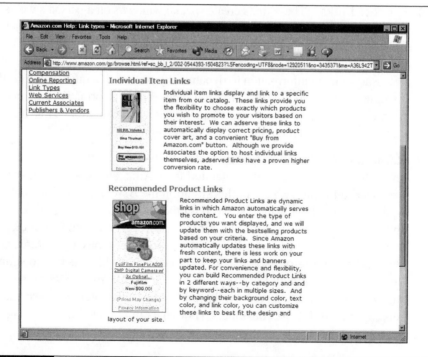

FIGURE A-2 Examples of Product Links and Recommended Product Links

- **Banner Links**   These links look very similar to the banner ads you've seen in most Internet marketing efforts. You can specify a banner ad that features different Amazon promotions or simply pick a banner ad based on one of Amazon's categories of products. They will provide the banner images and hyperlinks to bring customers to the given category specified.

- **Text Links**   If you're looking for a simpler way to refer customers to a given product, especially in devices like electronic newsletters or e-mail marketing, Amazon allows their Associates to build text links. These links allow the Associate to write their own text blurb for a given product, and then lets their customer click that custom text blurb and be taken to a specific product on Amazon's site. Unlike the Product Link, the text link given to the Associate upon its creation will stay the same and won't come with any cover images or buttons.

- **Search Boxes**   If an Associate just wants to give their referral customers the chance to search for a product on Amazon, instead of pointing that customer towards a specific category or product, Amazon offers a special Search box on the Associate's web site that can execute a search in Amazon's catalog and then take that customer to the Amazon web page containing the results of that search. This method allows Associates to refer people to Amazon without promoting or pushing a particular product or set of products.

With all these choices, you may be asking, "When would be the best time to use any of these?" The answer depends on what kind of web site you're hosting. Let's say, for example, you maintain your own blog diary on how to navigate through the hottest new video games on the market. You can use Product Links or Text Links to refer to the games you mention in your blog! That way, if someone reads about a new game they want to try out, they can instantly click a link on your web site to go to Amazon and purchase that game, thus earning you a commission.

As another example, let's say you maintain a directory of the best places to get musical instruments in your area. You can use a Recommended Product Link to advertise the newest musical instruments if your readers don't want to venture out to get these items. Text links are best used when embedding your product promotion within an article, while Search boxes work best when your site content is always changing, so you put the Search box on your home page for easy access.

How to Join the Associates Program

If you're interested in signing up for the Amazon Associates program, they've made the process quite simple. Access your Amazon account and then either click the Associates link from the See All 32 Product Categories screen, or go to this URL: www.amazon.com/associates.

Look for the orange Join Now button on the left-hand side of the page. Click it to go to the application page. In the first part of the application process, as shown in Figure A-3, you must enter your contact information (specifically, the name of the person or company that will receive the commissions generated from the Associates program) and the address for that person or company.

On the second part of this web page, as shown in Figure A-4, you're asked for the tax information regarding the person or company referred to in Part 1.

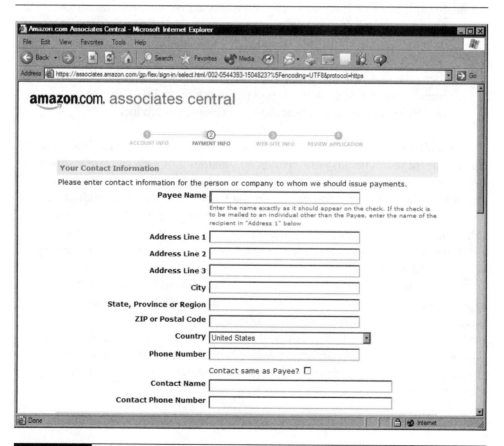

FIGURE A-3   Part one of the application process: your contact information

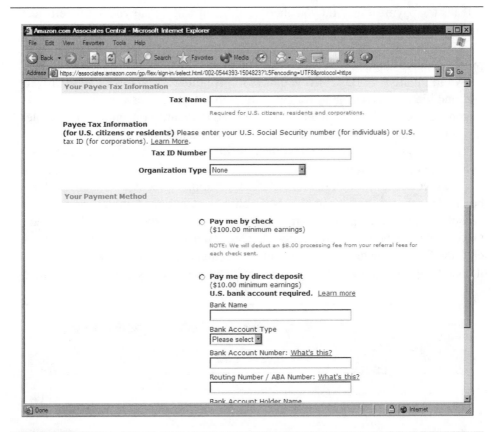

FIGURE A-4   Part two of the application process: your tax identification information

Since you're earning money through this program, once you earn more than $400 it's considered taxable income and needs to be reported.

Amazon will ask you for your tax ID name, tax ID number, and organization type. If you're an individual earning extra money, the tax ID name is simply your name, the tax ID number is your Social Security number, and the organization type is Individual. If you're doing these activities as part of your business or company, enter the appropriate information when prompted.

In the last part of this screen, you need to identify how you want to be issued your payments for this program. You can choose to receive paper checks, but you have to earn a minimum of $100 before a check is issued. You can also choose to have your funds direct-deposited into a bank account, which only requires a $10 minimum. If you choose the latter, enter your bank account information in the fields provided, as shown in Figure A-4. Lastly, you can choose to receive your funds in the form of an Amazon gift certificate, which also has a $10 minimum associated with it.

If that's the payment method you choose, Amazon will e-mail you a gift certificate with your proceeds.

Once all that's entered, click the Continue button to go to the third part of the process, identifying the web site where you plan to host your Associates ads, as shown in Figure A-5. Basically, you have to give the name and URL of your web site, and identify the category (or categories) that best fit your web site, in terms of content and/or customer interest. You'll need to identify the number of people in your organization (it can be one person—for instance, you, the owner/writer/ creator) and give a description of your web site as well as identify the main way you pull people into your web site.

Once you read through the Associates Operating Agreement and check the box that means you agree with the terms, click the Continue button to go to the last part of the application process—reviewing all the information you've submitted. Once you've read through everything and you're satisfied with what you've written, click the Continue button to submit your application to Amazon. Once they review it, they'll get back to you with either a confirmation e-mail welcoming you to the

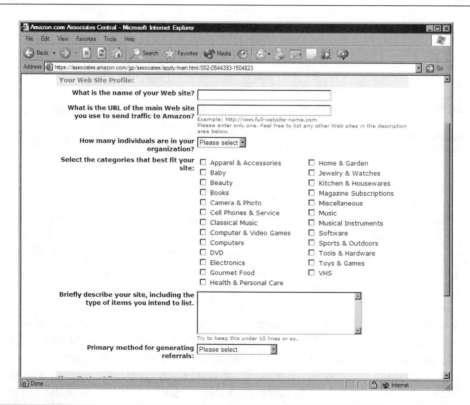

FIGURE A-5   Part three of the application process—your web site information

program, or an e-mail explaining why you're not eligible. Normally, the main reason someone might be rejected is if they're illegally piggy-backing onto an established web site, like eBay or Yahoo! Setting up an affiliates site like www.ebaysoftware.com would not be eligible for an Amazon Associates account because it infringes on the eBay name. Also, Amazon has an arrangement with certain merchants that says those brands cannot appear on any Associate's web site. Those merchants include Circuit City, Crabtree & Evelyn, Elisabeth, Godiva, Lands' End, Liz Claiborne, Lucky Brand Jeans, Nordstrom, and Sephora. Otherwise, your application should be approved, and you don't need to offer exclusivity to Amazon or have your business license yet.

That's it! Once you get your confirmation e-mail, go to http://associates .amazon.com. This time, however, log in with your account, and you'll see the Associates home page, like the one shown in Figure A-6. This is your home base for your Associates operations.

Once you've used your Amazon account to log in as an Associate, you can start to earn money by building these special links. In fact, let's talk about how to build your own product links for referral money!

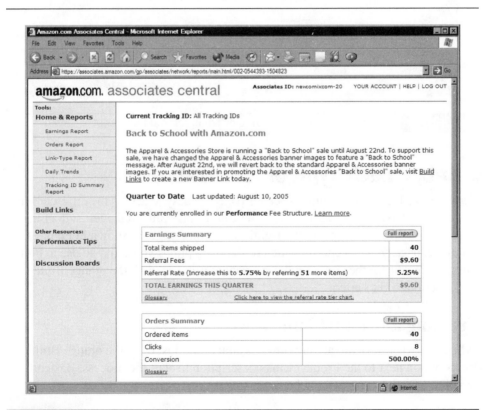

FIGURE A-6   The Amazon Associates home page: your base of operations starts here.

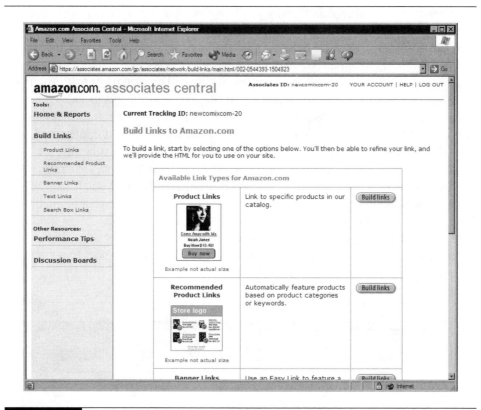

FIGURE A-7   Your home page for building different referral links

How to Use Each Type of Referral

Once you've logged into your Associates page, it's easy to access the different links you can build to refer traffic. Just click the Build Links link on the left side of the Associates home page to get to the Build Links home page, as shown in Figure A-7. From this page, you can choose which of the five options you'd like to use to build links. Once you see the type of link you want to use, just click the orange Build Links button to get started.

Creating a Product Link

When you want to create an individual product link, just click the orange Build Links button next to the Product Links description to start the process. Basically, building a product link works like this:

1. You're asked to search the Amazon catalog for the product you want to promote. You pick the category from a drop-down menu and enter either keywords or the Amazon ASIN or ISBN number in the box provided.

2. Click the Go! button and you're taken to a list of search results. Pick the product from that search list (or enter new search terms) and click the Get HTML button next to your chosen product.

3. You'll be taken to a screen where you can cut and paste special customized computer code, known as HTML, which you can add to your web page. This specialized computer code contains specific instructions that will contact Amazon for all the images and buttons necessary for your product link. It will also have your special Associates ID embedded in that link, so you get the commission credit when someone clicks that Product Link and then buys it from Amazon.

Creating a Recommended Product Link

The process for creating any other link will be very similar to creating a Product Link. Go back to the Associates home page and click Build Links on the left-hand side of the screen. Click the orange Build Links button next to the row for Recommended Product Link. You'll be taken to a screen like the one in Figure A-8, where instead of selecting an item from the catalog, you'll follow these three steps:

1. Pick a category from the drop-down list of categories within Amazon. Once you've picked one, you can either add keywords to narrow your ad or pick a given subcategory from the drop-down menu. Once you've made your selections, click the Continue button.

2. Choose the size of your Recommended Product Link. Amazon will show you up to ten different pixel sizes for your proposed link. Scroll through the list, and when you see the ad size you want, click the Select This Size button next to the ad. If you want to highlight one product very well, the 180×150 pixel size works great. If you're interested in highlighting up to four products, we recommend using the 300×250 pixel size ad. The best time to consider a 120×150 ad is when you're introducing something on a crowded web site but you're not sure you want this ad to be your focus yet.

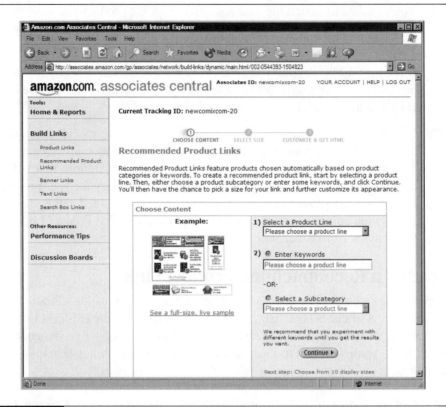

FIGURE A-8   Build your Recommended Product Link by selecting your category.

3. You'll then be taken to a screen like the one in Figure A-9, where you can copy the HTML code in the indicated box and paste that code into one of your web pages. The code will contact Amazon whenever someone looks at that web page, and Amazon will then display all the pertinent photos, buttons, and pricing information for best-selling products within the category and subcategory (or keywords) that you selected.

Creating a Banner Ad

Once again, go to the Build Links page from the Associates home page. This time, click the Build Links button next to the Banner Ad description, which will start a two-step process:

1. You'll be taken to a screen like the one in Figure A-10, where you can either choose an overall "promotional" banner, which will display various products on sale within Amazon that correspond with their promotional strategy, or you can choose from a variety of categories or special subject interests. You'll notice Amazon's standard categories as well as some custom ones, like Harry Potter and Target. Click any of the category (or the Easy Links) links to go to the second step.

2. At this point, you're presented with various sizes of banner ads, with the HTML code for each ad listed directly below it. Simply scroll through the page and pick the banner ad you like, preferably one that will fit well within your web page. Copy the indicated HTML code and paste it into one of your web pages. That's it! Amazon does the rest of the work.

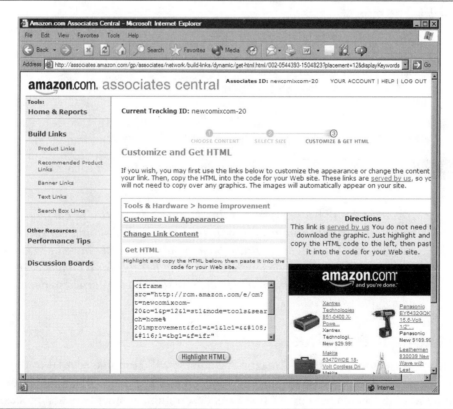

FIGURE A-9   Copy the HTML code from the text box on this screen, and paste it into one of your web pages.

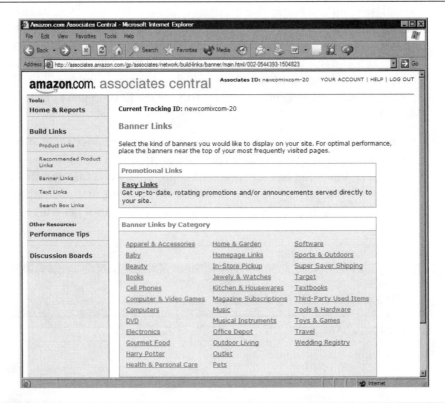

FIGURE A-10   Pick a category or a general promotional link for your banner ad.

> TIP
>
> *If your web site isn't currently using banner ads, or you're currently receiving very little money for your banner ads, you should consider switching to Amazon banner ads. Some small businesses have been known to replace their banner ads with Amazon banner ads for a month or two, and then measure the difference in commission money earned to decide which one works more effectively.*

Creating a Text Link

When you create a Text Link, Amazon Associates will combine several of the options you had with the other links into this creation process. When you click the Build Links button next to the Text Link description, another two-step process awaits you:

1. You'll be taken to the Name and Destination part of building a Text Link, as shown in Figure A-11. You need to tell Amazon where your Text Link will end up on Amazon's site, and what name you want to give this link (in other words, the "name" of the link is the words your customers see on the screen). You can set the destination by picking a product category and subcategory, by picking a category and various keywords, or by entering a specific URL web address within Amazon's web site. Once you've picked your destination and name, click the appropriate Get HTML button to go to the second step.

2. This step should be familiar to you. You'll see a big white text box with specific HTML code. Copy that code and paste it onto your targeted web page. Unlike some of the other links, this one doesn't make any calls to the Amazon site to retrieve pictures or buttons. It just sits there, waiting to get clicked. But don't worry, it'll have the same effect, or even a better one, than the others.

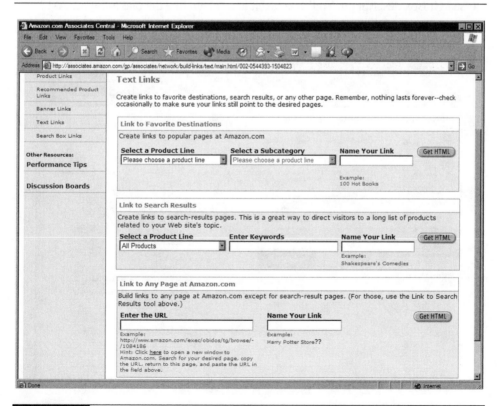

FIGURE A-11   Pick your destination and the name for your Text Link.

Text Links, along with the non-linked text URL example, also make excellent insertions into e-mail newsletters, not just web pages. You can consider adding this text link to your next newsletter or member update e-mail to attract people to products or categories within Amazon. Some ways businesses get more usage out of their Text Links are to offer people a special bonus if they buy a product through that link, or to promise to donate a percentage of the proceeds to charity if their users buy through that link. Newsletter members feel that they're getting a special benefit by belonging to this group, and sometimes the free offer or charity donation will spur them to buy the product even if they don't need the item right away.

Creating a Search Box

In this last case, the Search box is the easiest link to build, because there are no options to consider, no categories to select, and no products to highlight. The Search box just gives your customers an automatic window into Amazon's catalog, without leaving your web site to get to it. There's only one step: click the Build Links button next to the Search Box description. You'll be taken to a screen like the one in Figure A-12,

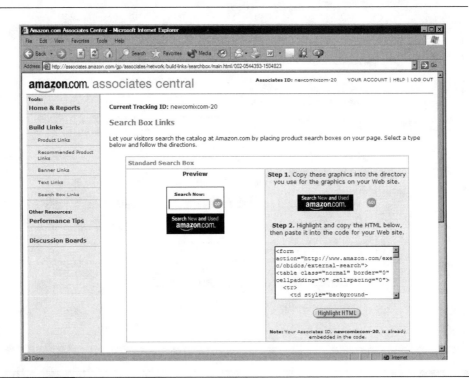

FIGURE A-12   The code is ready for you to put an Amazon Search box on your site.

where you can see and copy the HTML code necessary for the Search box to appear on your web page. Just paste it into a web page, and when that page is loaded into someone's browser, the Amazon Search box will appear, just like in the example. This will allow customers to type in their own keywords, select their own categories, and find products for sale on Amazon, giving you a commission on that sale.

> **TIP** *Try to place your Search box on your home page or an important category page. The value of the Search box is that it provides an easy window early on into the customer's browsing habits, so they'll learn to search from your web site instead of going directly to Amazon on their own.*

How to Track the Progress of Referrals

We've talked about how to build your links, and hopefully by now you've picked a test case or two to experiment with on your own web site, e-mail newsletter, and so on. Naturally, the first question you'd probably have is, "Well, how's it doing?" Amazon allows you to track your results in so many ways that it can become entertaining and educational for your bottom line.

Just go to the Associates home page, and you'll notice five links in the upper left-hand corner of the screen.

These five links basically take all your sales data and click-through results and present the information in different ways. They allow you to pick periods of time that you want to study, and either display the report on the screen or let you download the report as either a Comma Separated Value file (CSV) or an XML document for easy importing into other applications.

In short, the following lists what each report can show you:

- **Earnings Report** This report will give you a breakdown based on individual products purchased by customers using your various links. It will group all the times a particular product was viewed and purchased, and then show your average referral rate percentage and, finally, how much referral money you earned per product. An example of an earnings report is shown in Figure A-13.

- **Orders Report** This report will give you a breakdown of information based on each order placed by a customer through your referral links. You'll see how many clicks you got through an ad, and what product or products they ordered through that click. You'll see what items were ordered, and what items were added to a shopping cart but not eventually ordered. Finally, you'll see a conversion report showing Direct Clicks

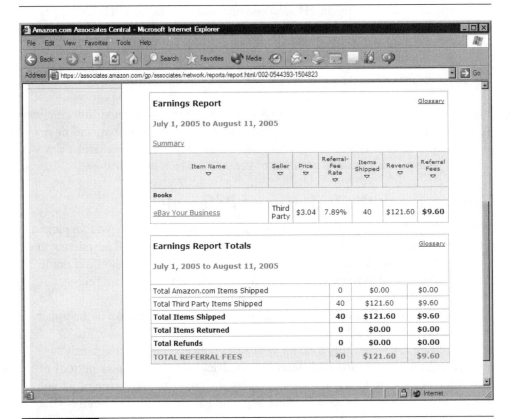

FIGURE A-13   The Earnings Report displays your referral money based on products sold.

(or orders resulting directly from a user clicking a targeted ad) and Indirect Clicks (or other products bought by customers who came to Amazon through a targeted ad for another product). An example of your Orders Report is shown in Figure A-14.

■ **Link-Type Report**   This report gives you some great analysis numbers on the different kinds of Product Links you're using. Whether you're stuck on one format, or experimenting with different types, this report will show you how many impressions your ad has had (how many times it was loaded onto a web page), how many people clicked each ad, the click-through rate (or number of clicks divided by the number of impressions), followed by your

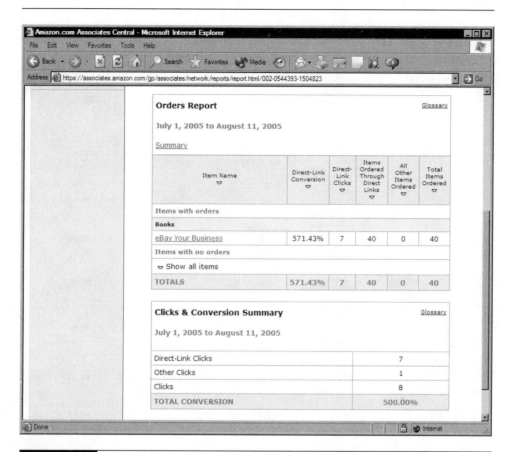

FIGURE A-14   The Orders Report displays your referral money based on orders made.

conversion rate, and the number of items ordered and shipped through each ad.
You can scroll down through the page to see breakdowns of all five ads. If
you're not using a particular ad format, you'll simply see 0% or N/A in the
various columns. An example of the beginning of this report is shown in
Figure A-15.

NOTE   *Sometimes, the conversion rate is over 100 percent if multiple items are
ordered through one order.*

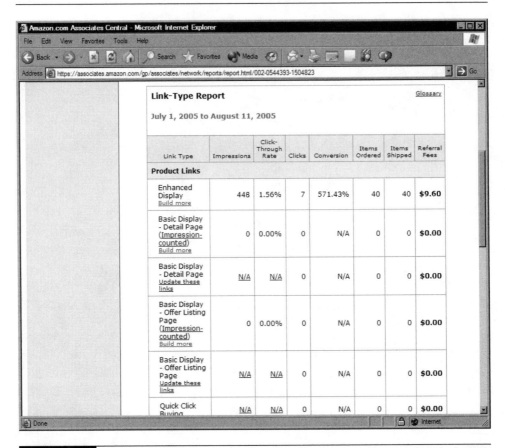

FIGURE A-15   The Link-Type Report displays the effectiveness of each referral ad.

- **Daily Trends**   This report adds up the effects of all your ads and displays the result based on daily summaries. You can see how much money your referral ads have generated on any given day. You can pick a range of dates, or a predefined period, like a quarter of the year. The results are presented in a table, showing the individual day, the number of clicks, visitors, and orders you got on that day, followed by the conversion rate for that day, based on that data. An example of this report is shown in Figure A-16.

- **Tracking ID Summary Report**   This report is great for people who have multiple Associates accounts or people who just want to see the overall performance of their Associates account for a given time period. You indicate the amount of time you want to study, and this report gives you a summary line report of the number of clicks your ads got, the number

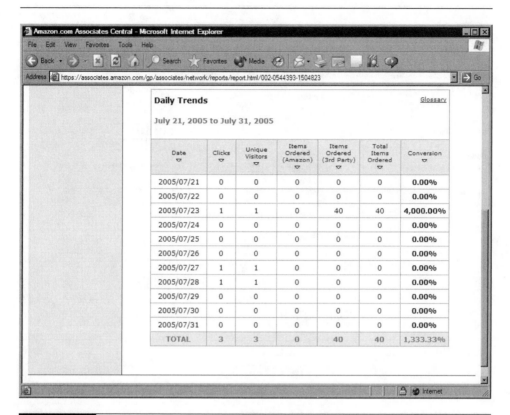

Date	Clicks	Unique Visitors	Items Ordered (Amazon)	Items Ordered (3rd Party)	Total Items Ordered	Conversion
2005/07/21	0	0	0	0	0	0.00%
2005/07/22	0	0	0	0	0	0.00%
2005/07/23	1	1	0	40	40	4,000.00%
2005/07/24	0	0	0	0	0	0.00%
2005/07/25	0	0	0	0	0	0.00%
2005/07/26	0	0	0	0	0	0.00%
2005/07/27	1	1	0	0	0	0.00%
2005/07/28	1	1	0	0	0	0.00%
2005/07/29	0	0	0	0	0	0.00%
2005/07/30	0	0	0	0	0	0.00%
2005/07/31	0	0	0	0	0	0.00%
TOTAL	3	3	0	40	40	1,333.33%

FIGURE A-16   Daily Trends shows your ads' performance each day of the year.

of items ordered through those clicks, the number of items shipped from those orders, the revenue generated from those shipped items, and finally, your referral fees from that revenue generated. An example of this report is shown in Figure A-17.

> **NOTE**   *In most cases, it takes at least 24 hours for the statistics pages to get updated, so don't expect to get "real-time" statistics. All the data will show up eventually.*

How to Get Paid for Your Efforts

In the past, Amazon used to set up a special Affiliate payment account that it would credit once a month with your commissions. However, they have now tied this program to your Amazon Payments account so you'll see those Payments show up alongside your Marketplace, Auction, and zShop payments.

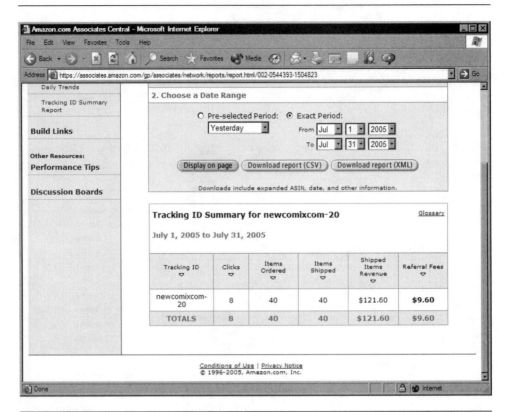

FIGURE A-17   The Tracking ID Summary shows a general summary of your results.

To Sum Up

In this Appendix, we've shown the powerful affiliate program known as Amazon Associates. You can earn a revenue stream just by referring people to products and stores within Amazon, and earn a commission each time a referral customer shops at Amazon. We've talked about some good scenarios and situations where you could benefit from this program.

We've explained the different types of referral methods that Amazon gives their Associates. We then walked through the process of joining the program and setting up your account, and then demonstrated examples for each kind of referral. We wrapped up by showing you the web pages where you can monitor your results and discuss how you get paid by Amazon.

Appendix B

Useful Web Links

In the next few pages, we provide you with both some helpful web sites and Amazon category paths that can provide assistance and information, and save you lots of time when used properly! Most of these links were mentioned throughout the book, but we've compiled a handy list for you here that you can refer to time and time again.

Evaluating Product Values

- **www.scoutpal.com**   ScoutPal is a very handy application that allows you to use your cell phone (and optionally, a bar-code scanner) to enter in ISBN and UPC numbers to find the value of particular items on Amazon.

- **www.abebooks.com, www.bookfinder.com**   Abebooks and Bookfinder are two excellent search engines for finding books online and their corresponding prices on various web sites.

- **www.pricegrabber.com, www.froogle.com**   PriceGrabber and Froogle are excellent shopping comparison sites that can give you estimates of what an item is selling for online, both on and off Amazon.

- **www.sothebys.com**   Sothebys.com is a good resource to bid on fine art, furniture, and decorations, as well as books, collectibles, and jewelry, which means the prices realized through these sales give you an idea of the upper value of the item. One advantage of this association with Sothebys is that the authenticity and condition of their sale items is guaranteed.

- **www.auctionbytes.com**   AuctionBytes has become one of the leading destinations for people who want to keep up-to-date on all online-auction news and events, including Amazon Auctions. Dave and Ina Steiner created the site, where people contribute interesting and helpful articles, tips, and tricks. Their e-mail newsletters are heavily subscribed to by people who use and sell items through online auctions. Their discussion boards are a great gathering point to ask questions and get help from leading experts.

- **www.hammertap.com, www.terapeak.com**   DeepAnalysis (from HammerTap) and Terapeak are two examples of data analysis programs that crunch through market data from eBay and other sources and show you different price points realized for an item online. Use these sites to get a ballpark figure of what the item will sell for on eBay, and then compare it to the price on Amazon.

Software Tools Available for Tracking Inventory

- **www.vendio.com**   Vendio.com is one of the leading online sales management tools. They help coordinate your online auctions and sales through various services like image hosting, web hosting, online storefront creation, online checkout, credit card processing, and more.

- **www.andale.com/corp/index.html**   Andale is an online Auction Business Management service for sellers on Amazon, Yahoo!, and eBay.

- **www.channeladvisor.com**   ChannelAdvisor offers multiple solutions, ranging from self-service auction management software to full-service, outsourced marketplace management solutions.

- **www.marketworks.com**   MarketWorks is another enterprise-level sales management tool that is adding Amazon to its roster of supported e-commerce sites. They offer a suite of tools to help you create new marketing channels and move all types of inventory.

Shipping Companies and Online Postage Printing

- **www.buyerzone.com/mailroom/online_postage/index.html**   BuyerZone provides a good general overview of the world of online postage and the small business shipping industry.

- **www.stamps.com, www.endicia.com**   Both of these sites offer ways to purchase postage online, thus avoiding the need to make trips to the Post Office or purchase a special postage printing machine.

- **www.usps.com**   Create shipping labels directly on the Post Office's web site, order a Carrier Pickup of your Express or Priority Mail packages, and track your packages online.

- **www.ups.com, www.fedex.com, www.dhl.com**   Set up accounts directly with the biggest shipping companies out there (UPS, FedEx, and DHL), and use their online tools to create shipping labels, order free supplies, and coordinate your shipping activities.

Packaging Supply Sources

- **www.uline.com, www.papermart.com**   Uline and PaperMart offer two of the most comprehensive packaging supply sources available online.

- **www.pbsb.com/company/company_main.htm**   This is the online listings in the PBSB, or Packaging Buyer's Source Book. Offers a very complete listing of packaging companies with a web presence. If you have a "hard to ship" item, this site will likely lead you to a company that can cater to your special needs.

- **http://shop.usps.com, https://www.ups.com/labels?loc=en_US, https://www.fedex.com/servlet/SuppliesOnlineServlet**   In addition to their other services, you can order free supplies from the U.S. Postal Service, UPS, and FedEx as well! And they'll send it free right to your doorstep!

Help with Amazon

- **www.amazon.com/exec/obidos/tg/browse/**   The seller Quick Start page, where you can find all the Amazon functions for sellers under one roof.

- **www.amazon.com/help**   This is the start page for Amazon's Help Guide. Look through the various subject categories to find the area you're looking for, and then click that category header to get more information. You can also scroll to the bottom of the Help page and type keywords into the Search box to go directly to the subject you're having questions about on Amazon.

- **www.elance.com**   e-Lance lets you hire professionals in the services areas you need help with when devising your strategy. You can post project proposals, collect bids, review performance histories, and hire your independent contractor.

And Finally...

- **http://forums.prosperotechnologies.com/am-USbuysell, http://forums.prosperotechnologies.com/am-UShelpnew**   At Amazon's Main Discussion Board and Help with the New Sellers Discussion Board, you can talk with other sellers and buyers who are "On the River." Ask questions, get answers, learn some new tools, and gain valuable contacts. There are several different discussion boards you can use as well. Search through past discussions, learn about new features, and don't be afraid to ask for help! There are a lot of great sellers who frequent these boards and are happy to help!

Appendix C

Glossary of Product Identification Terms and Grading Acronyms

Abbreviation/Term	Definition
1st Ed	First Edition
ACC	Accumulation (stamps)
ACL	Applied Color Label (wine or decorative bottles)
ADV	Adventure (books/movies)
AG	About Good (coins)
AIR	Air Mail (stamps)
a.k.a.	Also Known As
ANTH	Anthology (books)
AO	All Original
ARC	Advance Reader's Copy—usually a paperback edition of a book released for publicity purposes before the trade edition release
AU	About Uncirculated (coins)
AUTO	Autographed
BB	BB-sized hole drilled through record label
BBC	Bottom of Back Cover
BC	Back Cover; Blister Card
BCE	Book Club Edition
BIM	Blown in Mold
BIO	Biography
BJ	Ball Jointed Body (dolls)
BK	Bent Knee (dolls)
BKL	Booklet (stamps)
BLB	Big Little Book
BLK	Block (stamps)
BOMC	Book-of-the-Month Club Edition
BP	Blister Pack; stamps in a Booklet Pane
BU	Brilliant Uncirculated (top grade of coins)
BW	Black and White
C	Cartridge Only (video game); Cover (stamps or books)
C&S	Cup and Saucer
CART	Cartridge (video game)
CB	Club Book (stamps)

Abbreviation/Term	Definition
CC	Carbon Copy
CCA	Comics Code Authority
CCG	Collectable Card Game
CDF	Customs Declaration Form (stamps)
CF	Centerfold (magazines)
CFO	Center Fold Out (magazines)
CI	Cartridge and Instructions (video games, computer equipment)
CIB	Cartridge, Instructions, Box (video games, computer equipment)
CIBO	Cartridge, Instruction, Box, Overlay (video games, computer equipment)
CLA	Cleaned, lubricated, adjusted (cameras)
CM	Customized
COA	Certificate of Authenticity
COL	Collection
CONUS	Continental United States Shipping
CPN	Coupon
CPP	Color Picture Postcard; Color Postcard
CS	Cup and Saucer
CTB	Coffee Table Book
CU	Crisp Uncirculated (currency)
D	Denver Mint (coins)
DB	Divided Back (postcards)
DBL	Double (2-in-1: paperbacks)
DG	Depression Glass
DJ	Dust Jacket; Disk Jockey Copy (records)
DOA	Dead on Arrival (item was not working when received by buyer)
EAPG	Early American Pattern Glass
EC	Excellent Condition
EF	Extra Fine Condition; Extremely Fine (coins)
EG	Elegant Glass (Depression era)
EP	Extended Play (records, videotapes)

Abbreviation/Term	Definition
ERR	Error
EX	Excellent (condition)
EXLIB	Ex-Library Book
EXT	Extended
FAQ	Frequently Asked Questions
FB	Feedback
FC	Fine Condition; Front Cover
FDC	First Day Cover (stamps)
F/E	First Edition (books)
FE	First Edition (books)
FFC	First Flight Cover (stamps)
FFEP	Free Front End Page/Paper
FFL	Federally Licensed Firearms (dealer)
FN	Fine Condition
FOR	Forgery
FPLP	Fisher Price Little People
FS	Factory Sealed
FT	Flat Top (beer cans)
FTLO	From The Library Of
G	Good Condition
GA	Golden Age
GD	Good Condition
GF	Gold Filled
GGA	Good Girl Art (paperback book covers)
GP	Gold Plate; Gutter Pair (stamps)
GSP	Gold Sterling Plate
GU	Gently Used
GW	Gently Worn (clothes)
HB	Hard Back or Hard Bound (book)
HB/DJ	Hardback (book) with Dust Jacket
HC	Hand Colored (maps/engravings); Hard Cover (book)
HIC	Hole In Cover
HIL	Hole In Label

Abbreviation/Term	Definition
HIST	Historical (books)
HOF	Hall Of Famer (baseball memorabilia/autograph/trading cards)
HP	Hard Plastic; Hand Painted; Hewlett Packard computers
HS	Hand Stamp (stamps)
HTF	Hard To Find
HTML	Hypertext Markup Language
IBC	Inside Back Cover
IE	Internet Explorer
IFC	Inside Front Cover
ILLO	Illustration
ILLUS	Illustration; Illustrated
INIT	Initial; Initials; Initial Issue
IRAN	Inspect and Repair As Necessary
ISH	Issue
ISP	Internet Service Provider
JPG	The Amazon-preferred file format for pictures
JUVIE	Juvenile delinquency theme
L	Large
LBC	Lower Back Cover
LCD	Liquid Crystal Display
LE	Limited Edition
LED	Light Emitting Diode
LFC	Lower Front Cover
LFT	Left
LLBC	Lower Left of Back Cover
LLFC	Lower Left of Front Cover
LP	Long Playing record
LRBC	Lower Right on Back Cover
LRFC	Lower Right on Front Cover
LSE	Loose
LSW	Label Shows Wear (records)
LTBX	Letterbox (video that re-creates a widescreen image)

Abbreviation/Term	Definition
LTD	Limited edition
LWOL	Lot of Writing On Label
M	Medium; Mint; Mono (refers to audio quality)
MA	Madame Alexander (dolls)
MAP	Map back (paperback books)
MC	Miscut
MEDIC	Medical genre (paperbacks)
MIB	Mint In Box
MIBP	Mint In Blister Pack
MIJ	Made In Japan
MIMB	Mint In Mint Box
MIMP	Mint In Mint Package
MIOJ	Made In Occupied Japan
MIOP	Mint In Opened Package
MIP	Mint In Package
MIU	Made In U.S.A.
MM	Merry Miniatures (Hallmark)
MMA	Metropolitan Museum of Art
MNB	Mint—No Box
MNH	Mint Never Hinged (stamps)
MOC	Mint On Card
MOMA	Museum Of Modern Art
MOMC	Mint On Mint Card
MONMC	Mint On Near Mint Card
MONO	Monophonic (again, refers to audio quality)
MOP	Mother Of Pearl
MP	Military Post (stamps)
MS	Miniature Sheet (stamps); Mint State (coins in mint condition)
MWBMT	Mint With Both Mint Tags
MWBT	Mint With Both Tags
MWBTM	Mint With Both Tags Mint
MYS	Mystery (books/movies)

Abbreviation/Term	Definition
MWMT	Mint With Mint Tags
NAP	Not Affected Play (records)
NBU	Never Been Used
NBW	Never Been Worn/Wrecked
NC	No Cover
ND	No Date; No Dog (RCA record labels)
NDSR	No Dents, Scratches, or Rust
NIB	New In Box
NIP	New In Package
NL	Number Line (books)—a means of telling the edition; occurs on copyright page and reads "*1234567890*"; lowest number indicates the edition
NM	Near Mint
NORES	No Reserve
NOS	New Old Stock
NP	Not Packaged
NPB	Non-Paying Bidder/Buyer
NR	No Reserve
NRFB	Never Removed From Box
NRFSB	Never Removed From Sealed Box
NRMNT	Near Mint
NW	Never Worn (clothes)
NWOT	New Without Tags
NWT	New With Tags
O	New Orleans Mint
OB	Original Box
O/C	On Canvas (paintings)
OC	Off Center; Off Cut; On Canvas
OEM	Original Equipment Manufacturer
OF	Original Finish
OJ	Occupied Japan
OOAK	One Of A Kind
OOP	Out Of Package; Out Of Print

Abbreviation/Term	Definition
OP	Out Of Print
OS	Operating System (computers)
OST	Original Soundtrack
OTR	"On The River"—in other words, pertaining to the Amazon marketplace.
P	Poor Condition
PB	Paperback or Paperbound (books)
PBO	Paperback Original
PC	Picture Postcard; Postcard; Poor Condition
PD	Picture Disk (the record itself has a photo or images on it)
PF	Proof Coin
PIC	Picture
PM	Post Mark; Postal Marking; Priority Mail
P/O	Punch-Out (inventory that has been "declassified" with a hole punch)
POC	Pencil On Cover
POPS	Promo Only Picture Sleeve
PP	Parcel Post
PPD	Post Paid
PR	Poor Condition
PROOF	Proof coin
P/S	Picture Sleeve (records)
PS	Power Supply; Picture Sleeve (records)
R	Reprint
RBC	Right Side of Back Cover
RC	Reader Copy (books)—a copy of a book in good condition, not mint
RET	Retired
RETRD	Retired
RFC	Right Side of Front Cover
RFDO	Removed For Display Only
RI	Reissue (records)
RMA	Return Merchandise Authorization Number

Abbreviation/Term	Definition
ROM	Romantic (books)
RP	Real Photo (for Real Photo Postcards)
RPPC	Real Photo Postcard
RRH	Remade/Repainted/Haired (dolls)
RS	Rhinestones; Rubber Stamped on label (records)
RSP	Rhodium Sterling Plate
RT	Right
S	Small; Stereo (records)
SA	Silver Age
SB	Soft Bound or Soft Back (referring to large soft bound books)
SC	Slight Crease (hang tags, books, magazines); Sawcut (slice cut off record album jacket)
SCI	Science (books)
SCR	Scratch
SCU	Scuff (records)
SF	Science Fiction
SFBC	Science-Fiction Book Club
S/H	Shipping and Handling
SH	Shipping and Handling
S/H/I	Shipping, Handling, and Insurance
SHI	Shipping, Handling, and Insurance
SIG	Signature
SLD	Sealed
SLT	Slight
SLW	Straight Leg Walker (dolls)
snail mail	USPS delivery
S/O	Sold Out
SO	Sold Out
SOL	Sticker on Label (records)
S/P	Salt and Pepper (shakers); Silverplate; Silver Plated
SP	Sticker Pull (books)—discoloration or actual removal of cover color caused by pulling off a sticker price

Abbreviation/Term	Definition
spam	Unwanted or unrequested e-mail
SR	Slight Ring Wear; Shrink Wrapped
S/S	Still Sealed
SS	Stainless Steel; Still Sealed
ST	Soundtrack (records, CDs); Sterling
SUSP	Suspended; Suspense (books)
SW	Slight Wear; Shrink Wrapped
SYI	Sell Your Item form
TC	True Crime (books)
TE	Trade Edition (books)—standard paperback edition of a book
TM	Trademark
TMOL	Tape Mark On Label (records)
TOBC	Top Of Back Cover
TOFC	Top Of Front Cover
TOL	Tear On Label (records)
TOONS	Cartoon art (paperbacks)
TOS	Tape On Spine; Terms Of Service
TOUGH	Tough guy genre (paperbacks)
TRPQ	Tall, Round, Pyroglaze Quart (milk bottles)
U	Used
UB	Undivided Back (postcards)
UDV	Undivided Back (postcards)
ULBC	Upper-Left (corner) Back Cover (books, magazines)
ULRC	Upper-Right (corner) Back Cover (books, magazines)
UNC	Uncirculated (coins)
UPS	United Parcel Service
URL	Uniform Resource Locator (web address)
URFC	Upper-Right corner of Front Cover
USPS	United States Postal Service
VERM	Vermeil—gold plating on sterling silver, bronze, or copper
VF	Very Fine condition
VFD	Vacuum Fluorescent Display

Abbreviation/Term	Definition
VFU	Very Fine, Used (stamps)
VG	Very Good condition
VHTF	Very Hard To Find
V/M/D	Visa/MasterCard/Discover Card
W	West Point Mint/Depository (coins)
WB	White Border (postcards)
W/C	Watercolor (paintings, maps)
WC	Watercolor (paintings, maps)
WD	White Dog (RCA record labels)
WLP	White Label Promo
WOB	Writing On Back
WOC	Writing On Cover
WOF	Writing On Front
WOR	Writing On Record
WRP	Warp (records)
WS	Widescreen (same as letterbox)
WSOL	Water Stain On Label (records)
XL	Extra Large

Index